THE LAZY COOK

Also by Richard Ehrlich
The Cosmopolitan After-work Cookbook

Richard Ehrlich
THE LAZY COOK

BANTAM PRESS

LONDON · NEW YORK · TORONTO · SYDNEY · AUCKLAND

TRANSWORLD PUBLISHERS LTD
61–63 Uxbridge Road, London W5 5SA

TRANSWORLD PUBLISHERS (AUSTRALIA) PTY LTD
15–25 Helles Avenue, Moorebank, NSW 2170

TRANSWORLD PUBLISHERS (NZ) LTD
3 William Pickering Drive,
Albany, Auckland

Published 1993 by Bantam Press
a division of Transworld Publishers Ltd
Copyright © Richard Ehrlich 1993

A catalogue record for this book is available
from the British Library.

ISBN 0593 025962

Typeset in Palatino by Chippendale Type Ltd,
Otley, West Yorkshire.

Printed in Great Britain
by Mackays of Chatham Plc, Chatham, Kent.

For Norma Solway Ehrlich

An Unlazy Cook

Contents

Introduction

Now, there's no question that there are a handful of people doing genuinely creative things with food . . . But most cooking is based on elementary, long-standing principles, and to say that cooking is creative not only misses the point of creativity – which is that it is painful and difficult and quite unrelated to whether it is possible to come up with yet another way to cook a pork chop – but also misses the whole point of cooking, which is that it is totally mindless.

Nora Ephron, *Heartburn* (1983)

Many people have a love-hate relationship with food: they love to eat it but hate to cook it. This book is for those people. It is for people whom I call lazy cooks, and my qualification for writing it is that I am a lazy cook myself. Even though I love to cook – and sometimes get paid to do it – I don't like to spend any more time in the kitchen than I have to. And many of my waking hours are devoted to thinking of ways of spending even less time there than I do already.

The problem with cooking is that it has too many competitors for the time of busy people. If you're like me, by the end of the day you're usually tired and fed up; you long to have a meal set in front of you. But unless you have a particularly helpful housemate or a live-in cook, that isn't going to happen. So there's no choice but to cook for yourself.

That's the bad news. The good news is that, with practice, you can cook food that's as good as what you'd get in 90 per cent of the restaurants you're likely to visit.

That may sound implausible, but it isn't. When I cook for friends, I am often surprised to get compliments about the simplest, easiest aspects of the meal. These are techniques or ingredients that I use constantly to make ordinary meals seem special. *The Lazy Cook* aims to share these tricks. It won't teach you how to cook restaurant-style dishes, but it will teach you how to make excellent meals with relatively little effort.

Lazy cooking eliminates several time-intensive factors. One is the preparation of elaborate sauces that need close attention over long periods. You will not find in these pages the great sauces of French cuisine, wonderful though they are.

Another time-consuming task is the assembly and mixing of long lists of ingredients. If you have to measure out small amounts of ten or twelve separate items, you will soon find yourself spending many minutes in the kitchen before cooking even begins. Lazy cooking keeps the ingredients list to a minimum, concentrating instead on making maximum use of a few flavours which can combine to produce memorable dishes with little fuss. Please note, however, that in certain areas of cooking – especially braising – it is hard to keep the ingredients list in single digits without impoverishing the final result.

Finally, lazy cooking saves time by cutting down on shopping. Cooking begins not in the kitchen but in the shop where you buy your food. I think that lazy cooks have better things to do than spend a whole morning in the supermarket, or go out searching for 'exotic' ingredients sold only in specialist shops. Most of my recipes call for ingredients that are available in any good supermarket, delicatessen, or high street butcher, fishmonger, or greengrocer. You will not be stymied here by the unavailability of parrot fish, jicama or pomegranate juice.

Certain ingredients appear over and over again in *The Lazy Cook*. This is intentional. I have a few favourite ingredients which I probably use far too often. But this is part of my approach to home cooking. Just as a great singer can transform a well-known song with a subtle nuance of phrasing, home cooks can make simple dishes memorable by adding an unexpected flavour. Here are the items that I use this way, and which I always have on hand. Those marked with an asterisk are discussed in greater detail in the last chapter of the book.

*fresh ginger
*garlic
soy sauce
*sun-dried tomatoes
a jar of capers
a tin of anchovies
dried red chilis
a bottle of ruby port
a bottle of dry vermouth
a bottle of fino sherry
a bottle of cheapish cognac

a bottle of extra virgin olive oil
* a bottle of balsamic vinegar
* herbes de Provence
Parmesan cheese, in a whole piece (pre-grated is not worth buying)
onions, *spring onions, and/or shallots
an assortment of dried herbs and spices (replace them every 6 months regardless of whether there's some left)

Committed though I am to the goal of quick cooking, two important disclaimers are in order here. First, *The Lazy Cook* does not claim to hold the secrets for stunning repasts in 15 minutes. Other books make that kind of claim, and some of them are very good. But if you saddle yourself with a strict time limit, you eliminate a lot of good, simple cooking. You cannot roast a chicken in 15 minutes, or braise a shoulder of lamb.

You can, however, do either of those things with 15 minutes or so of *active* work. And it's active work that the lazy cook wants to avoid. Then, when the work is done, you can have a nap, or a shower, or watch TV – the kind of thing that lazy cooks would rather be doing while somebody else makes a *terrine de foie de volailles*.

The second disclaimer is that *The Lazy Cook* does not pretend to be a startlingly original collection of new recipes. Indeed, most of the recipes are only marginally related to the concept of culinary creativity, which I think Nora Ephron hits squarely (and fairly) on the head. Yes, there are a few people doing 'genuinely creative things with food'. But most cooking is not creative in the sense that, say, writing a piano sonata is creative. It is a process of elaborating on a small number of well-established culinary principles. And rather than try to leap to the heights of culinary innovation, most home cooks – except for the most dedicated and self-confident – would be much better off dealing in what's been tried and tested elsewhere.

That's where *The Lazy Cook* comes in. This book is based on my belief that people who have limited time for (or interest in) cooking should not be studying collections of recipes. What I aim to do is help you look at your cooking in a slightly different way. Most cooking is really a very simple matter as long as you understand a few basic principles and master a few basic techniques.

Thus, my approach has little to do with learning 'yet another way to cook a pork chop' and a great deal to do with cooking a really good pork chop in the first place. It is aimed at helping you learn a solid core of dishes which use your own imagination – and the materials at hand – to best effect. And the size of that core will keep growing steadily. For instance, if you learn the basics of making puréed soup, you can make hundreds of soups using whatever's available at the shops or the supermarket.

Similarly with braised meat. Boeuf Bourguignonne, Irish Stew, and Rabbit with Prunes are all the same kind of dish, using different ingredients. Make one and you can make them all.

My belief in mastering basic dishes explains why several chapters in this book concentrate on one or two techniques. Read the beginning of the chapter before proceeding to what look like recipes. The recipes are merely suggested variations on the theme, nothing more. More important are the explanations of basic principles. Understand those and you will be on your way to better cooking.

I am indebted for this 'theme and variations' approach to Julia Child, from whose many books – especially *Mastering the Art of French Cooking* – I have learned much of what I know about cooking. Mrs Child uses the 'theme and variations' method in a more recent book, *The Way to Cook*. She is a great cookery writer, and I do not claim to be anything like her equal. But I have learned this lesson from the master and am trying, in my more modest way, to apply it in this book.

Another book to which I am particularly indebted is *The Joy of Cooking* (Rombauer and Becker), less for its approach to cooking than for its method of presenting recipes and especially lists of ingredients. Readers of *The Joy of Cooking* will note the similarities. Non-readers would do well to buy a copy.

Other chapters in the book proceed in different ways, some of them quite unrelated to the standard cookbook format of introduction followed by recipes. I make no apologies for this eccentricity, but you should be warned.

'THE RULES'

This book takes a casual attitude towards rules. A home kitchen is not a restaurant kitchen; home cooks are not bound by gastronomic canons. The only rule is that the food must please. If you can do that using unorthodox methods, great. Use Chinese flavours in a 'French' dish of braised beef, and the leftover gravy from that beef on a piece of steamed fish. Use Indian spices in a pasta sauce. Most important of all, use your imagination and your intuition. Life has enough problems without adding to the list in the kitchen. When you settle down to cook, you should relax, experiment, and enjoy yourself.

Lazy cooking aims to minimize effort at all stages, and one way of doing this is to make good use of leftovers. By design or by accident, you can produce the basis of one or two extra meals every time you cook. A roast chicken will turn into a risotto or salad the next day, steamed vegetables into a soup, baked potatoes into bubble and squeak or galettes. Wherever possible I indicate variations using leftovers from the basic dishes.

HOW MANY WILL IT SERVE?

Portion sizes are a personal matter, influenced by several unrelated factors: the size of your appetite, the number of other dishes being served, how much you've eaten (or are planning to eat) in other meals that particular day. Though a greedy person by nature, I cannot eat too much without blowing up like a balloon. Disregarding nutritional advice, I choose to divide my daily feasting between a barely perceptible breakfast, a light lunch, and a substantial dinner. And since the dishes in this book are designed for the evening meal – i.e. the biggest meal of the day – I tend to regard any portion as a biggish portion. I also believe firmly in making 'too much' of everything because leftovers, as mentioned above, are an important part of lazy cooking.

If you do things differently, fine. I just wanted to let you know where I stood. If you find that one 4 lb chicken feeds 6, that's the way to plan your meal.

SALT AND PEPPER

Two ingredients you will see little of in this book are salt and pepper. These are the essential seasonings, but they are another matter of personal taste. When serving food to guests I tend to leave the salt- and pepper-ing on the skimpy side, for the obvious reason that while you can add more if you want them, you cannot take them out if you *don't* want them.

I do this even though I know I'm making a culinary mistake. Marcel Boulestin, one of the most influential cookery writers of the first half of the century, says that insufficient salt at the time of cooking can ruin a dish – and that 'no amount of salt added at the dinner table will correct it'.

But I'm more concerned with letting my friends choose for themselves than with obeying culinary rules. This is why I tend to err on the side of insufficiency. It means, of course, that I am never offended when someone asks for salt and pepper at the table; and neither should you be.

Where I have remembered to mention salt and pepper, however, do put them in at that point. There's always a reason for it. And if you feel confident adding those ingredients before or during cooking, keep it up. My way of doing things suits me, but yours suits you.

TASTE, TASTE, TASTE

Boulestin mentions salt and pepper in a discussion of tasting, which he calls one of the cook's 'most important duties'. He advises us to taste at the beginning, as we go along, and at the end. And he is right. Tasting a dish as it makes its way from raw to cooked will tell you, first of all, whether it's shaping up the way you want it to. More generally, it will teach you about the whole process of cooking. When you see chefs on television dip their fingers into a sauce and then lick them as they stir and season, they are not putting on a performance: they are carrying out the essence of their work. Follow their example, even if you use a spoon instead of your fingers.

A FINAL NOTE

I have already said that *The Lazy Cook* is not a startlingly original collection of new recipes, and that most good cookery ideas have already been thought of by someone else. Writing the book confirmed that belief in numerous ways, and one of them is particularly important.

Often, when thinking about recipe ideas, I had an idea that seemed like a good one. I tried it out, refined it as necessary, and then wrote it up. I felt very pleased with myself. Later, when leafing through a cookbook in my collection, I found that my idea had already occurred to someone else.

Several times I was certain that I had never looked at that book before, or at least not at the page in question. Where this happened – where I figured something out independently, as someone else had done before me – I have not cited the other guy in my text.

On other occasions I knew that I *had* read that page, and that the mysteries of the unconscious had made me 'forget' about the idea in question until I started writing this book. But for whatever reason, I had not remembered that I first saw the recipe elsewhere. So it came to me, in all innocence, as an idea of my own. And the discovery of my error came as a tremendous relief, since it enabled me to acknowledge my debt to another writer and avoid the sin of plagiarism.

Plagiarism is a touchy subject in the world of cookery writing, and plagiarism of recipes in particular is regarded – rightly – as a heinous crime. It goes on a lot; it is inexcusable. The writers who experiment, maintaining high standards of inventiveness and originality, see their ideas and often their very words used by other writers. There is nothing wrong with borrowing ideas as long as they are properly acknowledged, and I have often done that in this book. So much of what I know about cooking comes from cookbooks that I couldn't work without using their ideas.

What I have *not* done is look back through every single one of my cookbooks to check for other slips of the memory. Thus, it is possible that I have used ideas without giving credit to the source. If I have done this, and I fervently hope I haven't, it is entirely accidental. I humbly beg the pardon of any writer whose ideas I have filched.

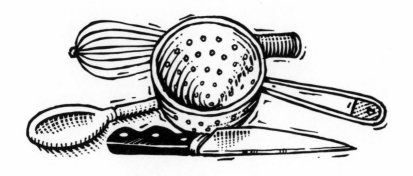

Timings,
Measurements,
Equipment

If you are going to be told exactly how much of everything to use, at precisely what stage each ingredient is to be added, plus cooking temperatures and timings down to the final minute, then you require to be told also the weight and dimensions of the cooking pot you are to use and the material of which it is to be made; variations for every type of fuel would have to be allowed for, not to mention qualifications such as the temperature of your kitchen and the altitude at which you are cooking; after all, you might want to know how long it takes to boil an egg when you reach the top of Mont Blanc.

Elizabeth David, *Spices, Salt and Aromatics in the English Kitchen* (1987)

There is a cookbook by an eminent French chef in which every step is timed with astonishing precision: 6 minutes for this, 3 minutes for that, 90 seconds for something else. I am sure that those timings reflect exactly how the recipe worked for him, and I admire his quest for exactitude.

In the real world, as Elizabeth David makes plain, such exactitude is unattainable. Do you use the oven and frying pans that this chef uses? Is the slice of lamb you're cooking exactly the same thickness and temperature as those he used? They are not. Nor are my cooker and pans and ingredients exactly like yours. Moreover, sometimes I use one pan to cook a particular dish and sometimes another. Those vessels have different thermic properties, and the differences will affect the time that the food needs to cook. If you're using the oven and cooking more than one dish at a time, timings are thrown off further.

In this book, most timings are given in two forms. One is a range, e.g. 20–25 minutes. The lower figure is the point at which the dish *might* be done; the higher figure indicates that by this point, the dish *should* be done. The other form of timing is an approximate figure, e.g. 'around 30 minutes'. In both instances I am trying to indicate the point at which you should test the stuff to see whether it's done. How do you tell whether something is done? By testing and experience. The two go hand in hand; there is no substitute for either of them.

Testing takes different forms. It can mean poking a steak to see how much 'give' there is – an essential means of determining the degree of toughening. It can mean pulling a piece of spaghetti out of the water to eat it, or to pinch it in half to examine the centre, or even – the traditional test – to throw it against the wall to see if it sticks. (If it sticks, it's done.) It can mean extracting a broccoli floret from the steamer and cutting off a section of stalk for tasting.

Whatever the ingredient, start testing at the lower figure in the range of timings – or even slightly earlier, just before you think the food might be done. By examining a dish throughout cooking, you will see how different amounts of heat affect it. And the more you develop your intuition through experience, the lazier you can be.

Measurements are another tricky business. In the USA, solid ingredients such as rice and flour are measured by volume. This has advantages and drawbacks. In the UK, solids are measured by weight and liquids by volume. This too has advantages and drawbacks, and the principal drawback is that many cooks lack scales that can precisely measure, for instance, 25 g (just under 1 oz) of flour. I use electronic scales which are accurate enough to do that, and I have found them to be a good investment.

But precision on this scale isn't needed in lazy cooking. When I specify ¼ of a teaspoon of thyme, what I really mean is a pinch. Half a teaspoon is a larger pinch, probably (though not necessarily) twice as large as a small pinch. If you feel confident using fingertips rather than a measuring spoon – or if you want a bit more or less thyme than I specify – you should proceed with your fingertips. You will not go wrong using the quantities I specify, but neither will you fail by using a bit more or less. Recipes are nothing more than a guideline. (The exception is pastry-making, but this book has only one pastry recipe, which is so easy as to be foolproof.)

One form of measurement that does crop up a lot in this book refers to the thickness of meat, fish and vegetables. In certain types of cooking, especially the pan-grilling discussed on pages 81–116, you have to pay attention to thickness or your timings will be wrong. But here, too, such precision is unnecessary. I had to be precise because I was writing a cookbook. In your own kitchen you can be more casual. But I do recommend that you try measuring a few times just to get yourself started. Then you will have a sure sense of how thick the chops or the courgettes are, and thus of how much cooking they need.

Here's a useful tip. I know, from measuring, that the distance from the tip of my index finger to the first joint is exactly one inch, and that my thumbnail is exactly half an inch long. Now I no longer need to use the tape measure because I can measure on equipment that I always carry with me, as it were. You should devise your own finger-based measurements.

Wherever possible, I have done away with measurements altogether. One of the things that take time in cooking is locating and then using the right measuring spoon from the collection in your kitchen drawer. And few measurements – in my kind of cooking, anyway – are truly critical. I would rather you spent your time reading a book than measuring a ¼ teaspoon of this and a ½ teaspoon of something else. For that reason, I have tried to give quantities based on the ingredients themselves rather than measurements in a spoon or jug – e.g. 'a small clove of garlic' rather than '1 tsp chopped garlic'. You will not go wrong, even if your garlic cloves are somewhat larger or smaller than mine.

Where quantities are specified more precisely, I have used both metric and Imperial/avoirdupois measurements. This is a standard procedure, widely used in both books and journalism, but it is not without its problems. The main problem is this: should you make the two sets of measurements exactly identical, or should you 'round off' one set so that the figures conform to the principal measurements on measuring spoons, commercial products, and scales? There are good arguments on both sides, but in lazy cooking there is really only one choice: round off whenever possible. This is what I have done. In the following recipes, therefore, you should stick to one set of measurements or the other. The metrically fastidious will note that, contrary to what my recipes think, 500 g does not equal 1 lb. But this doesn't make a great difference in the kind of cooking described here. Again, I would rather you spent your time doing something socially useful (or even just enjoyable) than weighing out 454 grams (1 lb exactly) of dried pasta. Don't worry if you notice that metric/Imperial equivalents occasionally vary from one recipe to another, for example that 4 oz is 100 g on one page and 125 g on another. This is unavoidable when rounding off, and you should just use the amount given in the recipe you are following.

Indeed, this book aims more than anything else to lead you away from finickety attention to grams and teaspoons, and to help you develop your own sense of how things should be done. Once you've roasted a few chickens, you will know *without measuring* how much thyme to put in the cavity; how much butter to smear on the skin; how much wine and stock are needed to make a gravy. Most cooking can be done by experience and intuition. Here is Elizabeth David, in the book quoted above. 'It is quite possible,' she writes,

> . . . to combine the exercise of one's five senses in the kitchen with the use of measuring devices as guides . . . the discipline of weighing and measuring does one's cooking nothing but good, provided that one does not . . . expect that precision will eliminate the necessity to keep one's head or train one's eye and palate.

Those words are more useful than all the recipes in this book.

EQUIPMENT

I would like to believe that, with one exception, nothing in this book calls for kitchen equipment that you're unlikely to own already. Of course, it's easy for me to say that. I know what lurks in my kitchen. You may not have the same things. And you won't feel like going out to buy them. For the record, this is what you need to cook these recipes. They are worth buying regardless of whether you use them in cooking from *The Lazy Cook*.

> A **grill pan** (griddle). See the chapter on pan-grilling (page 81) for more information about these.

> Good **knives**, which you should sharpen *little but often*. Buy the best you can afford. Sharp, well-balanced knives make slicing, chopping, and dicing easier by minimizing the effort you have to put into the operation yourself. Good knives are fairly expensive, and the cost makes some people buy cheap, but they're actually making their kitchen lives more difficult.

At least one large, heavy **frying pan**. Buy the best you can afford, and try to get one with a lid. (This is essential for some of the recipes in this book.) A wok is also useful.

At least one heavy enamelled cast-iron **casserole**, e.g. Le Creuset. You cannot make braises or pot-roasts without one. Be prepared to spend a lot of money, but regard that outlay – like the money you spend on good knives – as a long-term investment in your culinary happiness.

A **blender** for making puréed soups (see page 241). These are fairly inexpensive, and often come with a coffee grinder.

Apart from that it's just the usual assortment of bowls, whisks, wooden spoons, and assorted impedimenta that most cooks accumulate over the years. Everyone has his or her favourites. Mine include a bulb baster, a meat thermometer and a swivel-headed vegetable peeler. But you will have your own.

Having said that I don't want you buying new hardware, I must immediately add two items.

One is a food processor. This book mentions just one task that can *only* be done in a food processor. But these machines make kitchen life much easier and more pleasant.

The other item is an electronic digital timer with buttons for hours, minutes and seconds. It may seem bizarre to ask lazy cooks to buy such a thing, but we need them precisely *because* we're lazy. The timer replaces your memory, freeing you to do something truly important, such as read the paper or open a bottle of wine. It is also useful for high-heat cooking such as pan-grilling.

But timers do more than this: they remind you of what you should be doing. If you braise a piece of beef without a timer, it will be entirely up to you to remember when to check for doneness. If you get engrossed in something else, you may forget about the dish and overcook it. A timer does the remembering for you. The better you become at lazy cooking, the more your timers will help you avoid having to think about what you're doing. And the better you get at cooking, the less you will have to think about it.

One piece of equipment you will not see mentioned in these

pages is the microwave oven. This is a regrettable omission, and some might say a bizarre one, in a book aimed at lazy cooks. But since I don't know whether you *do* own a microwave, I finally decided to omit them from the book. Those who already have a microwave will recognize those tasks that can be carried out in the miraculous machine. Those who do not have a microwave should consider buying one: they are a useful tool for lazy cooking.

Roasting Chickens
and Other Birds

THE PRINCIPLE

You take a whole chicken, put flavourings inside the cavity, and roast it for just under an hour. The dry heat of the oven makes the skin crisp but – with care on your part – leaves the flesh moist and flavourful.

THE DETAILS

It's often said that you can judge a cook by the quality of his or her roast chicken, and there is a good deal of truth in that aphorism. The materials and technique are simple; the equipment is nothing more than an oven and a roasting tin. But the simplest things in cookery are often the trickiest. And this is certainly true of roast chicken. Producing a bird that's juicy on the inside (both in white meat and dark), and which has a crisp brown skin, requires skill, attention, and experience.

Experience is the most important of all these qualities. The French gastronomic philosopher Brillat-Savarin said that 'a man who can roast is born with the faculty', but I disagree: the basic technique becomes second nature once you've mastered it. And the result makes the trouble eminently worthwhile, for a good roast chicken is one of the greatest dishes in the world. It is also one of the most versatile, as it can be flavoured in any way you like – or simply cooked on its own, with nothing more than salt and pepper. And it's just as good when served cold or warm as it is hot.

The problem with chickens, and with turkeys too for that matter, is that they are really two different meats. The white meat is lean (i.e. dry) and relatively mild in flavour. The legs get much more exercise than the breast, and therefore have more fat and more flavour. Both these factors mean that the leg needs more cooking than the breast. As a result, the breast is often done before the legs; and if the legs are left in long enough to get fully cooked, the breast may be overdone. So the trick of roasting chicken is to cook both legs and breast to precisely the right degree. That's what makes the technique initially tricky to master. And it's probably why so many cooks and chefs devise their own personal technique: through trial and error, they have finally found the procedure that suits them best.

But which technique to use? A dozen cookery books will present a dozen different methods. To name but two: Nico Ladenis, in *My Gastronomy*, advocates cooking a 3½ lb bird on its back in a 180°C (350°F, Gas 4) oven for 45 minutes, then turning the oven off and letting the chicken sit for a further 45 minutes. The recipe given in the *Larousse Gastronomique* uses a temperature of 200°C (400°F, Gas 6), and calls for a cooking time of 15 minutes per pound, with the chicken lying breast-down for the first half of cooking and on its back for the second half.

I have tried both these techniques, and they both work. Neither is 'better' than the other. There is no definitive way to roast a chicken, just as there is no definitive way to play tennis. Every experienced chicken-roaster has a technique that he or she likes better than any other. You will succeed using the technique that suits you.

The one that suits me comes from Ken Hom, who in turn got it from Jacques Pépin. I use this one because (a) it has never failed me and (b) it requires less attention and less additional fat than many other techniques. But mostly I like it because I'm used to it. If you already have a technique that serves you well, stick with it. If you don't, or if your results with roast chicken are inconsistent, this recipe is a good one to master.

THE RAW MATERIALS

Because roast chicken is the simplest of chicken dishes, it cannot be made successfully without a good bird. Intensively reared chickens, given little opportunity for running around during their brief lives, have insipid flavour and soft, fatty flesh. Those shortcomings can be masked in a dish containing an abundance of pungent spices, but in a simple preparation they will be highlighted. To make a good roast chicken, you need a free-range bird which has fed on a high-quality feed like corn, and which has spent its life running, pecking and roaming at will.

At the same time, you should be wary of both the term 'free-range' and the term 'corn-fed'. The former is legally applicable to birds that have not had a much better life than their intensively-reared counterparts. But now the term 'free-range' has three internal classifications: 'free-range', 'traditional free-range', and 'free-range total freedom'. As a rule, birds in the second and third categories are best.

Feeding on corn is no guarantee that the bird is free-range, and I personally am unconvinced of the merits of a corn diet. It gives the skin and fat of the chicken an appealing yellowy tinge, but its effects on flavour are less tangible. The free-range distinction is much more important.

One item that I find immensely useful for roasting chickens (and for just about everything else in the kitchen) is a digital timer. Few of the lazy cook's kitchen tasks require split-second or even split-minute timing, but a digital timer acts as a little helper who sits there with you, reminding you when it's time to do something. My reasons for loving these contraptions are discussed more fully on page 17.

Finally, I urge you to buy a bulb baster, preferably one with a metal syringe. This makes basting immeasurably easier – no more tipping of the roasting pan while you insinuate a spoon that's inevitably too big into a space that's inevitably too small.

ROASTING

Here is the basic technique. It comes from *Ken Hom's Cuisine: East Meets West.*

Roast Chicken

a 1.5 kg (3 lb) chicken, preferably free-range
2 tbsp butter (optional)
salt and pepper
flavourings for cavity (see list below)

Remove the chicken from the fridge 45–90 minutes before cooking (or see note on Timing below). Arrange the shelves in the oven so that one of them is just below the middle point with at least 10 in clearance to the next shelf. Preheat the oven to 230°C (450°F, Gas 8).

Place the chicken BREAST SIDE DOWN on a rack in a

roasting pan. Smear it with the butter if you wish, and season the cavity and back with salt and pepper. Put your flavourings in the cavity and truss the chicken in the usual way, if you're so inclined (see note below). Put around 50 ml (2 fl oz) of water or wine in the roasting pan, then put the bird in the oven and roast for 15 minutes. Turn the heat down to 180°C (350°F, Gas 4). Roast for 35 minutes, basting once with any pan juices after 15 minutes. Take out the bird, turn the oven back up to 230°C (450°F, Gas 8), and baste again. Turn the bird over (see note below) and roast for 5–7 minutes to brown the breast skin.

Once the chicken is done, it will benefit – like all roasted meats – from resting for a while before you carve it. Put it either in the turned-off oven (with the door ajar) or in a warm spot in the kitchen. (On top of the cooker is a good choice, if there's space.) Many cookbooks recommend placing a large sheet of aluminium foil over the bird, loosely wrapped, to help retain heat. You can do this to minimize heat loss from the bird, but the foil will also trap steam, which in turn makes the skin less crispy. I usually prefer to leave the bird uncovered. It stays hot for a long time, and even if it is no longer oven-hot, it is still delicious. (Indeed, Nico Ladenis believes that a roast chicken is at its best when lukewarm. He may well be right.)

There are different views on the optimum resting time. Take 5 minutes as a minimum, 15 or 20 as a good target. But remember that the bird will hold its heat for quite a long time, and that roast chicken is good at any temperature. It's far better to have warm roast chicken than warm roast potatoes.

TIMING

If the bird has come straight out of the fridge, give it an extra 5 minutes in the first stage of cooking.

These timings are based on an ordinary oven, i.e. one that does not have an internal fan to circulate heat more evenly. If you have a fan-assisted oven, you will need to shorten these cooking times. But since you know your oven and I do not, the amount of shortening is best determined by you.

TRUSSING

Trussing roast birds makes them look nice, as the legs and wings are pulled tight against the body. But it does not affect the flavour one way or the other, and is by no means essential for the truly lazy cook.

TURNING

The best way to turn the chicken is by sticking a wooden spoon inside the cavity, picking it up, and rotating it with one hand held on the end of the drumstick. Take care not to break the skin when turning, as this will allow some of the juices to escape.

STUFFING

I am strongly opposed to stuffing roast chickens, and not just because making the stuffing can be time-consuming. When you stuff a bird, what you're doing is turning a hollow into a solid mass. The heat will take longer to penetrate to the centre, and the cooking time, especially with a stuffing that needs thorough cooking, will thus be increased. As a result, the chicken is likely to be *over*cooked by the time the stuffing is sufficiently cooked. If the chicken is cooked *à point*, as I think it should be, the stuffing will not be done. And if it contains pork or chicken livers, this can be dangerous. If you want to make a stuffing-like mixture, fine – but bake it in a separate dish.

TESTING

As long as you make sure the bird is at or close to room temperature before it goes into the oven, and observe the cooking procedure faithfully, I've never known this procedure to produce an undercooked chicken. But undercooked chicken can be a danger to your health because of the risk of salmonella poisoning; and some people just like to make sure. So here are some traditional techniques for testing the doneness of roast chicken.

First, a note on what is meant by 'done' in the context of roast chicken. Some people think that chicken should be falling off the bone before it is edible. I disagree strongly. When it's falling off the bone, it is the chicken equivalent of a roast beef that's grey right through to the middle – i.e. very well done. Roast chicken, as I have already said, should be what the French call *à point*. With red meat this means medium-rare. With chicken it means that the bird is cooked to precisely the moment at which it's appetizing and safe to eat, but no more. This is what the method above is designed to achieve. If you like chicken that's well done, you'll want to add 15 or 20 minutes to my cooking times – but don't invite me over for dinner.

Now, testing. One method is to pierce the skin of the thigh and examine the juice that runs out. If it's red or a deep pink, the bird is not cooked. If the juices run clear, the bird is cooked. I don't like this method. If the bird has to go back in the oven, the puncture will provide an efficient vent for the flavourful juices to escape. Even if it's deemed ready, precious juices will escape during the resting period.

Another method is to tilt the bird backwards so that juice runs out of the cavity. The same colour criteria apply as in the first method. The drawback here is that if the bird is tightly trussed, you'll have trouble getting the juice to run out. And in any case, I've known birds to produce bright pink juice from the cavity (where the bird's natural moisture tends to accumulate) yet be perfectly cooked.

A third method is to wiggle the end of the drumstick and see if the drumstick-thigh joint wiggles easily. If it does, the bird is done. But in my experience, this is really a test to see whether the bird is *over*done. And if there's nothing better than a perfect roast chicken, there's nothing worse than one that has cooked too long.

In short, there is no ideal method of testing a roast chicken for doneness. Again, the key word is experience; there is no substitute.

The method I use is unscientific and difficult to explain, as it depends on my own experience. The first aspect of the technique is poking the breast with your finger: if it has just a tiny bit of 'spring', i.e. resistance to the touch, the bird is probably done. If I'm in doubt, I take a close look at the legs of the chicken. Chicken skin is semi-translucent, so you can see what's going on underneath it. When the meat towards the inside of the thigh and drumstick reaches a certain temperature, the juices at the outside move around actively, rising as if heated from below. Active movement – i.e. a rapid rising of the juices seen through the chicken's skin – is usually a sign that the bird is done.

WHEN THINGS GO WRONG

No matter how experienced you are, you will sometimes make a mistake. There are two mistakes, overcooking and undercooking. Overcooking is a disaster and a waste. It should be disguised with plenty of gravy (see below).

If you become obsessed with the idea of cooking your chicken just right, you will probably more often find yourself undercooking it. Maybe the chicken was slightly bigger or colder than you'd thought, or the oven cooler. Happily, this mistake can be remedied. Here's what I do.

After the chicken has rested, I follow the standard carving procedure of slicing off one of the legs. (Only the legs are likely to be underdone, as they need more cooking time than the breast.) If they need more cooking, I immediately turn the oven back on to its highest setting. (Sometimes I leave the oven on throughout the resting period, just in case. It helps to be cautious.) I then carve off the other leg and pop both in the roasting pan (without the rack). Then I get them sizzling over a medium heat on the cooker. After a minute, I put them back at the top of the oven for an extra 3–5 minutes. In the meantime you can carve the breast and get the rest of the food ready.

If you follow these guidelines, I guarantee that you will produce a perfectly-roasted chicken 99 times out of 100; and in the other instance, you will not do anything that can't be remedied.

FLAVOURING ROAST CHICKEN

There are three ways of adding flavour to a roast chicken while the bird is being cooked.

1. Season the cavity.

2. Put aromatic vegetables in the roasting pan underneath the chicken. This flavours the run-off juices produced during cooking; if you then cook the vegetables in stock or wine, you will have an instant gravy.

3. Loosen the skin from the breast meat and stuff seasoned butter or other flavourings underneath. This moistens the skin, and can also be used to marinate the breast meat before cooking.

Except for special occasions, I use only the first and second techniques. The second remains more or less constant whatever else is being done with the bird:

Cut an onion, a carrot, and a celery stalk into ¼ in slices. Scatter these over the bottom of the roasting pan and season with salt and pepper. Moisten with around 50 ml (2 fl oz) of water or wine and proceed with the recipe.

The first method is the crucial one. As the flavouring ingredients heat up, their aroma penetrates the flesh of the chicken and their juices mingle with the chicken's. When the cavity juices are then poured off into the pan to make gravy, their perfume is concentrated and adds immeasurably to the flavour of the bird.

There are so many good chicken flavourings that you could spend a lifetime roasting and never have a dull meal. Because of this richness, giving recipes for 'Roast Chicken with This or That' strikes me as redundant. Yes, some combinations are classic: garlic, tarragon, and lemon is one of them. But looking down the list below, I can't immediately see any ingredient that wouldn't go well with any of the others. Use your imagination and apply it using whatever's available.

SUGGESTED FLAVOURINGS FOR ROAST CHICKEN

garlic, smashed, crushed or minced
parsley, chopped
fresh or dried tarragon
fresh or dried thyme
fresh or dried rosemary
ginger
spring onion
lemon, juice and zest
orange, juice and zest
lime, juice and zest
fresh mushrooms, cleaned and sliced
dried mushrooms, soaked for
  20 minutes in warm water and
  squeezed dry

fresh fennel, sliced thin or chopped
onion, chopped or sliced thin
shallots, sliced thin
rosemary
herbes de Provence (see page 338)
fresh coriander
extra virgin olive oil
whole coriander seeds
whole cumin
whole fenugreek
whole fennel seeds

Gravy

Gravy is not essential for roast chicken. If the bird has been cooked properly, the meat will be moist and juicy. But gravy is simple to make, and is useful for other dishes being served with the chicken.

When the chicken is cooked, remove it to a carving dish. Take out the roasting rack and skim off some of the fat from the pan. Put the pan over a low-medium heat and add around 225 ml (8 fl oz) of liquid, which may contain the following in any combination:

good chicken, beef, veal or vegetable stock
dry wine, red or white
port
sherry
water

While the gravy is coming up to heat, scrape the bottom of the pan with a wooden spoon to release the hardened cooking juices, which are full of flavour. (This is called *deglazing*.) Bring to a boil and simmer for 5–10 minutes, until the gravy is strong in flavour and very hot. Taste for salt and pepper, and serve separately in a gravy boat that allows you to pour off the fatless gravy.

A delicious variation on this technique is to deglaze the pan with something sharp and acidic, especially red wine, cider, or sherry vinegar. The more you use of this type of ingredient, the sharper the gravy will be. A combination of 3 parts stock to 1 part vinegar would be perfect. Even better is deglazing with balsamic vinegar (see page 344), which is sweeter than other types. It's also costlier, so this is a trick to use only for people you're really eager to please (or impress).

Roasting Vegetables with the Chicken

Many vegetables will roast well during the time needed by the chicken. If cooked in the roasting pan they will also absorb rendered fat from the bird as well as some of the cooking juices. This is a quick way of producing a one-step meal. Bear in mind, however, that the amount of space in the roasting pan will be limited.

> **New potatoes** (small): add after the first 15 minutes
> **New potatoes** (large): cook for the full cooking time
> **Large carrots**: add after the first 15 minutes
> **Whole medium onions** (around 2 in in diameter), topped and
> tailed but not peeled: add after the first 15 minutes

Roasting Vegetables Separately

Vegetables may also be roasted in a separate dish while the chicken is cooking. This keeps their flavours separate from the chicken flavours. And if the chicken is done before the vegetables (this is better than having it the other way round), the veg can continue cooking while the chicken is resting. Do note, however, that cooking other dishes at the same time will lower the temperature of the oven. If you're cooking a lot of veg, the chicken will probably need an extra 5 minutes in the final stage of roasting.

Here are a few suggestions for roasted accompaniments to

the chicken. Whichever you use, put them in a roasting pan with 1–2 tablespoons of oil or fat per 500 g (1 lb) of vegetables. I recommend:

plain oil
extra virgin olive oil
duck or goose fat
butter, preferably clarified

You can also add some stock or wine to the pan if you want to make sure the vegetables remain moist. Arrange the shelves in your oven so there's room for another one at the top of the oven, and time them as follows:

New potatoes (small): add after the first 20 minutes
New potatoes (large): cook for the full cooking time
Large carrots: add after the first 20 minutes
Whole medium onions (around 2 in in diameter), topped and tailed but not peeled: add after the first 20 minutes

For more detailed guidelines on roasting vegetables, see pages 146 and 180.

Small Turkeys and Larger Chickens

The technique above can be used for birds up to 3.5 kg (7 lb) in weight; beyond that, turning them is difficult. Baste at least five times during roasting to keep the skin and breast meat from drying out. These cooking times are a good guide, but you'll need to keep your wits about you after the second stage: sometimes the large birds need more time, sometimes they are nearly done.

2.5 kg (5 lb) bird
25 minutes at 230°C (450°F, Gas 8)
45–50 minutes at 180°C (350°F, Gas 4)
15–20 minutes at 230°C (450°F, Gas 8)

3.5 kg (7 lb) bird
35 minutes at 230°C (450°F, Gas 8)
50–60 minutes at 180°C (350°F, Gas 4)
15–20 minutes at 230°C (450°F, Gas 8)

Guinea Fowl

Smear the skin with 1 tbsp or so of butter to compensate for the leanness of the bird, then give it

> 25–30 minutes at 230°C (450°F, Gas 8)
> 30 minutes at 180°C (350°F, Gas 4)
> 5 minutes at 230°C (450°F, Gas 8)

Duck

Not suitable. See page 129 for a better technique.

Pheasant

Pheasant is often a tough bird both to cook and to eat. I like it best when pot-roasted (see page 40), but it can be roasted dry if you like. Smear the skin with 1 tbsp or so of butter to compensate for the leanness of the bird. Timings:

> 5 minutes at 230°C (450°F, Gas 8)
> 25 minutes at 180°C (350°F, Gas 4)
> 10 minutes at 230°C (450°F, Gas 8)

Pigeon

Pigeon can be either domesticated 'squab' pigeon, which is plump and tender, or the commoner wild 'wood pigeon' which is small and needs careful cooking. Wood pigeon isn't really suitable for this technique. See page 130 for some better ideas. Squab pigeon, if you find one, should be timed as for guinea fowl (see above).

Wild Duck

This is perfect for the basic technique but may need more basting because it's not very fatty, having had such an active life. Bacon or goose fat are both good for basting; butter will do perfectly well. Timings:

10 minutes at 230°C (450°F, Gas 8)
25 minutes at 180°C (350°, Gas 4)
10 minutes at 230°C (450°F, Gas 8)

Poussin

These little birds, usually weighing around 500 g (1 lb) tend to be leaner than older chickens so extra fat is usually needed. Pot-roasting might be a good alternative (see below). For ordinary roasting, here are the timings:

5 minutes at 230°C (450°F, Gas 8)
20 minutes at 180°C (350°F, Gas 4)
5 minutes at 230°C (450°F, Gas 8)

Quail

Quail are so small – and cook so fast – that they don't need special treatment for roasting. To roast them dry, smear each bird with 1 tbsp of softened butter or wrap it in a slice of bacon seasoned with black pepper and a small pinch of herbes de Provence (see page 338). Roast them, breast side up, in a very hot oven (230°C, 450°F, Gas 8) for 20–25 minutes. Another good technique is discussed below under pot-roasting (see page 39).

POT–ROASTING

Because the heat is moist, pot-roasted chicken can be cooked longer than ordinary roasted chicken. Please note: this is not because pot-roasting slows down cooking. On the contrary, it speeds it up. But the juices are retained in the pot, producing a delicious gravy which is served with the bird. And some people prefer it that way, thinking that the chicken isn't done till the leg meat is 'falling off the bone'. Again, I prefer all chickens to be cooked à *point*, but in deference to the falling-off-the-bone contingent, here are cooking times for both styles of pot-roasted chicken.

	À point	Well done
1.5 kg (3 lb) bird:	40–50 minutes	60–70 minutes
2 kg (4 lb) bird:	50–60 minutes	70–80 minutes
2.5 kg (5 lb) bird:	60–70 minutes	80–90 minutes
3.5 kg (7 lb) bird:	80–90 minutes	100–110 minutes

Two notes about equipment are in order here. First, pot-roasting a very large chicken requires a very large casserole. If the sides of the bird are too close to the sides of the casserole, they may cook too fast. If they are touching the sides, the skin will stick. Second, the casserole itself must be very heavy, preferably of enamelled cast iron, and must have a tight-fitting lid. If the casserole is too thin, or is made of a highly conductive metal like aluminium, the intense heat may overcook the outer sections of flesh and skin. Le Creuset cookware, made of enamelled cast iron, is the best choice for pot-roasting (as for many things).

Pot-roasted chicken needs a little more attention than the ordinary variety. The bottom of the casserole is very hot, hot enough to cause the chicken to stick to it. You should check it every 20 minutes or so to watch for this, and add a little water or stock or wine if the chicken is sticking.

If the chicken has stuck to the bottom at all during cooking, there will probably be some delicious bits left in the casserole. These should be deglazed as in the main recipe.

Pot-roasted Chicken

The same basic ingredients are used as in roast chicken:

2 tbsp butter, oil or extra virgin olive oil
salt and pepper
flavourings for cavity (see list on page 29)
a 1.5 kg (3 lb) chicken, preferably free-range

The only major difference here is that the oil or butter is no longer optional, as it's needed to brown the chicken and keep it from sticking to the bottom of the casserole. Use less if you're watching calories, more if you're pre-eminently concerned with ensuring that the chicken doesn't stick.

Preheat the oven to 180°C (350°F, Gas 4). Melt the butter gently in a heavy lidded casserole. Put seasonings and flavourings in the cavity and truss if desired. When the butter begins to bubble, put in the chicken and cook on all sides till it is lightly browned. The chicken should finish on its back, and should stay there for the main cooking. Cover the casserole and cook in the oven for the times given above, basting a few times with butter and the cooking liquid. You can also add a little liquid to the pot (around 110 ml/4 fl oz) for flavour and lubrication. The ones I suggest are:

dry vermouth
dry white wine
fino *sherry*
chicken stock with a splash of Cognac

But you should improvise with whatever you've got lying around the kitchen. A splash of vinegar, especially balsamic, would certainly not go amiss.

Roasting Vegetables with the Chicken

A perfect one-dish meal. Cut the vegetables into smallish pieces (no more than 2 in on any side) and time as follows:

New potatoes: add after the first 15 minutes
Large carrots: add after the first 15 minutes
Whole medium onions (around 2 in in diameter), topped and tailed but not peeled: add after the first 15 minutes

Please note that only new potatoes (or a waxy type of main-crop potato) should be cooked with a pot-roasted chicken. Floury potatoes will disintegrate in the pot.

Chicken with 40 Cloves of Garlic

The name of this recipe terrifies people who fear its effects on their breath. I won't lie: if the garlic used is particularly pungent, your breath may suffer from a hangover. But long, slow cooking drastically moderates the effect of the odoriferous compounds in garlic, and the after-effect is not nearly as powerful as you would imagine. And the taste makes it worthwhile, for this is truly one of the great dishes of French cuisine. Make it on a Friday or Saturday night so your colleagues at work won't suffer if your breath is garlicky.

The technique is the same as the one for pot-roasted chicken, except that you don't brown the chicken but colour it very lightly in the oil. No other flavourings are needed apart from salt and pepper, but fresh herbs of your choice make a lovely addition. Try tarragon, sage, thyme, or rosemary. Scatter them around the bird rather than sticking them in the cavity. The ingredients you'll need, apart from a good chicken, are:

6 tbsp extra virgin olive oil
4 or 5 heads of garlic
a small handful of fresh herbs of your choice (e.g. rosemary or tarragon)
salt and pepper

Separate the heads of garlic into cloves. Remove the papery husks but do not peel. Heat the oil in the casserole over a medium heat. When it's hot, roll the chicken in it on all sides, turning it well to make sure the oil covers every bit of skin. Add the garlic and flavourings (optional) and toss in the oil. Now cover the casserole and cook the chicken on its back, timing it as detailed in the chart above (page 34). Putting a sheet of aluminium foil under the lid will ensure a tighter seal, which locks in the garlic-scented steam.

Note: if you're using a very large chicken, begin the cooking without the garlic and herbs. Add them when the bird is 40–50 minutes from being done.

This dish should be served with French bread and steamed vegetables such as French beans. If your guests want to avoid the garlic, that's their loss. Sensible eaters will squeeze the cloves on to the bread, smash it down a little, and enjoy themselves.

Pot-roasted Chicken with Chinese Flavours

'Red-cooked chicken' is a Chinese dish in which the whole chicken is poached or braised in a liquid dominated by soy sauce. This pot-roasted version uses the same flavours but in smaller quantities. The ingredients you'll need:

2 tbsp plain vegetable oil (peanut, corn, safflower or sunflower)
around 50 ml (2 fl oz) each of beef or chicken stock, soy sauce, and dry sherry
ginger, spring onion, and garlic, all coarsely chopped

Heat the oil in the casserole and lightly brown the bird as uniformly as possible. Then pour in the remaining ingredients and proceed as in the basic recipe.

Pot-roasted Chicken with Indian Flavours

Indian spices have an affinity with chicken, as you'll know if you've eaten Murgh Masallam in a really good Indian restaurant. This is not a true Indian dish: the spices are used merely to give a standard pot-roast the unique pungency of those remarkable flavours. Use any combination of 5 or more from the following spices, figuring on a total of 2 tbsp for a whole chicken:

whole cumin   *ginger*
whole coriander   *garlic*
whole fenugreek   *garam masala*
whole mustard seeds   *whole cloves*
dried or fresh chili   *cinnamon sticks*

Proceed with browning the chicken as in the basic recipe. When it's finished browning, add the spices to the oil and let them sizzle for 30 seconds or so. Add around 50 ml (2 fl oz) of water water or stock, and proceed with the rest of the recipe.

Pot-roasted Chicken Pieces

Chicken pieces can be roasted dry or in the pot. For tips on dry roasting, see the chapter on flash-roasting (page 117). Pot roasting is more like true roasting, so I am explaining the technique here.

Chicken pieces are particularly good for pot-roasting because they don't take very long to cook. The problem with them is that they need a casserole which will accommodate all the pieces in a single layer. When the pieces get stacked up, those on top will cook unevenly unless they're covered with liquid – and then the dish will be a braise rather than a pot roast. But if you have a wide, flat casserole or baking dish, the chicken pieces sold at supermarkets and butchers make this an easy dish to prepare. Any of the flavourings on page 29 can be used, and small carrots, onions, or turnips would cook very well alongside the chicken pieces. Use:

2 tbsp vegetable oil
1.5 kg (3 lb) chicken pieces, preferably free-range
salt and pepper
flavourings (see page 29)

Preheat the oven to 180°C (350°F, Gas 4). Heat the oil in the casserole over a high heat and brown the chicken pieces a couple at a time, so they don't crowd each other in the pot. The browning will take 3–4 minutes per side. When all the pieces are browned, bung them all in the casserole with the other ingredients. You may also add at this point:

75 ml (3 fl oz) stock, wine, vinegar, or a combination
small carrots or new potatoes or 2 in pieces of onion

Cover the casserole and put it in the oven. Let it cook for 30 minutes, checking a couple of times to see that the chicken isn't sticking and the liquid is not evaporating.

Quail

Pot-roasted Quail

Pot-roasted quail are delicious. And because they take so little time to cook, they're a good choice for after-work dinner parties when you want to impress but don't have much time for anything elaborate.

The drawback is that their short cooking time won't cook any but the tiniest morsels of anything else that's in the pot. For this reason, I like to pot-roast them with a selection of vegetables which are pre-cooked in butter or oil, then added to the browned birds for cooking in the oven. If you're hungry, allow 2 birds per person. More abstemious eaters will be satisfied with one. Here's the way to cook them.

3 tbsp butter or extra virgin olive oil
a few stalks of celery
2 small onions (or one large), or 2 small, young leeks
a couple of carrots
any of the flavourings on page 29
8 quail

Chop the vegetables in chunks around ½ in square. Heat 2 tbsp of the butter or oil in a casserole large enough to hold the birds in one layer, and toss in the vegetables. Add flavourings of your choice. (See page 29 above for possibilities.) Sweat the vegetables slowly for a few minutes, then add any good stock (except fish, of course) to come up about half-way to the height of the vegetables. Cover the pan and simmer for 10–15 minutes. Remove the lid and boil rapidly until the liquid is reduced to a few spoonfuls. Remove the vegetables and wipe out the casserole.

Add the remaining butter or oil and heat it till bubbling, then put in the quail and brown them lightly all over. Return the vegetables to the casserole and cook either on the stove or in the preheated oven (180°, 350°F, Gas 4) for 20–30 minutes.

Guinea Fowl

These delicious birds are very slightly tougher than chicken, so they need just a little more time in the pot than a chicken of the same size. On the other hand, they are smaller than most chickens – rarely more than 3½ lb and sometimes less than 3. See the timings for small pot-roasted chickens (page 34) for guide times.

Pheasant

Pheasant is another good choice for pot-roasting, as it can be tough. Like most game birds, it needs either very quick cooking (see the chapter on pan-grilling, page 81) or very long cooking in liquid. As pot-roasting doesn't provide quite enough lubrication, I prefer to give these flavourful creatures a straightforward braise if I'm not going to joint them and roast the breasts separately. See page 80 for a braise recipe, page 130 for instructions on flash-roasting.

   The same limitations apply with wild pigeons (wood pigeons), which are small and powerful in flavour.

THE REST OF THE MEAL

Roasted and pot-roasted birds go well with any number of vegetable dishes. For the ordinary roast chicken, try serving a vegetable dish that's on the moist side, as the bird itself will not have a lot of liquid. (There's more liquid if you make a gravy, but the advice still holds.) If you're trying to eat on the light side, serve it with a green salad or steamed, boiled, or stir-fried beans or broccoli. For the starchy dish, I would suggest

a potato gratin (see page 186)
a pasta gratin (see page 196)
charred potatoes (see page 174)

If you're willing to do a bit more checking-up during cooking, the first two of these suggestions can be cooked at the same time as the chicken. Put them in the bottom of the oven when the chicken goes in, and leave them there throughout the changes of oven temperature. I have found that the timing works out just about right, as using a lower position in the oven means that the effective cooking temperature is lower than that of the chicken. But because you're cooking two dishes at once, the chicken itself may take a little longer. Fear not: you can compensate easily by leaving the chicken in longer at the final stage.

If you'd like a more elaborate, hearty vegetable to go with the chicken, consider the following:

charred celery (see page 171)
courgettes á l'étuvée (see page 161)
braised chicory, celery, or carrots (see pages 164–5)

Accompaniments to pot-roasted chicken don't need to be so moist, as the main dish is itself moist. Any charred or stir-fried green is a good idea, as are braises. For the starch dish, I like eating pot-roasted birds with rice, plainly boiled or cooked with herbs, spices, or a whole clove of garlic. Garlicky rice is a delicious dish which lazy cooks should know about: boil the rice in your usual way, but cook it in chicken stock with a whole clove of garlic added at the beginning of cooking. The same thing can be done with a few slices of onion, either cooked in oil first or just whacked into the pot with the rice.

CHICKEN LEFTOVERS

Whenever you cook chicken you should aim to end up with some leftovers. You can make so many good dishes from them that it seems a waste not to make more than you need. The same principle applies with any other bird, though the smaller ones (like quail and guinea fowl) are less likely to leave anything over.

When cooking leftover chicken, or any other bird, there is only one rule to remember: don't overcook. The chicken is already cooked perfectly, or possibly even slightly *over*cooked. Your aim at this stage should be to do nothing more than heat it through; anything more than that and the chicken will dry out.

Curried Potatoes and Chicken

250 g (8 oz) cooked chicken
500 g (1 lb) waxy potatoes
150 g (6 oz) onions
1–2 tbsp vegetable oil
1–2 tsp mild curry powder or Indian spice mix
150 g (6 oz) button mushrooms.

Cut the chicken off the bone and into pieces around ½ in square; don't worry if they're larger, smaller, or uneven in size. Chop the potatoes and onions into pieces of around the same size. Heat the oil over a fairly high heat in a large pan – ideally one that's large enough to take the potatoes in a single layer. Put in the potatoes and cook, stirring once, for 2 minutes. Put in the onions and stir thoroughly, then add the curry powder or spice mix. Turn the heat down a little and cook for 15–20 minutes, stirring and tossing regularly, till the potatoes and onions are browned in places and almost soft enough to eat. While they're cooking, clean the mushrooms and cut if necessary into pieces around ½ in in size. Put the mushrooms and chicken in the pan, *without stirring*, and cover. Cook for 5 minutes exactly, by which time the chicken will be heated through and the mushrooms cooked *al dente*. Serve with a green salad.

Here are a few more suggestions, decribed in general terms rather than in detail.

Chicken and Rice

Cut the chicken into small pieces around ½ in thick. Boil some rice using your usual method, perhaps with some of the extra flavourings described above. When the rice is cooked, fluff it up and stir in the chicken with a handful of fresh herbs. Put the top back on, leave the pot to sit for 5 minutes, then dig in. Eat it with a green salad.

Chicken Salad

I got into trouble with a dietician for referring to chicken with mayonnaise as 'chicken salad'. But that's what I call it, being an American, and I make no apologies. Even less do I feel the need to apologize for this excellent combination. When made with the remains of a well-roasted chicken, it is one of the best things ever. Use:

2–4 tbsp mayonnaise per 250 g (8 oz) of chicken

– just enough to coat the chicken without drowning it. Mix in flavourings, whatever's around. Here are some of my favourites:

ginger, garlic and spring onion
spring onion on its own
finely chopped celery
crisply fried bacon, shredded (2 rashers per 250 g (8 oz) of chicken)
fine dice of red or green peppers
fine dice of red, ripe tomatoes
toasted sesame seeds

If you use sour cream instead of mayonnaise, with a few drops of balsamic vinegar per tbsp of sour cream, you will make a tangier and more refined dish. Combine this with some of the bits listed above, wrap a large spoonful in a lettuce leaf, and you have a dish that's elegant enough to serve for an informal summer lunch.

Chicken in Soup

Pages 241–67 of this book are about puréed soups. If you make one of these delicious things, especially one that has chicken stock as a base, skinless bits of leftover chicken can be puréed with it for a fuller flavour and substance. Chop the meat into small pieces, taking special care to cut across the grain. Add to the soup when you put it in the blender, and give the soup an extra-long time in the blender so the meat is well blended. Chicken in soup goes especially well with leeks, potatoes, fennel, rice and onions.

Chicken and Vegetables à l'Étuvée

Here's a really soothing dish to make for 1 or 2 people. Cut every bit of skin and flesh off your leftover chicken, and chop the carcass into pieces with poultry shears, a cleaver, or a heavy knife and a wooden kitchen mallet. Prepare for cooking *à l'étuvée* (see page 157) a combination of the following:

carrots
celery
onions

and cook them with the carcass sitting on top of the vegetables. Every last bit of flavour will leave the bones and enrich the vegetables. Just before serving, remove the bones and put in the chicken meat. Continue cooking just long enough to heat the chicken through. Served with noodles or boiled rice, this is a good dish for a Sunday hangover.

Braising Meat

THE PRINCIPLE

You take some meat either in a whole piece or in chunks, brown it, then cook it slowly, for a long time, in liquid with flavourings. The result is tender meat and a good quantity of gravy.

THE DETAILS

Braising is a cross between roasting and poaching. Because the dish is covered and the meat is not subjected directly to the dry oven heat, braised meats produce their own gravy which can then be served with the dish.

Braising is a perfect cooking method for lazy cooks because it's eminently forgiving. Where roasting can demand split-second timing if ruination isn't to ensue, many braised dishes may be cooked an extra 10, 20, or even 50 per cent without suffering unduly. Requiring little attention while the cooking is in progress, they are excellent for cooking in advance, and tend to be better when reheated. They are also good for slimming, as extra fat is rarely necessary. And, as with roast chicken, the range of flavouring possibilities is endless.

Incidentally, it is often supposed that braising cooks meat more slowly than roasting. This isn't true. Moist heat cooks faster than dry heat. But braising is still a more forgiving cooking method than roasting because any dryness in the meat – which is often technically 'overcooked' – is masked by the braising liquid. Of course, I'm not suggesting that you go out of your way to overcook *any* meat. Try to stick to the timings given below.

Flavourings apart, there are two important variables in braising: the type of meat and the form in which it's used. In general, the meat can be cheaper and tougher than roasting meat, since long cooking in liquid will soften both gristle and muscle tissue. Having said that, I should add immediately that more tender meat will cook faster than the tough cuts; and that the results are better with better meat. Use the cheaper, tougher cuts for everyday meals and serve the fancier stuff to guests – as long as you can afford it.

Best cuts for braising are:

Lamb: shoulder, leg, breast, chump
Beef: shoulder (clod), topside, silverside, brisket, rump, shin,
   flank, short ribs, oxtail
Pork: shoulder, hand, belly
Veal: shoulder, shin, breast

TO CUBE OR NOT TO CUBE

The form of presentation is crucial in braising, and there are
two basic choices: in pieces or whole. Both have a lot to
recommend them. What's best for you will depend on the type
of meat and what kind of dish you're planning. Cubed meat
produces something approximating to most people's idea of a
stew, and many people love this kind of dish. Just remember
three things. First, cubed meat is usually trimmed of all or most
of its fat, and it therefore tends to dry out quite a lot in cooking.
Compensate for this by ensuring that there's plenty of cooking
liquid in the dish. Second, it is vital that cubed pieces of meat be
roughly equal in size. Don't cut them smaller than 1 in square, as
they may fall to bits and lose too much of their flavour to the
cooking liquid; 1½ in is a better target size. Third, try to ensure
that the pieces are cut along the natural contours of the meat. If
a cube contains a section of connective tissue, it may fall apart
or deform during cooking. The best way to be sure of good
cutting is to do it yourself: this takes just a few extra minutes,
and it's worth the extra trouble even for the laziest of cooks.
Cubes of 'stewing steak' sold by butchers tend to be scrappy and
gristly.

All these considerations apply also to slices of braising meat.
You can make a very good braise from 1 in slices if you have a
casserole wide enough to hold them in a single overlapping
layer.

Personally, I prefer to braise whole pieces of meat. They look
nice when you bring them to the table for carving, and they
retain a lot more of the meat's natural juices. There's also – and
this is an important point for lazy cooks – less work involved in
preparation, and especially in the browning phase.

THE BRAISING LIQUID

A good braise should include stock in the cooking liquid. And as it happens, making stock is possible even in the lazy kitchen. Many cookery writers give stock recipes which seem forbiddingly fiddly and time-consuming, but it needn't be quite so painful. In particular, all the careful skimming can be dispensed with if you're careful about cooking over a very, very gentle heat. There is a stock recipe for lazy cooks in the chapter on soups (see page 245), and I urge you to try it out at least once.

BROWNING

Browning is the preliminary process in which meat is sautéed over a high heat to colour the outside. This process is still sometimes called 'sealing', even by some knowledgeable cookery writers, and I think it's important to understand that browning has nothing whatsoever to do with sealing.

The concept of sealing has a long and noble history. Beginning in the nineteenth century, it had long been believed that browning meat turns the outside tissue into an impermeable barrier through which the meat's juices cannot escape. Harold McGee, in his great book *On Food and Cooking*, has shown conclusively that this effect does not take place – that browned meat does not retain its juices better than un-browned. As McGee points out, you need only listen to the sputtering of a well-browned steak or joint to know that the juices aren't 'sealed in'. The sputtering, he points out, is caused by the rapid evaporation of watery juices. And if they were sealed inside the meat, they wouldn't be sputtering. When you see the term 'sealing' in a book, magazine or newspaper, sit back and enjoy the satisfaction of knowing that you know something the writer does not.

But even if it doesn't provide a moisture-proof seal, browning is useful in meat cookery. When you cook any food over a very high heat without liquid, chemical reactions take place in the surface portion which gets exposed to the high temperature. The reactions are complex, but in practical terms what you need to know is that they change the flavour and texture of the food. Browned meat tastes different and feels different to the bite. It is tougher and often crunchier than unbrowned. It looks appetizing, with a colour that can range from deep brown to solid black. And it tastes delicious, at least to meat eaters. So even if browning isn't needed for sealing, it may still be worth doing for gastronomic reasons. Here is the basic browning technique, if you don't already know it:

> Heat some oil in a thick, heavy frying pan or casserole, or in a wok if you use one. If you have a nonstick frying pan, the oil may be omitted – especially if the meat itself is fairly fatty. Just use a somewhat lower heat or you may damage the nonstick coating. Pat the meat dry with kitchen towels to remove excess surface moisture (which will slow down the browning process).
>
> When the oil (or pan) is very hot, put in the meat and step back: there will probably be some splattering. Let the meat fry over this high heat for a minute or so, then check to see if it needs turning. It needs turning when it has reached a deep, caramel-brown colour. Don't let it blacken deeply, but don't worry if it's black in spots. Keep cooking till the meat is browned all over, or as near to this ideal as possible, then transfer it to your casserole.

Incidentally, you may get as impatient as I do with recipes that tell you to 'brown the meat all over'. This is fine with cubes or with a cylindrical joint of beef, but with irregularly shaped cuts like a leg of lamb or chicken pieces it is impossible. Don't worry if the meat doesn't get uniformly 'browned all over'. Just give it your best shot.

BROWNING CUBES OR CHUNKS

When you're using the meat in chunks, browning is a little more difficult as it must be done in an uncrowded pan. If the pan is too crowded, the temperature in the pan will fall and the meat will take longer to brown. More important, close proximity will cause the meat to cook partly in steam rather than in the ferocious heat of the pan bottom.

Apart from that, it's simple. Follow the instructions above but:

add the meat, enough pieces at a time to keep them at least 2 in apart. Don't move them around for at least 1 minute after putting them in, as the surface may stick to the pan and get torn.

STOVETOP OR OVEN?

Meat can be braised either on top of the stove or in the oven, and there's something to be said for both methods. **Stovetop** cooking makes it easier to monitor the progress of your dish, and to adjust the heat if necessary. It also eliminates stooping and lifting everytime you want to have a look at the dish. (This is no joke if you have a dodgy back, as so many people do nowadays.) **Oven** cooking frees up space on the hob for other dishes. It also, more importantly, provides a uniform, all-over heat: the dish is heated not just from underneath but from the sides and the top. This may produce slightly more even results, and will prevent sticking.

In the end result, there is little to choose between the two. If you are going to cook on the stove, however, there is one important rule to remember:

use a low heat

so the dish doesn't cook too energetically. The liquid should simmer gently rather than boil rapidly – small bubbles rising to the surface in what appears to be a leisurely, lazy manner are the sign of correct heat. If you are cooking in the oven, use a medium- to medium-hot temperature. I usually use

180°C (350°F, Gas 4)

and that is the temperature on which all timings in this chapter are based. If you use a lower or higher heat, the timings will have to be adjusted. This is somewhat tedious, but it's nothing you can't master given a little experience. But the difference in terms of results will not actually be all that great. Remember, braising is an eminently forgiving cooking method. When I'm in a hurry, I sometimes braise at the very un-gentle temperature of 230°C (450°F, Gas 8), and while the results can be somewhat tougher than you get with a gentler heat, no one has complained yet. To begin with, however, try to use 180°C (350°F, Gas 4) as your braising benchmark.

SERVING A BRAISE

I've already mentioned that many braised meats are even better
if you cook them in advance and then reheat them. Needless to
say, this makes them a good bet for dinner parties. The hard,
dirty work is done in advance and final preparations are just a
matter of heating and serving. To serve, slice the meat and lay it
on a big platter, then make a healthy border of any vegetables
you've cooked with the meat and spoon some of the braising
liquid over the whole assemblage.

When you know you're going to be reheating a braised dish,
it's easier and often better to let the meat cool and slice it. Then
you put the slices back in the liquid before reheating. The
liquid gets more opportunity to permeate the flesh this way,
and your last-minute work is reduced even further.

DEGREASING

Removing the meat from the braising liquid makes it easier to
perform a simple but essential task: degreasing. This refers to
the removal of the rendered fat that rises to the top of the
liquid. The quantity of fat will depend on how lean the meat is,
and how much fat you've removed during trimming. If you're
not going to let the braise cool and then reheat it, this step
should be carried out before reducing or serving.

There are several degreasing techniques. By far the easiest is
to use a special jug or gravy boat, designed for this purpose,
with at least one spout fed through a channel leading directly to
the bottom of the vessel. The fat, which rises to the top, is left
behind and can then be discarded. These are widely available,
and a good investment.

If you don't have one of these contraptions, you can use a
ladle. Remove the meat from the liquid and wait for the fat to
rise to the top. Stick the ladle into the liquid gently, just until
the fat starts to seep into the bowl of the ladle. When the ladle is
full, pour the fat into a clean jug or bowl. Repeat this process as
many times as you have patience for, until most of the fat is
gone.

A variant on the ladling method, even easier in some
respects, is to transfer the cooking liquid to a clear jug or bottle

with a fairly narrow neck. This concentrates the fat in a deeper layer and makes it easier to get to.

Yet another method is to refrigerate the liquid, wait till the fat has hardened, and pull it off in a neat block. The problem here is that you won't always have time to refrigerate the liquid. Also, I personally have rarely found that the fat comes away with the surgical ease described by other cookery writers.

A final method is to lay paper towels on top of the liquid. These soak up and retain the fat while any adhering liquid falls away. I don't like this method because it uses up half the paper towels in the house, and seems much more time-consuming than any other method. But it is useful for getting out the very last vestiges of fat.

LAMB

The first recipes here are for a whole boned shoulder of lamb, which happens to be my favourite braise (and one of my favourite dishes of any description). Do bear in mind, however, that the techniques and flavourings suggested for lamb – as well as the variants that follow – are appropriate to beef and pork as well.

Braised Shoulder of Lamb

1 tbsp vegetable or olive oil
a shoulder of lamb weighing 1.25–2 kg (2½–4 lb) (boned weight)
2 cloves of garlic, chopped in half
a bay leaf
whatever herbs you want
a 400 g (14 oz) tin of tomatoes, roughly chopped
225 ml (8 fl oz) good stock, or more as needed
a squirt of tomato purée
100 ml (4 fl oz) dry vermouth, or white or red wine

Preheat the oven to 180°C (350°F, Gas 4). Heat the oil in a casserole and brown the meat all over, then add the remaining ingredients. There should be enough liquid to come about half-way up the meat. If there isn't, add more stock and/or wine.

Now put the casserole in at the top of the oven and cook for 90 minutes, turning every half-hour. The dish should now be done.

It's hard to overcook this dish when you follow these instructions. If the joint is on the larger side, the meat will be on the rare side, which is fine: if it's smaller, it will be more well-done. This too is fine. Moreover, the dish will also be perfectly acceptable if you fall asleep watching TV and cook it for an extra half-hour; or even an extra hour, as long as you don't mind that the meat is falling apart. (Indeed, some people like it better this way.) And again, it is even better, like most braised meats, when cooled off and reheated the next day.

If you like, sliced onions make a good addition to this dish at the cost of around 2 minutes' extra work. Use them in any quantity you like, up to 500 g (1 lb) or so, and brown them in the casserole after the meat has finished browning. (Remove the meat to a separate plate while browning the onions.) To simplify your life, you can also simply add the onions with the remaining ingredients. They will cook to limp rags by the time the cooking is finished, but never mind: they add flavour to the liquid and make a pleasantly gooey side dish for the meat.

But onions are just the beginning of what you can do with a braised shoulder of lamb. This is a dish that can be improved in a hundred different ways, and with little extra fuss. Here are just a few of the possibilities.

Braised Lamb with Balsamic Vinegar and Herbes de Provence

This makes excellent use of two of my 'all-purpose ingredients' (see pages 338 and 344). For the wine in the braising liquid, substitute:

50 ml (2 fl oz) ruby port
50 ml (2 fl oz) balsamic vinegar

For the herbs use:

1 tbsp herbes de Provence (see page 338)

And proceed as in the master recipe.

Braised Lamb with Rice

When the meat has been cooking for 1 hour, put in enough rice to fill a measuring cup to

225 ml (8 fl oz)

Add around the same quantity of stock or water and stir in well to blend. Set the timer for 15 minutes. When it goes off, stir the rice and add more liquid if needed. Check again after 15 minutes. It should almost be done at this point. You should try to check every 5 minutes if it's still not done, but don't worry if your mother rings or there's something on the radio that you can't tear yourself away from. It's hard to overcook this dish.

Braised Lamb with Vegetables

If you're feeling truly lazy, you can use the basic braising technique to produce a one-dish meal containing one or more vegetables. The vegetables will flavour the cooking liquid and absorb flavour from the basic ingredient. And because the meat cooks for a long time, you can add vegetables at different points in the cooking process so that each of them is cooked just the way you want it. Here is a table of *approximate* cooking times for an assortment of vegetables. But see my plea below for separate cooking of the vegetables.

> **Large carrots**: add after 45 minutes
> **Small carrots** : add after 60 minutes
> **Courgettes**, cut into 2in lengths: add after 75 minutes
> **Whole or halved button mushrooms**: add after 75 minutes
> **Whole medium onions** (around 2 in in diameter), topped and tailed but not peeled: add after 45 minutes
> **Small turnips**, peeled but left whole: add after 75 minutes

Whole small parsnips, halved: add after 45 minutes
New potatoes (small): add after 60 minutes
New potatoes (large): add after 45 minutes
Main crop potatoes (large): add after 45 minutes

Note that main crop potatoes, or any potatoes of the floury variety, may tend to break apart during cooking. Waxy types or new potatoes are preferable for this type of cooking.

Note also that I have said you should add vegetables, except those intended primarily to flavour the cooking liquid, fairly late in the cooking process. This complicates life somewhat, but it is important. Vegetables cooked in simmering liquid for long periods will lose all their flavour to the liquid and fall apart. They will not be disgusting, but neither will they be worth eating on their own merits.

This is why I usually prefer another technique altogether: cooking the vegetables separately and adding them to the braised meat for the last stage of cooking. Most of the braised meat dishes I make are served on their own, with vegetables cooked and presented separately. This makes life even more difficult for lazy cooks. It also flies in the face of the popular image of a steaming casserole stuffed with various items to form a one-dish meal. But it has the distinct advantage of being superior to most of those dishes. Moreover, while cooking meats and vegetables together may seem the laziest of procedures, it requires precisely the kind of careful timing that we lazy cooks are anxious to avoid.

There's no question that separate cooking does take a little more work. For one thing, it means you're going to have more pots and pans to wash up. But the results really are better. If you check out the classic braise recipes in Julia Child's great *Mastering the Art of French Cooking*, you will see that she follows this technique; the vegetables are cooked in butter and stock and then added to the braise for the last few minutes only.

There are two ways of approaching the separate cooking of vegetables. One is to braise them (see page 162) to completion and then add them to the main dish just a few minutes before serving. This has the advantage of allowing complete control over the vegetables, and has a lot to recommend it. The other approach is to half-cook them, either by braising, stir-frying, or *à l'étuvée* (see page 157), and add them for the final half-hour or so of cooking. I've used both techniques to good effect, and you should do whichever fits in with your schedule.

Braised Lamb with Beans

Dried beans make one of the classic combinations with braised lamb. This dish is French in origin, so that types such as flageolets are preferred when braising beans with lamb. But dried butter beans, kidney beans, or Italian cannelini beans are also good. Red kidney beans are least attractive from the visual point of view, but lazy cooks place good eating and convenient cooking over matters of presentation. If you can find only red beans, use them. And incidentally, this would be just as good if you substituted pork for the lamb. (See page 71 for a bean recipe that's tailor-made for pork.)

Presoak

250 g (8 oz) dried beans

overnight or preboil them for 1 hour and drain. (Dried beans double their weight, approximately, in soaking.) You could also, if you're pressed for time, use

500 g (1 lb) tinned beans

This is easier, if somewhat more expensive.

Prepare the meat for cooking as described in the master recipe. Drain the beans well and add to the lamb at the very beginning of cooking.

BEEF

What you can do with lamb you can also do with beef. Indeed, you could substitute a piece of topside or top rib for the shoulder of lamb in most of the recipes above and they would be just as good.

Moreover, with beef there are other possibilities. Some people love cold lamb, but in my view it is not very appetizing.

Braised beef is better for serving cold, and is often done that way in French cuisine. The recipe that follows is a simplified version of the classic French *boeuf braisé*.

Braised Beef, Hot or Cold

When this dish is served cold it benefits from the presence of a wonderfully flavoured jelly produced by the pig's foot. Serve it with a *salsa verde* (see page 325) if you wish to. Whether you're serving it hot or cold, make it the day before.

a 2.25 kg (4½ lb) piece of brisket or shin of beef, boned and tied
500 ml (18 fl oz) red or white wine
2 bay leaves
4 large sprigs of parsley
4 cloves of garlic, roughly chopped
1 tsp herbes de Provence (see page 338)
1 large onion, roughly chopped
2 carrots, roughly chopped
2 celery stalks, roughly chopped
1 whole clove
plenty of salt and pepper
If serving cold: 2 pig's trotters; or a 6 in square section of skin from a joint of
*   pork*

Place the meat in a heavy casserole just large enough to hold it and add the remaining ingredients (except the trotters or skin, if using). Marinate it for as many hours as you can be bothered; overnight in the fridge is ideal. Turn it a few times, as the mood takes you, to let the marinade come into contact with as much of the meat as possible.

When you're ready to cook, preheat the oven to 180°C (350°F, Gas 4). You can now brown the meat if you want to get serious; I often skip it. To brown the meat, remove it from the marinade and dry it well on paper towels before proceeding as described for lamb above (page 53). If you're going to serve the dish cold, add the trotters or skin to the casserole along with enough water barely to cover the meat. Bring it to a boil, then cover and place it in the oven. Now sit back and relax: the cooking will look after itself. The dish will be done in anywhere from 3–4 hours, and by this I really do mean that it will be done whether you take it out after 3 hours or after 4. All you need to do is check it once or twice to make sure the meat is still well covered by liquid.

If serving cold, remove the meat from the casserole and put it on a platter; cover it with aluminium foil and let it cool, then put it in the fridge overnight. Meanwhile, strain the cooking liquid into a clean bowl. This may be done through a fine strainer, but using muslin (cheesecloth) will produce a clearer jelly. Let the liquid cool and put it in the fridge. The next day, just before serving, lift the solidified fat off the top of the bowl and serve the jelly – which will be delicious – with the thinly-sliced meat.

If serving hot, remove the meat from the casserole and degrease the cooking liquid (i.e. remove the fat) as thoroughly as possible. Return the meat to the casserole, if not serving immediately, and let it sit in a cool spot till needed. (Unless the weather is exceptionally warm, it should be perfectly safe left overnight in the kitchen.) Forty minutes before serving, pick off any noticeable globs of fat and bring the dish back up to a simmer over a gentle heat. Let it simmer for half an hour, then slice as thin as possible and serve with the cooking liquid as a gravy.

To make the gravy more concentrated in flavour you may remove the meat to a platter, then bring the liquid to a rapid boil and boil it away as far as you feel like. You may also thicken it with

1–2 tbsp cornstarch, arrowroot or flour

Take a few spoonfuls of liquid from the casserole, whisk into the starch till well blended, then return to the casserole. I personally think this is unnecessary, but it does keep the sauce from slopping about quite so freely.

Braised Beef with Chinese Flavours

A delightful surprise to most people. Make it exactly like the Braised Beef above, but with the following flavourings:

4 cloves of garlic
4 thick slices of peeled fresh ginger
1 large onion, roughly chopped
2 carrots, roughly chopped
2 celery stalks, roughly chopped
1 whole piece of star anise
1 tsp Sichuan peppercorns (optional)
110 ml (4 fl oz) soy sauce
225 ml (8 fl oz) dry sherry or Chinese rice wine
50 ml (2 fl oz) oyster sauce
1 dried red chili (optional)

Some chopped fresh coriander adds a nice touch to this dish. Sprinkle it on to the slices on the platter, or on to each plate, before serving.

Braised Beef with Italian Flavours

Again, proceed as in the basic Braised Beef recipe but use these ingredients for the marinade:

500 ml (18 fl oz) red or white wine
2 bay leaves
4 large sprigs of parsley
4 cloves of garlic, roughly chopped
1 large onion, roughly chopped
2 carrots, roughly chopped
2 celery stalks, roughly chopped
1 tsp dried oregano
a 400 g (14 oz) tin of Italian plum tomatoes

Braised Topside of Beef

Many people regard topside as a roasting joint, but I personally have never understood this. Roast beef should be tender, and topside is fairly tough stuff – lean and stringy. It does have an excellent flavour, however, which lends itself to braising. Because it's half-way in the toughness stakes between true roasting joints and the cheapest cuts like brisket, it needs less cooking time than brisket. And being more expensive than brisket, it's best for small dinner parties where you want a reasonably hefty dose of elegance.

Here's an extravagant braise that I serve on those occasions. The cost isn't all that much higher than for a regular braise, apart from the cut of beef plus the wine and Cognac. But it does take more time, and extravagance with time, for lazy cooks, is just as important as extravagance with cash. Be comforted by the knowledge that if this looks time-consuming, you ought to see the superb recipe on which it's based: the *boeuf braisé* in Julia Child's *Mastering the Art of French Cooking*. My version is slimmed down from the original, and by quite a margin. Please note that it should be started at least 24 hours in advance – but it can also be completed in advance and then reheated when the gang arrives. The juniper berry and clove, though listed as optional, are a very nice addition to the marinade.

a 1.5–2 kg (3–4 lb) piece of topside, or of rolled top rib
2 large carrots
1 or 2 stalks of celery
1 large onion
2 large cloves of garlic
5 peppercorns, lightly crushed
1 juniper berry (optional)
1 whole clove (optional)
100 ml (4 fl oz) Cognac or Armagnac or Calvados
100 ml (4 fl oz) extra virgin olive oil
a 75 cl bottle of red wine

Put the beef in a very large bowl or in the casserole in which you'll be cooking it. Peel the carrots and slice them around ⅛ in thick with the celery and onion; add to the bowl or casserole. Give the garlic cloves a good whack with a large knife, so they're roughly crushed, and add to the bowl or casserole. Put in all the remaining ingredients and leave to marinate for a minimum of 6 hours (if cooking that day) or preferably overnight. If leaving overnight, refrigerate or put outside (assuming that the weather is good and cold). If the beef isn't fully covered, turn it at least once during marination.

Two hours before you're ready to cook, bring the beef back to room temperature (if necessary). Remove from the marinade, let it drain for a minute, then pat thoroughly dry with paper towels. Heat a frying pan or grill pan till very hot, and add around

1 tbsp vegetable oil

Brown the meat as well as you can on all sides. Pour in the marinade, bring to the boil, and cook for 2–3 hours as described above.

BEEF IN PIECES: A BASIC BEEF STEW

I must confess that beef stews, except in their most sophisticated French incarnations, are not my favourite dishes. Julia Child sums up my objections succinctly: 'The better the meat, the better the stew.' And the beef sold in Britain as 'stewing meat' is never, in my experience, either choice or well butchered. I know many people love them, and normally I try to accommodate everyone's taste. But what the hell, this is my book.

So my basic beef stew recipe is for oxtail, and this is something that I *am* crazy about. Oxtail has tremendous depth of flavour, and the cartilage-rich bones give an oxtail braise a melting, tender succulence which is rarely found in ordinary beef stew. Naturally this recipe can be used for chunks of beef off the bone. But it's much better with oxtail. If you haven't discovered the joys of this cheap, delicious cut, do something about it soon. You'll never look at beef stew in the same way again.

Remember that while whole pieces of meat do not need to be browned before braising, cubed meat is much better if browned. This takes a few extra minutes but it's worth it.

Braised Oxtail with Red Wine

1 oxtail around 1.5 kg (3 lb) in weight
100 ml (4 fl oz) beef stock
a 400 g (14 oz) tin of tomatoes
8 cloves of garlic, separated but unpeeled
200 ml (7 fl oz) red wine
stock to cover

Oxtail often has a lot of fat, if the butcher hasn't made the effort to trim it away. You may want to trim it off. On the other hand, it's easier to leave the fat on and remove it by skimming when the dish is cooked. Also, if you leave the fat on you can do the browning without extra oil or fat: heat a nonstick frying pan over a low heat, and put in the oxtail pieces with at least 1in between them. Let some of the fat render out and turn up the heat so the meat browns briskly. Turn each piece when it's browned on the bottom and repeat the process till it's browned all over. Put the browned pieces in your casserole and continue till the rest are done.

Now preheat the oven to 180°C (350°F, Gas 4) and put the remaining ingredients in the casserole. The stock should be added in quantities just sufficient barely to cover the meat; you can top it up as needed. Bring it to the boil, turn down the heat to a simmer, and let it cook for an hour. Give it all a good stir and cook for another hour. Stir again. Because oxtail is a very tough cut (just think of all that swinging and fly-swatting), this will need a good 3–4 hours in the oven. But the results are worth it.

TIMING FOR CUBES OF BEEF

Oxtail, being very tough stuff, takes somewhat longer to cook than cubes of so-called braising steak. At these temperatures, you should start testing cubes of beef at

2 hours

and 3 hours should be the most that's needed.

Braising beef pays off in unexpected ways. The day after you've eaten the oxtail dish above, you will be left with a thick, densely flavoured liquid which reaps rich dividends. To wit:

Braised Leeks in Oxtail Gravy

Trim and slice in half lengthwise:

2–3 large leeks

Keep the halves intact, as they will be tied with string after cleaning. Rinse them well under cold water, put the two halves together again, and then tie them up with kitchen string. For ease of serving, they can be cut into 3 in lengths (each length tied with string). Put the leeks in the casserole with the gravy and bring to the boil, then turn down the heat and let them simmer very gently – turning occasionally to prevent sticking – for 30–40 minutes. These are as good cold as they are hot – and they're pretty good hot. For more detail about braising vegetables, see page 162.

The next day, the gravy will still be there. Now's the time to turn it into a pasta sauce.

Pasta with Oxtail Gravy

Shred any leftover meat and/or leeks and heat with the gravy over a very gentle flame while you boil

250 g (8 oz) penne or fusilli

until barely cooked. Drain well, then toss in the hot gravy for a minute or so, to let the pasta absorb the gravy well. Serve immediately with grated Parmesan. This is just about as good as any purpose-made pasta sauce you can think of.

There: three dishes for the effort of one. This is the essence of lazy cooking. And the same thing can be done if you braise beef in a whole piece. Lazy cooks never throw anything away – they recycle it.

Another nifty recycling trick for leftover braising liquid is to use it as a sauce for other dishes. Strain the liquid if necessary and reduce it (if you feel energetic) till it has a concentrated flavour and syrupy texture. Then pour it over any of the following:

plainly cooked vegetables
plainly cooked fish
plainly cooked steaks or chops
boiled rice or potatoes

This is a totally painless way of adding depth and character to an everyday dish.

Embellishing a Beef Stew

There are so many variations on this simple theme that I could list them all day. Here are just a few of them.

Braised Beef as a One-dish Meal

The ultimate in lazy cooking. While the beef is bubbling, wash and prepare any 3 of these vegetables:

8–12 new potatoes
2 large carrots (peeled and cut into 2 in lengths)
3 medium leeks (peeled and cut into 2 in lengths)
4 medium turnips (peeled and chopped into 2 in chunks)
250 g (8 oz) Brussels sprouts
250 g (8 oz) green cabbage

Add them to the casserole after

2–3 hours

and continue cooking for another 30–45 minutes or so, until the vegetables are well cooked but not falling apart.

Beef Stew with Rice

If you happen to have some leftover rice lying around, you can use it up by adding it to braised beef. Use

250 g (8 oz) cooked rice

and add it around 10 minutes before you serve. The rice need do nothing more than heat through, so it doesn't need any more time than that.

Braised Beef with Balsamic Vinegar

For the beef stock, substitute an equal amount (100 ml/4 fl oz) of balsamic vinegar. This is one of the best braises I've ever made.

Braised Beef with Mushrooms

Clean and trim

250 g (8 oz) fresh mushrooms or
50 g (2 oz) dried black mushrooms which have been soaked in hot water and cleaned

and add them to the casserole. Return to the oven and cook till the mushrooms are just done – around 20–30 minutes.

Braised Beef with Olives

A simplification of a French classic. Put in:

100–150 g (4–6 oz) stoned green olives, preferably French or Italian olives with a herb and garlic flavour

and continue cooking. You can cook the olives for as little as 30 minutes or as much as a couple of hours. Longer cooking times will make them disintegrate somewhat, but the flavour will still be there. I personally prefer them to be cooked for around 45 minutes.

Sweet and Sour Braised Beef

This isn't a Chinese dish but an ultra-simple liquid for giving a rich, deep tang to braised beef. For around 1 kg (2 lb) of beef, use as braising liquid:

200 ml (around 7 fl oz) ruby port
50 ml (around 2 fl oz) wine vinegar
400–500 ml (14–18 fl oz) stock
1–2 tsp sugar

Beef Stew Like Chili con Carne

This one deserves a recipe of its own because it's somewhat more elaborate and unusual. We all know the dreary chili con carne of substandard pub lunches, but this version is delicious and precisely seasoned. I owe the inspiration to the Thundering Herd Buffalo Tail Chili served at Tarantula Jack's of Seattle, Washington, a winner in the World Cook-off of the International Chili Society. Tarantula Jack's recipe would not use beans, but they're swell in this version. You could just as easily use chunks of beef, or even mince if you insist.

2 kg (4 lb) oxtail
2 medium Spanish onions, grated
2 large cloves of garlic, minced
800 ml (28 fl oz) chicken stock (2 cubes will do fine)
two 400 g (14 oz) cans plain tomato sauce
7 tbsp mild chili powder
2 tbsp ground cumin
250 g (8 oz) presoaked kidney beans
½ tsp cayenne pepper

Brown the oxtail as in the master recipe and transfer to the casserole. Cook the onions and garlic gently in the pan, then add to the casserole with all the remaining ingredients except the beans and cayenne pepper. Cook gently, covered, for 3 hours. Add the beans and continue cooking for another 45 minutes. Add the cayenne and cook for another 15 minutes or so. Serve with rice and some cold beer.

The next recipe is somewhat Spanish in inspiration, with a rich liquid coloured and scented by saffron. You could use white wine instead of sherry, but sherry tastes much better.

Beef Stew with Saffron and Orange

2 kg (4 lb) oxtail
1 tbsp extra virgin olive oil
4 large cloves of garlic, halved
1 medium onion
1 carrot
500 ml (18 fl oz) beef or chicken stock (a cube will do fine)
225 ml (8 fl oz) dry (fino) sherry
1 large strip of orange peel
1 very large pinch of saffron, rubbed to a powder
2 bay leaves
1 good squirt of tomato purée

Brown the oxtail and transfer to the casserole. In the same frying pan, heat the oil and quickly brown the garlic, onion and carrot. Add to the casserole with the remaining ingredients, bring to the boil, then turn the heat right down and simmer gently for 3–4 hours, as in the master recipe. Serve with rice and braised or charred cabbage.

PORK

Most people think of pork for roasting or quick cooking (e.g. grilling or stir-frying). It *is* good for those methods but it's also a good braiser, especially when you use one of the cheaper 'red' cuts – not the expensive loin and leg but hand, shoulder, or belly. These are just as flavourful – more flavourful, in my book – and they are much better suited to long, slow cooking.

All the braising ideas on the preceding pages for lamb and beef can easily be adapted for use with pork. I have therefore given fewer pork recipes than lamb and beef recipes, and have confined myself to some of the dishes that I've made using pork with particularly notable success.

The chief difference between pork braises and those using other red meats is that pork will not, on the whole, need quite as much cooking time. Since this may come as a surprise to people who think pork needs more cooking than anything else, I'll explain it quickly.

Pork needs less braising time for two reasons. One is that the micro-organisms called *trichinae* – which cause the illness trichinosis – are killed at a fairly low temperature, when the meat is still rare. But we like pork to be cooked till any trace of pink is removed, so that's no problem. The other reason is that most pork joints used for braising are in themselves very tender, and therefore do not need the long cooking that you would need, say, for brisket or braising steak.

There are numerous pork braises in French, Italian and Chinese cuisine; in one way or another, these have inspired most of my favourite approaches to the problem. Julia Child's *Mastering the Art of French Cooking* gives a recipe in which pork is marinated in a 'dry' marinade, and this too is stunning. And perhaps the best of all is Marcella Hazan's recipe for pork braised in milk. Hazan notes that this idea sounds peculiar to many people, but she also notes that it's delicious – and she's right. I have given a few of my variations on the theme below.

Before proceeding any further, however, I have to warn you that braised pork lacks one dimension that many British eaters consider indispensable: crackling. I too love good crackling, and I eat it as greedily as anyone when it's placed before me. But British eaters are virtually *unique au monde* in insisting on crackling with their pork: Chinese cuisine prefers to render the skin slowly till it's melting and gelatinous. French cooks remove it from the pork and use it for adding texture and body to other braised meats. You can use either method, but try it at least once with the skin on. The skin is truly luxurious, and you can cut it off the underlying fat. In any case, once you've eaten good braised pork, you won't miss the crackling.

If you leave the skin on, you can't really brown the joint all over: the skin wouldn't brown, and it would tend to stick even in a well-oiled pan. This means that the dish is not an authentic braise, since braising always involves browning, but who cares?

Here is the simplest pork braise I know, and one of the best. It uses some of the wonderfully fragrant spices of Indian cooking but leaves them whole, so each mouthful contains little explosions of spice. There is no pork in Indian cooking, so this dish bears no relation to the authentic cuisine of that nation. But it is delicious.

Braised Pork with Whole Indian Spices

a large piece of hand or shoulder of pork, around 1.5 kg (3 lb)
1–2 tbsp vegetable oil (not olive oil)
1 medium leek
1 tsp whole cumin
1 tsp whole fennel
1 tsp whole fenugreek
½ tsp whole coriander
1 bay leaf
1 dried red chili or ½ tsp chili powder
2 cloves of garlic
800 ml (28 fl oz) chicken stock

If the skin has been removed from the joint, heat 1 tbsp of oil in the casserole or in a frying pan and brown the meat as described on page 50. Remove and set aside, and proceed as follows.

Clean the leeks if necessary and cut into 2 in discs. Heat 1 tbsp of oil in the casserole and gently cook the leeks for 1 minute. Add the spices and cook for another minute. Now add the remaining ingredients and bring to the boil. Cover and cook for 1½-2 hours, either on the stove or in a 180°C (350°F, Gas 4) oven.

Pork, like lamb, goes very well with most pulses. The American Pork and Beans is a New England dish of substance, smoothness, and rich, satisfying flavour. Here is a version using a whole piece of pork. It's very satisfying on a cold winter's night, especially if you use belly of pork – the cheapest cut of all. But the flavour will be more authentic if you use a piece of smoked knuckle. Otherwise just substitute bacon as described in the recipe. Like all braises, this can be made well in advance and will improve if it is. And since it's an excellent freezer item, losing nothing in the way of quality, I've given it in large quantities so you can freeze some. This recipe will easily serve 8–10 people. Be warned: it is very sweet, and not to everyone's taste. If you don't like the idea, reduce the amount of sugar and/or syrup, or add a few tablespoons of wine vinegar to counteract the sweetness.

Pork and Beans, New England Style

500 g (1 lb) dried red or white beans
1 large onion (around 200 g/7 oz)
2 small carrots
3 fat cloves of garlic
4 slices of ginger
300–750 g (10 oz–1½ lb) smoked pork knuckle or 300–750 g (10 oz–1½ lb)
  belly of pork and 125 g (4 oz) smoked bacon
1 tsp whole cumin
1 tsp dried thyme
50 g (2 oz) demerara sugar (enough to fill a measuring cup to the 100 ml mark)
200 ml (7 fl oz) maple syrup or golden syrup
30 ml (2 tbsp) Worcester sauce

Soak the beans in water overnight, or for at least 8 hours. If you're pressed for time, you can boil them unsoaked for 1 hour, let them sit for another hour, and then drain well. Chop the onion, carrots, garlic and ginger; this can be done as fine or as coarse as you fancy, and is easiest in a food processor. Put everything in a large casserole and add enough water or stock (from a cube will do fine) to cover the beans and pork. You will need around 1 litre (2 pints) of liquid.

The dish is now ready for cooking, and here the lazy cook has a particularly easy ride. You can do the cooking relatively quickly, say for

3–4 hours at 180°C (350°F, Gas 4) or
2–3 hours at 200°C (400°F, Gas 6)

The dish is done when the beans are good and soft, and the meat is fork-tender.

An even easier alternative is to do the cooking at a very low temperature for a very long time. The last time I made Pork and Beans I cooked them as follows:

overnight (12 hours exactly) at 140°C (275°F, Gas 1)

followed by

2 hours at 180°C (350°F, Gas 4)

I love the slow method because (a) all the flavours really have a chance to get to know each other, (b) it's so ridiculously simple, and (c) the latitude is so generous. Using the slow method makes it impossible to overcook pork and beans – and it's nearly impossible even using the faster method.

The cuisines of China, where pork is cheaper yet more highly valued than almost any other meat, probably do more great things with the stuff than any other of the world's great cuisines. One of my favourites for home cooking is Red-cooked Pork, so called because the cooking liquid contains soy sauce. Here is a simplified version. I find that this works better on the hob than in the oven, so that's the technique specified in the recipe. To do it in the oven, follow the cooking times given for Braised Pork with Whole Indian Spices (above, page 70). This is not a true braise, as the pork isn't browned first – but that makes it easier, so who cares about definitions. NB: if you leave the skin on, it will end up being gelatinously succulent. Some people don't like this, but it's delicious.

Red-cooked Pork

a large piece of hand or shoulder of pork, around 1.5 kg (3 lb)
225 ml (8 fl oz) soy sauce
110 ml (4 fl oz) dry sherry
3 cloves of garlic
3 thick slices of ginger
1 piece of star anise, 1 tsp five-spice powder, or (failing those two) 1 small stick of
   cinnamon

Put the pork in a heavy casserole and add cold water to cover by an inch or so. Put it on the hob over a high heat, adding the other ingredients in the meantime. When the liquid has come to a boil, turn the heat right down and put the lid on so the pot

is half-covered. It can now cook almost without further attention other than the occasional peek to make sure the liquid is
still covering the pork (or nearly covering it). If necessary, turn
the meat once to ensure that every bit gets cooked. The cooking
time is generously flexible. Figure on:

1½–2½ hours at a gentle simmer

This dish needs nothing more than plain boiled rice and some
plain vegetables to accompany. Charred French beans would be
a good bet.

Finally, here is a recipe for belly of pork. Belly has long been
one of my favourite cuts of pork, not only for its low cost but for
its excellent flavour and texture. You can grill it or fry it, but
because it has a lot of toughish connective tissue, it is a prime
choice for braising. And it doesn't need to be browned first, so
it's good when you're feeling lazier than usual. Look for lean
pieces cut around 1 in thick, but be warned: even lean belly of
pork is fairly rich stuff, and not for people who are trying to
lose weight. You could just as easily make this dish with pork
shoulder, hand or leg cut in 1 in strips, but I do think that belly
is best. This recipe serves 4.

Braised Belly of Pork with Whole Shallots

You could use cloves of garlic or small onions instead of
shallots. (You could also use shallots *and* garlic, if you're not
worried about your breath.) Just remember to top and tail
them, but do not peel.

500 g (1 lb) belly of pork
8–10 shallots (around 250 g/8 oz)
around 400 ml (14 fl oz) chicken stock
around 100 ml (4 fl oz) dry white wine
1 heaped tsp dried rosemary

Preheat the oven to 180°C (350°F, Gas 4). Cut the strips of meat
in pieces around 3 in long and put them in a single layer in a
casserole or roasting pan. Top and tail the shallots and/or cloves

of garlic or onions, and add to the pan. Pour in just enough stock to cover the meat, plus the seasonings. Cover the casserole with its lid or the roasting pan with aluminium foil, and bake for 1½–2 hours. Try to do some careful skimming here: belly of pork tends to be very fatty.

The same recipe can be used for chicken breasts (30 minutes), chicken legs (40 minutes), or long strips of shoulder of lamb (40 minutes). Serve with mashed or boiled potatoes.

RABBIT

There are two kinds of rabbit, and they need very different forms of treatment. Farmed rabbit is pale, delicate, and fairly tender. Wild rabbit is tougher, darker, and much more substantial both to the tooth and to the palate. It needs longer cooking than farmed, but this makes it well suited to braising: the long, slow cooking will soften up those tough, lean muscle fibres and produce a reasonably succulent main course. Though not a great rabbit fan myself, I can see its attractions for people who really like braised meats.

   If you have the opportunity to buy rabbit in pieces rather than a whole beast, jointed, take it. The leg quarters are much more tender than the rest of the animal, and you get a higher proportion of meat to bone. Here is a rabbit braise based on a French classic. Note that I've included a little flour to thicken the gravy; you can skip this if you want.

Rabbit with Prunes (Lapin aux Pruneaux)

8 haunches of rabbit
1 tbsp plain flour (optional)
1 large onion
1 tsp herbes de Provence (see page 338)
1 clove of garlic
1 bay leaf
300 ml (10 fl oz) beef stock
200 ml (7 fl oz) red wine
250 g (8 oz) prunes, pitted if you feel like it

Clean the haunches and remove any stray bits of fur. Heat around 1 tbsp vegetable oil in a frying or grill pan and brown the rabbit as evenly as possible on all sides; you may not be able to brown every inch of meat because the joints are so irregular in shape. Remove to the casserole and top up the oil in the pan if necessary. Cook the flour for a few seconds, then add the onion, herbs, garlic, and bay leaf. Brown well and add a little water to dislodge all the bits sticking to the pan. Pour into the casserole and add the stock and wine. Bring to the boil, and cook in the oven or on the hob for 1½ hours. Now add the prunes and cook for another half-hour or so, till the prunes are soft.

Rabbit also goes well with green olives in a lighter sauce. This recipe is based on one for sautéed rabbit in Patricia Wells's *Bistro Cooking*, though it differs in cooking the rabbit for a longer time. If you're using farmed rabbit, the cooking time will be closer to the 30 minutes specified by the estimable Ms Wells.

Braised Rabbit with Olives

8 haunches of rabbit
1 tbsp plain flour (optional)
1 large onion
1 tsp herbes de Provence (see page 338)
2 cloves of garlic
1 bay leaf
300 ml (10 fl oz) chicken or vegetable stock
100 ml (4 fl oz) dry sherry or white wine
250 g (8 oz) pitted green olives

Prepare and begin cooking as for Rabbit with Prunes, with the rabbit, sliced onion, and flavourings all going in at the same time. While the dish is cooking, cut the olives in quarters. After 1½ hours, test the rabbit by poking it with a fork. If the muscle tissue still feels very tough, let it cook for another 30–45 minutes before adding the olives. When the flesh is soft enough to separate easily, add the olives and continue cooking for another 30 minutes. This dish goes well with a gratin or with plain boiled rice or noodles.

CHICKEN

I have problems with long-cooked poultry. My idea of proper treatment for most birds is to cook them as briefly as possible, so that every bit of their natural juices is retained intact. Needless to say, braising represents the antithesis of this approach.

But if the bird is chicken, and specifically either the wings or the thighs, I am willing to make exceptions. Both these items take well to long cooking, and they can be absolutely delicious.

Wings especially are a peerless braiser. They're just as good after 45 minutes of cooking as they are after 2 hours, and their flavour seems to bear out the old saying that 'the closer to the bone, the sweeter the meat'. If you find some cheap wings in suitably large quantities, snap them up without delay: they're an excellent choice for a large, informal dinner party. I specify informal because chicken wings must be eaten with the fingers, so you won't want to serve them to your grandmother or your boss.

Here is a recipe for braised chicken wings which is inspired by one in the excellent Chinese cookbook by Craig Claiborne and the late Virginia Lee.

Chinese-style Braised Chicken Wings

1.5 kg (3 lb) chicken wings
1 large onion
a 400 g (14 oz) tin of Italian plum tomatoes
3 cloves of garlic
1 dried red chili (or more to taste)
3 thick slices of ginger
2–3 tbsp peanut or vegetable oil
60 ml (4 tbsp) soy sauce
30 ml (2 tbsp) oyster sauce
500 ml (around 18 fl oz) chicken or beef stock
60 ml (4 tbsp) dry sherry or Chinese rice wine
30 ml (2 tbsp) Worcester sauce

Cut off the wing tips and cut the remaining wing at the joint. If you want to, you can use some of the tips to add gelatin and extra flavour to the dish; otherwise, chuck them or save them for stock. Cut the onions in half lengthwise and then into thickish slices (anything from ¼–½ in will do). Coarsely chop the tomatoes and mince the garlic with the chili and ginger.

Get the oil fairly hot in a wok or your casserole, and brown the chicken pieces in batches for around 3–4 minutes per batch. This may take as much as 20–25 minutes, but it's by far the most time-consuming aspect of the cooking. When they're all browned, drain off any remaining oil and put in the garlic, onion, ginger and chili. Stir-fry for a minute or so, just to colour the stuff lightly. Then put in the wings and tomatoes and toss everything well. Add the remaining ingredients, bring to the boil, then turn down the heat and simmer gently for

1–1½ hours

either on the stove or in a 180°C (350°C, Gas 4) oven. This can easily be done well in advance, with the dish left to cool its heels for up to 6 hours and then reheated at the last minute. Serve in bowls, with boiled rice and stir-fried or pan-grilled vegetables on the side.

The dish above can be made in exactly the same way with chicken thighs, though it really is better with wings. If you can't get wings, however, by all means use thighs. Thighs will also taste fine in a European-style braising liquid such as the next one, which is based on one of the great flavour combinations: chicken, garlic and tarragon.

Chicken Thighs with Garlic and Tarragon

2 tbsp extra virgin olive oil
1 kg (2 lb) chicken thighs
4 plump cloves of garlic
110 ml (4 fl oz) dry white wine
110 ml (4 fl oz) chicken or vegetable stock
a few sprigs of fresh tarragon

Heat the oil in a large frying pan or casserole. Brown the thighs in batches of 4 or 5 at a time, then transfer them to a large casserole if you haven't used it for browning. While you're doing this, peel the garlic and chop each clove in 4 pieces. When all the chicken is in the casserole, lightly brown the garlic in the oil and scrape every bit of oil and garlic on to the chicken. Pour in the wine and stock, sprinkle on the tarragon, and cook in the oven or on top of the stove for 45 minutes–1½ hours. If the thighs were very fatty, you might want to degrease the liquid before serving the dish with boiled rice or noodles.

DUCK

Duck too presents problems for the would-be braiser, but the problems are different from those that crop up with chicken. One problem is that it's expensive: a 4–5 lb duck costs at least £5–£7, and it will not easily feed more than 3 people. The other problem is that it's an extremely fatty bird, with most of the fat concentrated under the skin. If you're lucky and skilled enough, you can roast out most of the fat to leave crisp skin and succulent flesh.

When you braise duck, the fat renders out into the braising liquid and the skin does not crisp up. Some people assume that duck has to be crispy, and will be unpleasantly surprised to get one with soft skin. To hell with them. Braised duck is an excellent dish, especially if made with duck legs and a powerfully flavourful braising liquid. I would suggest that you buy 2 whole ducks and cut both legs and breast off the carcass. Use the breasts for pan-grilling (see page 100) or flash-roasting (see page 130). And stick the legs in the freezer till you are ready to cook the following braise, which is one of the most delicious I've ever cooked.

Braised Duck Legs with Apricot and Cinnamon

4 duck legs
1 large onion
1 large clove of garlic
16–20 dried apricots
2 bay leaves
1 tbsp herbes de Provence (see page 338)
a 1 in piece of cinnamon or a large pinch of cinnamon powder
400–450 ml (14–16 fl oz) chicken stock
110 ml (4 fl oz) ruby port

Preheat the oven to 180°C (350°F, Gas 4). In a nonstick frying pan, brown the duck starting with the skin side down and without using extra fat; the duck skin will release copious quantities of the stuff. Brown for 4–5 minutes on the skin side and 2 minutes on the flesh side. Transfer to a casserole, preferably one that will hold the legs in a single layer. Slice the onions and garlic thin, and add to the casserole. Pour some boiled water over the apricots and add to the casserole along with the remaining ingredients. Bring the contents to a boil and put the casserole in the oven. It will need

1½–1¾ hours

at 180°C (350°F, Gas 4), but can be turned off after

1½ hours

and left in the oven for another hour. Eat with new potatoes and some French beans.

PHEASANT

Pheasant is perhaps the best of all birds for braising. Indeed, it is far better cooked in wet surroundings than in the dry heat of an open pan. The duck recipe above would be a good way of proceeding, with the bird browned just as the duck legs are. You could also brown the bird, plonk it into a pot of braised cabbage (see page 165) that's around half-way cooked, and then finish cooking for 45–60 minutes. Or, for something completely different, try this recipe using the venerable combination of pheasant and bacon. Try to get a hen pheasant, which is usually the more tender variety.

Braised Pheasant with Bacon and Fennel

4–5 strips of streaky bacon
1 pheasant, oven ready
2 bulbs of fennel
1 tsp herbes de Provence
150 ml (around 7 fl oz) dry white wine
150 ml (around 7 fl oz) chicken stock

Cut the strips of bacon in half. Put them in a casserole that will accommodate the pheasant, and heat gently for a few minutes till they've released a good-sized slick of fat. Remove from the casserole, turn up the heat a little, and gently brown the pheasant as uniformly as you can manage. In the meantime, trim the fennel and slice it around ½ in thick. When the pheasant is browned, add all the other ingredients to it and bring to the boil. Turn down the heat and simmer gently for

45–60 minutes

turning two or three times. If you wish, you can remove the bird, fennel and bacon at the end of cooking, and reduce the liquid by boiling hard for 3–4 minutes. This dish cries out for mashed potatoes and some charred celery (see page 171).

Pan-Grilling

THE EQUIPMENT

If I could take only one piece of kitchen equipment to a desert island, I would take my grill pan. Of all the pieces of kitchen equipment I've bought in recent years, this is the one I use most – and with most pleasure. Since acquiring it I have found myself using the ordinary grill less and less.

THE DETAILS

A grill pan – sometimes called a griddle – is essentially a frying pan; the cooking action is roughly that of frying. But there are two principal differences. One: pan-grilling is usually done at a fairly high heat whereas frying can use any heat. Two: the bottom of the grill pan is not smooth but ridged. Those parts of the food lying on the ridges get a higher level of heat than those over the troughs, so they are marked with black lines while the rest of the food gets lightly browned or retains its natural colour. By turning the food through an angle of 45° you can make a diamond-shaped crisscross pattern, which looks even better (but is not essential unless you cook in a restaurant). The lines look nice, the browning reactions at the surface make the food taste delicious. And cooking by this method is fast, easy, and fun. What more could a lazy cook ask for?

You can use the grill pan to cook meat, vegetables, or even fruit. There are few better meals – and few that are simpler for lazy cooks to make – than those cooked entirely on a grill pan.

Grill pans are available in a variety of metals, including aluminium, stainless steel, and cast iron. Some have nonstick surfaces, but I strongly advise buying one that's made from cast iron *without* a nonstick coating. Nonstick pans are not suitable for very high heat, which is essential to the kind of cooking described in this chapter. And cast iron, if well preheated, reaches and retains a consistent, steady heat.

The pan should be thick and heavy: thin ones don't allow for good heat control. The one I use is made of cast iron by Le Creuset, better known for their casseroles and pots, and has a single coating of matt black enamel. (This prevents corrosion, to which plain cast-iron cooking materials are subject, and facilitates cleaning.) There are three shapes: square, rectangular, and round. Those with straight edges make more efficient use of space, but the round varieties distribute heat more evenly. The choice is yours. The most important things to remember are: no nonstick and very thick. Of all those I've seen or used, Le Creuset is by far the best.

There are also ordinary frying pans with ridged bottoms which serve exactly the same purpose. These have the advantage of catching some of the spluttering oil that's inevitably produced when you pan-grill meat or well-oiled vegetables. (A useful pan-griller's tip: roll up your sleeves and wear an apron, preferably one that's made from a plasticized fabric.)

The main drawback of the grill pan is that it's suitable only for foods of roughly uniform thickness which will lie flat in the pan. If part of the piece being cooked doesn't come into contact with the surface, it won't get as much heat as the rest; if it's significantly uneven in thickness, the thinner parts will get overcooked. This eliminates most poultry on the bone and large whole fish, for instance, as well as vegetables like broccoli and cauliflower. But you can press the food down with a spatula to aid even cooking. And in any event, this drawback is a minor one when you consider the other advantages.

One other word of warning about grill pans: they produce a lot of smoke. If you have an extractor fan (and every kitchen should have one), turn it on to full power before you start grilling. If the weather is fine, it's also advisable to open the windows in the kitchen.

THE TECHNIQUE

However and whatever you cook on the grill pan, the procedure is essentially the same. To wit:

> Preheat the grill over a moderate heat for at least 3 minutes. This is necessary because cast iron, though an excellent retainer of heat, is not quite so efficient at conducting. You will notice that even after a few minutes over the flame the centre of the pan is significantly hotter than the peripheries. Thorough preheating will even out the heat and eliminate most cold spots, though inevitably the heat will be highest directly over the flame.

When the pan has reached uniform heat, you may either leave the heat source at the original setting or turn it up higher for another minute before cooking. **High heat** is best for meat dishes, which need to cook a little faster. **Medium heat** is better for vegetables.

It's easy for me to talk about 'medium' heat and 'high' heat: I know what these things mean on my cooker and using my grill pan. For your cooker, here are a few guidelines to use:

Medium heat will be produced by one of the middle settings on your most powerful hob or burner. If you have a gas cooker (and I hope you do), set the flame so the jets are around half-way between the lowest and the highest. To test the grill pan, put a few drops of water on it. If the drops skitter around for a second before disappearing, the heat is right.

High heat is attained with the hob or burner at or near its highest setting. I usually use a setting that's just below the fiercest flame: the very fiercest tends to char the exterior before the inside is cooked. To test the grill pan, put a few drops of water on it. If the drops disappear immediately with a violent fizzing sound, the grill pan is at the right heat.

When cooking on the grill pan, remember that the heat is high and the pan surface has no nonstick properties. This means that food will stick initially, regardless of whether you've oiled it (see below). After a time, however, the surface of the food will build up a hard outer layer which will not stick. So the only unalterable rule of pan-grilling is:

do not turn or move the food too soon

Too soon can roughly be defined as under 30 seconds (high heat) or a minute (medium heat). The way to test whether you can turn is: gently push the food in the direction of the ridges. If it slides along easily, with no sign of resistance, it is ready for turning or rotating.

TESTING PAN-GRILLED FOODS

When you pan-grill any food, you are using a heat that ranges from very high to downright ferocious. This means you need to be on your toes, as the stuff can overcook if you're not careful.

The good news is that you don't need to be on your toes very long, as the short timings in this chapter suggest.

But let me say again, because it can't be repeated too often, that my timings are a guideline and nothing more. To tell whether the food is cooked you need to test it by sight and by touch. Here are the best techniques.

Meat: Raw meat is soft, so soft it will hold the imprint of your finger if you press down on it hard. As it cooks, it gets more resistant to the touch. And the degree of resistance is the best gauge of doneness. Press the meat at the centre of the chop or steak with your index finger. If it feels soft, the meat needs more cooking. If it feels springy, it is probably cooked just right. If it feels rock-hard, it is probably overcooked – and you've ruined a good piece of meat.

At the risk of encouraging you to waste your money, I must say that the touch method is better in the long run than the other doneness test for meat – cutting into it with a knife. As soon as you do this you are releasing tasty juices from the interior. Try to build up your confidence by using the touch method only. Even if you have problems to begin with, you will soon gain the experience that tells you easily whether the meat is done.

I would also urge you to err on the side of underdoneness in timing and testing meat. You can always correct undercooking. You cannot correct overcooking.

Fish: This too can be tested by touch, using the same criteria as described for meat. But a small, sharp knife is more reliable – even if it means that a little bit of moisture escapes from the interior. Stick the knife half-way down to the centre of the steak or fillet and pull it back so you open a little gash in the flesh. The flesh should be truly opaque, with not a hint of translucence; it should release a mild-mannered little spurt of liquid on being cut; and the knife tip, when inserted and then pressed against your finger, should feel well and truly hot. If your testing satisfies all these criteria, the fish is done.

Vegetables: These are slightly trickier, because doneness in vegetables means different things for different people. If you like vegetables well cooked, they are done when a small, sharp knife slides easily into the centre. The knife will feel as if it's sliding into soft butter. If you like vegetables fully cooked but still retaining a hint of crunch – and this is the best way to eat most vegetables, with notable exceptions – the knife should encounter some resistance as it goes in. Some resistance, but not too much.

Sounds vague? It is! But one or two vegetable-grilling sessions will easily teach you how to tell whether you've reached the crucial point of 'soft but crunchy'. Honest.

MENU PLANNING WITH THE GRILL PAN

When I'm feeling acutely lazy, which happens a lot, I cook entire meals on the grill pan. Just thinking about the washing-up I won't have to do – a frying pan, a saucepan or two, etc. – makes me believe in the existence of a higher power. But the best thing about pan-grilled meals is that they are delicious. This is serial cooking: you do the vegetables first (one, two or even three of them) anywhere up to a few hours in advance, and dress them before serving with a vinaigrette. Then you wipe down the grill and cook some meat or fish just before serving. A few suggestions for entirely pan-grilled meals follow at the end of the chapter.

ENTERTAINING WITH THE GRILL PAN

The grill pan is a real show-stopper when you're cooking for friends. They see the characteristic black lines on meat, fish or vegetables and think you're cooking like a pro. (Which, in a sense, you are.)

The drawback of the pan is that it can accommodate only a limited amount of food at any one time. Most will have trouble accommodating more than 6 chops or 4 large steaks, and if you're basing your whole menu on it then you may run into space problems.

There are two ways round the problem. One is to cook the vegetables in advance and then serve them lukewarm, and this is by no means the cheater's way out. Many vegetables are delicious served at room temperature. The second method, for meats only, is to combine the grill pan method with flash-roasting (see page 117). Page 124 gives instructions for browning meat before flash-roasting it. This can be done well in advance using an ordinary frying pan or the grill pan, and the results will look spiffier on the grill pan.

MEAT AND POULTRY

Pan-grilled meat is a wonderful thing. The intense heat of the pan browns the meat more quickly than an open grill, and little or no extra fat is needed, so all the so-called health advantages of regular grilling apply equally.

Because the heat is so intense at the surface, there is a limit to the thickness of meats you can cook successfully. If the meat is too thick, the outside will burn before the inside gets done. One inch is the optimum thickness, though thinner cuts will also do well. (They'll just need more careful watching to avoid over-cooking.) Anything over 1½ in is extremely tricky unless you finish the cooking by flash-roasting the meat (see page 117). And again, pieces of poultry on the bone will not lie flat, so some areas of bird won't come into contact with the pan; they will therefore remain uncooked. If you want to cook chicken or other poultry, use boned and trimmed pieces.

MARINATING

If you want to, you can marinate the meat first. The problem here is that some marinade ingredients can be burnt by the fierce grill heat, so you have to choose carefully. But there's no doubt that long marinating adds flavour, and with very little extra work.

Here are a few marinade possibilities which are well suited to the grill pan method. When using aromatic ingredients (garlic, onion, etc.), chop them in fairly large pieces which can be wiped off the meat before cooking: that way they won't burn in cooking and spoil the flavour. All quantities are for 500 g (1 lb) of meat cut ½–1 in thick.

Marinade 1

(for poultry, red meat, offal, or fish)

1 tbsp soy sauce
1 tbsp dry sherry or Chinese rice wine
1 clove of garlic, sliced around ⅛ in thick
4 in cube of ginger, sliced around ⅛ in thick
1 spring onion, sliced around ⅛ in thick

Marinade 2

(for red meat or offal)

1 clove garlic, sliced around ⅛ in thick
1 small onion or 1 spring onion, sliced around ⅛ in thick
1 tbsp red wine
1 tbsp extra virgin olive oil
1 tsp red wine vinegar
1 tsp herbes de Provence

Marinade 3

(for poultry or fish)

1 tbsp lemon juice
1 tsp balsamic vinegar (see page 344)
1 clove of garlic, sliced around ⅛ in thick
1 tsp dried tarragon

If you're cooking after work and are therefore both short of time and long on hunger, long marinating is out of the question. But even 15 minutes in a marinade affects the taste of meat, so it may be worth doing. The marinade's flavour is also affected by grilling, and the uncooked marinade can be poured on at the end.

BEEF

Pan-grilling beef means two things above all: steaks and burgers. The steak can be sirloin, rump, skirt, or fillet. Larger cuts like T-bone can also be used, though there may be a space problem if your pan isn't one of the largest sizes. And since the meat needs to lie perfectly flat to ensure even cooking, a steak with the bone in must be expertly sliced by the butcher: a protruding bone may raise some of the meat off the surface of the pan. Boneless cuts are better. Whichever cut you use, either steak or burgers, the procedure is essentially identical.

Remove the beef from the fridge half an hour before serving, or even an hour before. Get the grill pan really well preheated. Just before cooking, brush the meat with oil (optional) and season with salt and pepper. You can also sprinkle on a fine dusting of

herbes de Provence

to make it taste even better.

Take the steak or burger and, in a single confident motion, put it on the hot pan. DO NOT MOVE IT FOR AT LEAST ONE MINUTE, so the meat has a chance to form a crust which will not tear or stick. Use the timings below as a guideline, but remember: you will need to keep an eye on the cooking, and these timings are necessarily approximate. I do not know how hot your pan will be, how cold the steaks will be, or exactly how you like your meat to be cooked. These timings are for rare steaks made with beef at true room temperature. If the meat is fridge-cold, the timings might have to be increased by 50 per cent or even doubled. Again: watch the cooking with an eagle eye, especially when you're starting out.

1 in thick: 2 minutes first side, 1–2 minutes second side
¾ **in thick**: 1–2 minutes first side, 1½–2 minutes second side
½ **in thick**: 90 seconds first side, 30 seconds–1 minute second side

These timings may seem very short. They are. But quick cooking is essential if you don't want to overcook the beef – a sacrilege second to none. Remember that the meat will continue to cook even after it comes out of the pan, as the heat equalizes between surface and centre. And while you can always return an underdone steak to the pan, you cannot uncook it if it's overdone.

If you're using fillet steak, well trimmed of every bit of fat, you want to try another trick which is more usually used for salmon. This involves cooking the beef on one side only, so that the cooked side is deeply browned and the other side is rare-to-raw. NB: you should only do this if (a) you like very rare beef and (b) the steaks are ½ in thick. Cook them for

2–3 minutes on one side only

and be sure to let them rest for a minute or two before serving.

Hamburgers

There are many ways of cooking a good burger, and pan-grilling is just one of them. But it is one of the best. Use whatever flavourings you usually use in burgers, if you use any at all. I usually leave them out and add them at the end, when the burger is cooked.

A word of caution is in order here. First-rate hamburgers cannot be made with second-rate meat, and that is precisely what most butchers sell as 'mince'. If you want to be sure that your burger will be distinguished, buy whole pieces of braising steak and get them trimmed to order; don't bother with expensive cuts like sirloin or rump, which in any case are too lean to make a good burger. Then your butcher can mince them specially for you or you can do it at home in a food processor. More work, but worth it.

Once you've got your mince, form it into patties 1 in thick. They should not be packed too tight: press firmly but lightly between your hands. To cook the burger, season it on one side with salt and pepper, and cook for around

4–6 minutes (rare)
6–8 minutes (medium-rare)
9–10 minutes (medium)

Again, these timings are necessarily approximate. If you prefer a thinner burger, they should be reduced considerably.

If you like beef well done, cook the burger as long as it takes to burn off every bit of moisture and make the meat uniformly grey, dry, and chewy. I assume that people who like well-done beef consider these qualities to be a virtue.

VARIATIONS

I like burgers on their own, with nothing more than a gurgle from the ketchup bottle (Heinz only, please) and maybe a few shavings of cheese. The grill pan will not melt cheese satisfactorily.

But it's nice to have something fancier on occasion. For an all-pan-grilled burger of great distinction, first cook 1 slice of onion (see page 106) per burger and set it aside; cook the burger, and top with the onion before you dig in. Slices of pan-grilled red pepper work well in the same position. You can also serve burgers with *confits* of onion or shallots (see page 177), or mix other seasonings into the meat before cooking. Here is a wet mix, for use with 500 g (1 lb) or so of minced meat:

1 tbsp Worcester sauce
1 tsp soy sauce
1 tbsp minced onion or spring onion

Minced meat is also a popular basic in Middle Eastern cooking, and here is an idea for adding some of those flavours to your basic burger. Per 500 g (1 lb) of meat:

1 tsp ground cumin
1 tsp ground coriander
1 tsp minced ginger
2 tbsp minced onion, or more if you like a lot of onion
1 tsp lemon juice

Grill a burger with these flavourings and then top it with some pan-grilled aubergines and courgettes. This is a fairly fancy burger which could be eaten with knife and fork rather than on a roll.

Sliced Beef

Beef on the pan grill needn't be either steaks or burgers. If you're feeling in the mood for some instant, split-second cooking, you can also cut the beef into strips or shreds around ⅛–¼ in thick and cook them very quickly. This needs your close attention, but there's nothing too intimidating about it. It's best for those occasions when you're eating alone, or with one other person, as you can't fit too many slices on the grill at one time. The nicest thing about it is that the slices need be cooked on one side only, as long as you like your beef rare or medium-rare. Here's how:

> Slice the beef and marinate it briefly in any of the marinades above. Have it in a dish that allows easy, rapid access – a large plate would be ideal. Get the grill pan hot and put the shreds on one at a time, proceeding in an orderly fashion. By the time you've finished putting the last shred on, the first one will be cooked. Take them off in the order in which you put them on, and transfer them to a plate. Serve immediately.

LAMB

If the grill pan itself is my desert island cooking vessel, pan-grilled lamb would be my desert island dish. Lamb tastes better on the grill pan than just about any place else. Chops, slices, and burgers; slices of boned loin or fillet from the best end (neck); lamb brochettes (kebabs), alternated with button mushrooms and chunks of pepper and onion. These are all things of beauty. (Beware, however, that it's a little bit tricky to turn skewers in a way that ensures uniform cooking on all sides of the meat. It can be done, but you need to pay attention.)

With lamb there's an additional option: slices or chunks of shoulder. I am a great believer in the virtues of shoulder of lamb, and buy more of this cut than any other red meat. Its taste is arguably superior to that of leg and loin, and it is much cheaper.

Shoulder pieces can be cut in several ways, either from the boned joint or through the bone, and can then be marinated (see page 89) or coated in a herb coating. Here's a good money- and time-saving tip:

> Get the butcher to bone you a shoulder of lamb, then take it home and cut it in ½ in chunks or slices. Put 100 g (4 oz) of the pieces in a freezer bag and seal tightly. Repeat with the remaining lamb. Freeze it all. You now have small servings of lamb which will defrost quickly and provide a good meal for yourself, yourself and a friend, or even for an impromptu dinner party.

All the techniques described for beef can be used with lamb, but the timings are somewhat different: lamb should never be cooked rare. It should be medium-rare to medium. Well-done lamb is not *quite* as disgusting as well-done beef, but it is not particularly appetizing if the meat is grilled. Here are the timings: they apply to all cuts of lamb.

½ **in thick**: 4–5 minutes
¾ **in thick**: 5–6 minutes
1 **in thick**: 6–7 minutes

Grilled lamb takes well to marinades, and all-purpose marinades 1 and 2 (see page 89) are both excellent. Here's another one, which also works well with chicken. It is only for those who like spicy foods.

Spicy Yogurt Marinade

This quantity is sufficient for 4 lamb chops, loin or shoulder.

½ tsp ground cumin
½ tsp ground coriander
½ tsp ground black pepper
2 tsp cayenne pepper
2 tsp turmeric
1 green cardamom pod
3 thin slices of ginger
2 small cloves of garlic
150 ml (6 fl oz) low-fat yogurt or low-fat fromage frais
1 tbsp vegetable oil

Mix the spice powders. Split the cardamom pod, remove the seeds, and add to the powders. Mince the ginger and garlic and mix into the spices with the yogurt and oil. Stir well to combine thoroughly, then smear on to the lamb and marinate for a minimum of 2 hours. Pan-grill as for beef on page 89.

PORK

Pork is often divided into 'red' and 'white' cuts, the colour being determined by the amount of myoglobin in the tissue. 'White' pork, especially the loin, is considered best by many people, but I must confess to a deep-seated opposition to loin pork chops. The loin of pork is the leanest and neatest part, but it's also the driest and the mildest in flavour. If I am forced to eat loin of pork, I prefer it braised – more flavour, more moisture. To counteract the dryness and lower flavour content, try marinating it first in any of the marinades on page 89.

For grilling, frying, and pan-grilling I much prefer the so-called spare rib chops. These have redder meat, a little more internal fat for natural basting, and a far richer flavour. They're also a lot cheaper than loin chops, and you're not paying for the thick layer of fat between meat and skin. If using them, please remember to

remove all the bones

as this will make the meat lie flatter.

Spare rib chops can also be cut into strips, like beef, or into 1in cubes for cooking *en brochette* (kebabs). Alternate with button mushrooms and chunks of pepper and onion. Here are approximate timings for all these pork possibilities:

Loin or spare rib chops, ½ in thick: 2 minutes per side
Loin or spare rib chops, ¾ in thick: 3 minutes first side, 2 minutes second side
Loin or spare rib chops, 1 in thick: 3 minutes per side
Pork brochettes, 1 in thick: 6–10 minutes total, turning at least 3 times
Pork strips, ⅛ in thick: 1 minute per side
Pork strips, ¼ in thick: 90 seconds per side

Pan-grilled Belly of Pork

Belly of pork is one of the tastiest cuts of pork, and usually the cheapest. It can be pan-grilled from raw, but its toughness and layers of sinew make it fairly chewy. Far better to simmer it first (preferably when making Lazy Stock, see page 245), stick it into a marinade, and *then* pan-grill it. This is a really delicious dish, and very cheap for an evening at home with your spouse, housemate, or spouse-equivalent.

Take

2 or 3 strips of lean belly of pork

Slice off the rind, which doesn't cook very well on the grill pan, and cut the strips into 3 in lengths. Put in a saucepan with cold water to cover by 2 in or so. Bring to the boil, skimming if you can be bothered, and simmer for at least 1 hour. (If you've used the meat to make a stock, you can skip this step.) Now put them in marinade 1 (see page 89) and let them sit for at least 20 minutes. If you do this step in the evening, the pork can easily sit in the marinade overnight. When you're ready to eat, cook the pork on the pan grill for

6–7 minutes

turning several times so all sides are well browned. Serve with a salad and plain boiled rice.

If you don't have time to marinate, make a dipping sauce instead from:

1 tbsp soy sauce
1 tsp dry sherry
1 tsp Chinese oyster sauce
½ a small clove of garlic, minced
1 thin slice of ginger, minced

and dip the pork in it. Two minutes of work for a mealful of pleasure.

OFFAL

OK, this is a contentious point. Some people love organ meats and many people hate them. I will refrain from proselytizing, but I am one of the enthusiasts. For those who agree with me, here are some timings for liver, kidney and heart. *Liver* can be chicken, duck, calves' or lamb's. *Kidney* can be calves' or lamb's.

Heart can be ox, duck, calves', or lamb's. In all cases, they should not be sliced too thick – aim for a target of around ¼ in.

Liver, ¼ in thick: around 1 minute per side
Kidney, ¼ in thick: 1–2 minutes per side
Heart, ¼ in thick: 1–2 minutes per side

Sweetbreads

Sweetbreads are not brains, as is sometimes thought, but the thymus and pancreas of a calf, lamb or (very rarely) pig. Veal sweetbreads are the best and costliest, while the lamb variety are milder but no less delicious. And sweetbreads are truly a delicious thing. Even people who don't like offal seem to like sweetbreads – as long as you don't tell them in advance what they're eating.

In the classic preparation, sweetbreads are a major pain in the neck. Soaking is followed by blanching in salted water or bouillon, then a fine network of membrane and fibres has to be picked and snipped off. Finally they are pressed under a weighted board before cooking.

Happily, lazy cooks are not excluded from cooking these delicious nuggets. You can fudge most of the tiresome prelims apart from blanching, which takes around 2 minutes of active work (and can be done well in advance). And if you then cook them on the grill pan, you have a dish worth dying for. Here's how.

Pan-grilled Sweetbreads

Soak

500 g (1 lb) lamb's or veal sweetbreads

in a few changes of water for at least 6 hours (or overnight). (If the sweetbreads are not very bloody, you can even skip this stage – though it's so little trouble there isn't much point in skipping it.) Boil a large saucepan full of salted water and blanch the sweetbreads for 5 minutes. Drain, refresh under the cold tap, and dry. Trim off any fat or straggly bits, and cut into chunks around 1 in square. You can now marinate them in marinade 2 (see page 89), or in

2 tbsp extra virgin olive oil
juice of ½ a lemon
salt and pepper
1 spring onion, chopped fine

Or you can just brush them with oil. Thread them on to skewers if you feel like it, brush generously with extra oil, and put them in the pan. It's important not to move the sweetbreads for

2 minutes

because the membranes stick easily. Grill for a total of

9–10 minutes,

turning every couple of minutes and basting with the marinade. The outside should get well browned while the inside stays tender and juicy. Serve immediately with pan-grilled courgettes, mushrooms, and spring onions. In all the cooking I did for this book, that combination was perhaps the single most delicious meal my wife and I ate. You could also serve one of the *confits* on page 176 with this dish.

CHICKEN

Chicken and duck can be delectable on the grill pan as long as you treat them right. We've covered the point about boning and trimming already, but it needs a little clarification. After boning the bird (or buying ready-boned pieces), cut it into slices or chunks of uniform thickness. This can be anywhere from ⅛ in (for quick-cooking strips) to 1 in (for kebabs). If you can find minced chicken, or if you own a food processor and feel like spending the 60 seconds it takes to mince it yourself, you can also make chicken burgers.

The white meat of chicken is fatless and therefore dry, so strips or chunks of breast meat will need to be brushed with oil before cooking. If you're mincing the chicken, try making

Chinese-flavoured burgers (recipe below). Dark meat is some-what fattier (and a lot more flavourful, in my view), so you can get away without using fat. Here are some timings for the various forms of chicken.

Cubes or slices of chicken, 1 in: 5–6 minutes, turning regularly
Strips of chicken, ⅛ in thick: 1–2 minutes, turning once
Strips of chicken, ¼ in thick: 2–3 minutes, turning once
Chicken burgers, 1 in thick: 6–8 minutes, turning once.

If you've got some chicken breasts and are feeling too lazy to mess with them, they can be pan-grilled with fairly good results. Two provisos apply here: (a) you can't worry if the thin end of the breast gets cooked more thoroughly than the thick end, and (b) you have to pay more attention during cooking. The breast of a chicken is actually two sections of meat, and these have a tendency to separate during cooking as they're connected by nothing more than a thin, delicate membrane. And the whole breast, even from a relatively small bird, can be very thick. So you may need to move it around during cooking, and adjust the heat, to ensure even cooking. Cook the skin side first unless you prefer to remove the skin altogether, and again, make sure the chicken is well oiled to prevent sticking. Approximate timings for breasts from a 1.5–2 kg (3–4 lb) bird:

6 minutes first side, 4 minutes second side

Chicken Wings

It's a well kept secret that chicken wings are the tastiest part of the bird. If the secret were better known, every supermarket and butcher would sell the wings separately at a high price. Instead of which they are found only intermittently and at a reasonable price. If you're lucky enough to find some, try cooking them on the grill pan. Cut off and discard the wing tips, and joint the rest of the wing. Marinate it in marinades 1 or 3 (see page 89), and then grill for

4–6 minutes

turning a few times and brushing with more marinade if you wish. The 'drummet' joint will cook a little unevenly, as it's not of uniform thickness, but no matter. The skin crisps up and the succulent meat will be delicious. If you're a wing fan, see page 76 for another (better) way of treating these delicacies.

DUCK

Sautéed duck breasts are delicious, and pan-grilled duck breasts are even better. My technique for cooking them is derived from Nico Ladenis's *My Gastronomy*, in which Mr Ladenis recommends cooking them almost entirely on the skin side, with only a brief spell with the flesh side down. This has the effect of crisping the skin and rendering out its copious underlayer of fat, while the flesh remains properly moist.

My experiments with duck on the grill pan have led me to modify the high heat principle for meat and poultry. Using a high heat makes the skin cook too fast. Instead, use a *medium* heat, and proceed as follows. It's impossible to be precise about timings, so you'll have to pay attention during cooking.

First you can marinate the duck if you want to. Here's a simple marinade that I like, in quantities sufficient for 2 breasts of around 125 g (5 oz) apiece:

1 shallot or ½ a small onion
1 tsp vinegar
1 tbsp ruby port
½ tsp herbes de Provence
salt and pepper

Cut the shallot or onion into very thin slices and mix with the remaining ingredients in a dish that's large enough to hold the duck in a single layer. Put the duck breasts in, skin side *up*, so that only the flesh is in the marinade. Leave for an hour or so.

Preheat the grill pan over a high heat and put in the duck breasts, skin side *down*. Immediately turn the heat down to medium and let the duck cook until the skin is well browned. It's important not to let it blacken, so I would check it after

5 minutes

and would expect it to be ready for turning within

6–8 minutes

As soon as the skin is properly crisped and a deep mahogany colour, turn the duck. If the rendered fat is threatening to overflow, spoon a little of it out.

The amount of cooking needed to finish the breasts will depend on how deeply they got cooked during the first stage, but on the whole it should not take much more than

3–5 minutes

on the second side. You will cook the breasts more evenly if you press them down with a metal spatula a couple of times during the flesh-side-down cooking. The meat is done when the flesh side feels quite firm to the touch; but the best way to check is to cut half-way through the flesh side with a small, sharp knife.

This sounds a bit complicated for lazy cooks, but once you've done it, it's actually very easy.

GAME

Game on the grill pan is a tricky proposition. Only the tender varieties are suitable, and tenderness in game is hard to predict. I've had most success with two types: pheasant and venison (which is farmed nowadays anyway, and therefore isn't always considered to be game).

Pheasant

I love pheasant but not when it's roasted whole: the breast tends to dry out before the legs get done. A braise is often the best way forward (see page 80), and flash-roasting is also good (see page 130).

Pan-grilling is another excellent method, though it takes a bit of fuss: this shouldn't be the first thing you cook if you're new to pan-grilling. You can cook whole pheasant legs on the grill pan because (a) they're thinner than chicken legs, and (b) they lie fairly flat in the pan. This is an expensive dish, as the main ingredient is expensive: make it for small dinner parties.

The best way to deal with pheasant is to joint the bird yourself. Slice down the breast bone and remove the 2 breasts in a whole, boneless piece. Or get the bird cut in quarters by your butcher or fishmonger and then do the final boning at home. The breasts should be completely bone-free; the leg portions should have all the carcass trimmed away so that they lie perfectly flat. If you can't be bothered with this fine work (which takes only a few minutes – honest), and if you can't get your game dealer to do it for you, forget about pan-grilling pheasant.

When your pieces are ready, either oil them or (better still) marinate them for a while. Marinade 2 (see page 89) will work very well, but better still is this simple sweet-and-sour game marinade (similar to the duck marinade on page 100). This quantity is sufficient for one plump pheasant.

1 tsp honey
½ tsp vinegar
2 tsp ruby port
½ tsp herbes de Provence (see page 338)
2 tsp vegetable oil

Get the legs cooking first, as they will take longer than the breasts. As with chicken, you'll need to press down with a spatula to ensure close contact between pan and meat. Approximate timings are as follows:

Legs: 7–8 minutes
Breasts: 6 minutes

Game goes splendidly well with all pulses, and I like to serve this pheasant with Lentils with Sun-Dried Tomatoes (see page 342).

Venison

Haunch (leg) and loin of venison work beautifully on the grill pan, as long as you cook them nice and rare. Venison is one of the leanest of meats, and one of the chewiest when overcooked. Even if you cook it perfectly, however, you'll still need something to moisten it. Here are some approximate timings, plus an instant sauce that goes particularly well with the rich taste of the meat. I think the best thickness is ½ in. It calls for split-second timing and careful observation, but the extra effort is worth it.

½ in thick: 1 minute each side
1 in thick: 3 minutes each side

Instant Mushroom Sauce for Venison

This is enough for around 500 g (1 lb) of venison.

250 g (8 oz) button mushrooms
1 spring onion, 1 shallot, or ½ a small onion
1 tbsp extra virgin olive oil
1 thick pat of butter
½ tsp herbes de Provence
4 tbsp (60 ml) red wine
1 tbsp balsamic vinegar

Clean the mushrooms and slice them around ⅛–¼ in thick.
Mince the onion. Heat the oil and butter in a small pan and
sauté the mushrooms with the herbs for 4–5 minutes, till the
mushrooms are just cooked but still retaining a lot of bite. Put
in the wine and vinegar, season with salt and pepper, and stir
well; remove from the heat till needed. Just before serving,
reheat thoroughly and pour over the cooked meat.

VEGETABLES

Pan-grilling may be my favourite way of cooking vegetables,
and it's always a hit with guests. Best to use a *medium heat*, which
ensures that the slices or chunks don't burn before the centre is
fully cooked. Don't worry if they get a bit blackened; this only
enhances their charm. The vegetables may be served straight
from the grill or left to cool. Leaving them to cool makes life a
lot easier for lazy cooks, as it means you don't have to co-
ordinate the vegetables with your other dishes. This is the way
forward if you're planning a pan-grilled meal. Pan-grilled
vegetables are also particularly good in assembled salads (see
page 269).

Aubergines

Slice ½ in thick either across or lengthwise. Salt them first and
leave for 30 minutes, then dry thoroughly and grill over a
medium heat for 4–6 minutes.

Carrots

Slice on the bias around ¼ in thick. Brush with oil and cook for around

6 minutes per side

or more if you want them very soft. I like them with quite a bit of crunch.

Courgettes

One of the best vegetables for pan-grilling, and possibly even better at room temperature than straight from the pan. You must buy small, very firm specimens, otherwise the grill pan is unsuitable. Wash them well, and top and tail, but do not peel them; salting is optional, and unnecessary in my view. Then slice ½–1 in thick either across or lengthwise. Cook for

4–8 minutes

depending on how crunchy you want them. May be served with a dressing, but the flavour of the oil plus a sprinkling of salt will be sufficient for most purposes.

Fennel

Fennel tastes great on the grill pan, as it does on the barbecue (and charred – see page 167). Trim off the base of the bulb, leaving enough of the core so that the slices hold together. They will still need careful handling, but with extra stem they are less likely to fall apart. Slice ½ in thick lengthwise, again trying to keep the slices whole. Take care when turning the slices. Holding them with one hand when you're turning helps keep the slices whole. Timings depend on how soft you want them, but

5–8 minutes

should be about right.

Mushrooms

Unfortunately, mushrooms are not just mushrooms: they are button mushrooms, big mushrooms, wild mushrooms, field mushrooms, shiitake mushrooms, and so forth. The various types need somewhat different treatment because of their differences in shape. While it's difficult to generalize, the point to bear in mind is that flattish mushrooms cook more quickly and evenly on the grill pan than the roundish varieties. Oyster mushrooms are particularly good from this point of view, though I've never been all that impressed by their flavour-to-price ratio.

The large, very flat field-type mushrooms with fine black gills have excellent flavour. But because the gills are so fragile, it's best to cook them on the cap side only – and serve them with the cap up. If you can get only roundish button types, keep an eye on them and turn them regularly. They *will* get cooked; it just takes a little more effort. Larger mushrooms do particularly well on the grill pan, either whole or in thick slices. It's easy to cook them just to the point of perfection – hot and juicy yet still retaining a hefty bit of bite – and the tops can look very impressive with their scoring of blackened lines.

The mushrooms can be oiled, either with a brush or by dribbling a few drops (extra virgin olive oil, *please*) on to the gill side when you've turned them over. But because they have such a high water content, you can also cook them without fat. This leaves a pure mushroom flavour which will drive mycophiles crazy with delight. Here are some approximate timings for different types:

>**Small button mushrooms**: 4–5 minutes, turning regularly
>**Large mushrooms** (2–4 in in diameter): 3–4 minutes per side
>**Mushroom slices** (around ½ in thick): 1 minute per side
>**Oyster or shiitake mushrooms**: 1 minute per side

For a slightly more complicated version, as a garnish for pan-grilled meat, larger flat mushrooms can be flavoured in a variety of ways and cooked either in advance or alongside the meat. Here's the procedure.

Pan-grilled 'Stuffed' Mushrooms

Oil the gill side of 2–4 in mushrooms and cook at the centre of the pan for 2 minutes, turning once through an angle of 90° so the top gets that attractive criss-cross pattern. Then turn them gill side up and place in the 'cup' any of the following (or a combination):

> *a large pinch of grated Parmesan*
> *a few paper-thin slices of Gruyère, Pecorino, or Manchego cheese*
> *a tiny bit of minced garlic or spring onion*
> *a large pinch of minced fresh herbs*
> *2 small chunks of anchovy fillet*
> *a tiny piece (around the size of your thumbnail) of lemon*

Season with salt and pepper and move the mushrooms over to the edges of the pan, and let them cook over this slightly lower heat while you cook the main dish at the centre of the pan. The mushrooms should be done when the meat is done. If they aren't, move them back to the centre of the pan for a few seconds to complete cooking. The combination of cheese and herbs is particularly scrumptious, as is anchovy, garlic and lemon.

Incidentally, this recipe flies in the face of one of the most famous battle-cries of the lazy cook: Shirley Conran's statement that 'Life is too short to stuff a mushroom.' She's got a point. But if you regard stuffing as an ornamental anointing with a dab or two of simple ingredients, the procedure looks much less daunting.

Onions

Thick onion slices (around ½ in) do beautifully on the grill pan, though careful turning is needed because the rings tend to separate. Tiny pickling onions are also very good, but lazy cooks will shy away from the tiresome job of peeling them. Spring onions, topped and tailed, may be the best of all. They cook in no time, and the contrast between blackened exterior and moist interior is a delight. They are also good as a garnish for grilled meat or fish. Here are some approximate timings:

Spring onions: 3–6 minutes, turning 2 or 3 times
Onion slices (around ½ in): 2–5 minutes per side
Small (pickling) onions, around 1 in in diameter: 6–10 minutes,
turning regularly to blacken uniformly

It's hard to be precise here because the timing will depend on whether you want a fresh, raw taste or a blackened exterior and melting interior.

Peppers

Red and yellow have a better flavour than green, unless they're from Holland. In that case they will have hardly any flavour at all, and will need jazzing up with *salsa* (see page 323), lemon juice, or vinaigrette. It doesn't greatly matter if the pieces aren't perfectly flat. Cut them into 4–8 pieces depending on size, and start cooking with the skin side down, pressing the pieces flat with a spatula occasionally to bring more of the skin into contact with the pan's surface. They will need

5–8 minutes

depending on how crunchy you want them. By all means let them brown and blister thoroughly, but don't let the skin get so black that it chars. If it does, the skin will have to be peeled off – and this is a major pain in the neck.

Potatoes

Pan-grilled potatoes are a very good alternative to chips, tasty and much lower in calories. They do need to be brushed with fat of some kind, but you'll still end up with much less than you get from a plate of chips.

You can use either floury or waxy potatoes on the pan grill, but the cardinal rule – don't move the food around too soon – is particularly important. If the exterior doesn't get a chance to form a tough crust before you turn or move the slices around, they will tear and stick.

Vegetable oil is the most sensible type of fat to brush on potatoes as its smoke point (the temperature at which it starts to produce smoke) is higher than any animal fat. Having said that,

I must add immediately that bacon, chicken, and especially duck or goose fat are exceedingly delicious with potatoes. If you're using a medium temperature, you can just about get away with animal fat. If too much smoke is being produced, just turn the heat down a little bit.

It's particularly hard to be precise about timings for potatoes because each type cooks differently. But you should be all right using these guidelines. Don't use slices that are more than around ¼ in thick or they'll be susceptible to burning before the inside is cooked. Brush well with oil, season with salt and pepper, and allow around

5–6 minutes per side

whichever type of potato you're using. But check small new potatoes after 3 minutes or so.

'Stir-frying' Vegetables on the Grill Pan

In true stir-frying, the food in question is kept in near-constant motion in a frying pan. You can use a variant of this technique, perfect when you're cooking for yourself, on the grill pan. Cut into thin shreds:

1 small onion
1 small red pepper
around 125 g (4–5 oz) French beans

Toss them in a bowl with

1 tbsp extra virgin olive oil

Put the whole mess on the grill pan over a medium heat and cook for

4–5 minutes

tossing and turning 3 or 4 times. When everything is cooked, remove to a bowl and toss with 1 tsp balsamic vinegar. Let them sit while you proceed with a steak, chop, or piece of fish. A complete light meal in 10 or 15 minutes.

FISH

Fish is a little tricky on the pan-grill. The delicacy of its flesh makes it liable either to stick or to break up when being turned; and because overcooking kills fish stone-dead, the cooking has to be watched carefully.

But it can be done. If you're a barbecuer, you know the rules to follow: use firm-fleshed fish, or fish that has its skin on; don't move it around any more than you absolutely have to; and make sure any flesh that gets exposed to the fierce heat of the grill surface is well lubricated with oil or marinade.

The fish that I've had most success with on the pan-grill are salmon, halibut, monkfish, and tuna. Swordfish is also a good choice, if you like it. (I think it's wildly overrated.) The other prime choices are shellfish – expensive but delectable – and whole small fish.

Salmon

The best way of cooking salmon, whether in a grill pan or ordinary frying pan, is to get the pan pretty damned hot and then cook the fish on one side only. (In France, where this technique originated, it is called cooking *'d'un coté'*.) For this reason, choose salmon fillet rather than steaks. Heat the pan medium-hot and brush the skin side of the fish with oil. Slap the fish on and leave it for

4–8 minutes

depending on how rare you like the fish to be. (You can see exactly what's happening to the fish, so there's no way to undercook it.) I like it very pink at the top, so that it's effectively around 60–70 per cent cooked. If you like it more completely cooked, just give it more time.

When the fish has been cooking for around 5 minutes, gently lift one end of the fillet and check out the skin. If it's getting blackened, turn the heat down. You want the skin to be deep brown and crispy (this is the best part of the dish), but it shouldn't look as if it's been coated with coal dust. Eat with a squeeze of lemon, *salsa verde* (see page 325), or a yogurt-based dipping sauce (see page 116).

Halibut

Everything I say about salmon applies to halibut, with one exception. Because it has firmer flesh than salmon, it can be turned without fear of sticking or tearing. If using fillets, cook the skin side first, then apply the oil to the flesh side with a free hand before turning. Approximate timings:

1 in thick: 4 minutes first side, 2 minutes second side
1½ in thick: 5 minutes first side, 2–3 minutes second side

For reasons I do not understand, the skin of a halibut rarely survives pan-grilling. Probably this has something to do with the absence of scales, such as those on salmon. In any event, don't worry if it shrivels up like the Wicked Witch after Dorothy throws the water on her. You don't really need the skin.

Monkfish

Monkfish has excellent flavour and very firm, fibrous flesh. It needs careful trimming to take off the pinkish membrane, and this is the kind of work that lazy cooks hate. If you're in the mood for microsurgery, or if you can buy the fish already trimmed, monk is a good choice. Slice it either into medallions (roughly disc-shaped pieces) around ¾ in thick or into neat strips around ¾ in thick at the most. Timings:

¾ in pieces: 2–3 minutes first side, 1–2 minutes second side

WHOLE FISH

To cook a whole fish on the grill pan you must first choose the right fish: nothing over 1½ in will do. In practice this is a rather restrictive limitation. Trout is one possibility, though I personally have never had much time for the cheap farmed trout that British fishmongers sell all year round. Much better are small whiting, small bream (especially black bream), and especially red mullet. The head should be left on all these fish except perhaps the whiting, which may be too long if it isn't decapitated, and the heat should be in the medium range or the delicate skin may break and tear. Target timings are as follows:

1 in thick: 4 minutes first side, 2–3 minutes second side
1½ in thick: 5 minutes first side, 3–5 minutes second side

Pan-grilled fish can be served straight from the pan with nothing more than a lemon wedge. They're even better, I think, if plunked straight into a marinade or vinaigrette and left to cool. Use a plain vinaigrette with a sliced clove of garlic or one of the marinades on page 89. This is an excellent way of cooking for a summertime lunch when you don't feel like barbecuing.

SHELLFISH AND SQUID

Here the only problem, apart from cost, is shape. Shellfish doesn't always come in neat packages, and major disparities in thickness will result in uneven cooking. But this is not an obstacle with my favourite pan-grilled seafood: prawns, squid, and scallops.

Prawns (Shrimps)

Uncooked prawns are exquisite on the grill pan. They are likely to have been frozen before you buy them, and this is a shame: there are few foods more delicious than a really fresh prawn or shrimp. But it is not a disaster, and it's better to have a defrosted prawn of good quality than no prawns at all. Do remember, however, that the prawns must be uncooked. Those bags of cooked prawns (their weight boosted by the spraying of water before freezing) are totally unsuited to pan grilling – and to most other uses, for that matter.

Shrimps and prawns take next to no time to cook, and it's a terrible waste to overcook them. But in a way this is an advantage with the grill pan, as the rapidity of the cooking method is really shown off. It's best to use unpeeled prawns: the shell acts as a casing to keep the juices inside while protecting the delicate flesh from the fierce heat of the pan. And it can then be either discarded or eaten as you and your guests choose.

For further protection against drying out, try marinating the prawns for a few minutes in a mild vinaigrette-type dressing. Here is a simple one that I use, in quantities suitable for 500 g (1 lb) or so of prawns.

2 tbsp extra virgin olive oil
4 tbsp vegetable oil
1 tbsp white wine
1 tbsp wine vinegar
a few sprigs of parsley, minced
salt and pepper

Mix the marinade ingredients and toss the prawns well in it. Leave to sit for 15–30 minutes before grilling, then use the following cooking times as a guideline.

Very large prawns: 90 seconds per side
Large prawns: 1 minute per side
Small prawns: 30–45 seconds per side

If you've marinated them, no other flavouring is needed for these delectable morsels. If they've been cooked on their own, serve them with lemon wedges or maybe a *salsa* (see page 323).

Squid

Squid too is excellent on the grill pan, especially if it's fresh squid of fairly modest dimensions. (The larger ones have much thicker sacs and a coarser flavour.) Look for squid around 6–8 in long.

There are two ways to approach pan-grilled squid, and both have their merits. One is to cut them into rings, of the type you find battered and fried in Greek restaurants. The rings shouldn't be more than ¼ in thick or they'll be hard to cook. Brush them lightly with oil, and cook them over a high heat for

30–60 seconds per side

Serve straight from the pan with a *salsa* (see page 323) or just lemon wedges.

The other way, which I think I prefer by a small margin, is to stuff something light and tangy into the sac and then grill it whole. The stuffing shouldn't be bulky or the squid will be hard to cook. For a single squid with a 4–5 in sac, here's a suitable stuffing (which may be varied endlessly):

4 sprigs of parsley, minced
1 slice of garlic, minced
1/2 tsp extra virgin olive oil
salt and pepper

Mix the ingredients well and spread them inside the sac with your fingers. (This can be done many hours in advance.) Brush the squid with a little more oil and grill over a high heat for

3–4 minutes

turning once and pressing down with a spatula so the sac doesn't swell up like a balloon and lead to uneven cooking. Serve with a *salsa* (see page 323) or just lemon wedges.

If you're having friends over and want to go to a little more trouble, here's a slightly more complicated recipe of real distinction.

Pan-grilled Stuffed Squid

Use fairly large squid, preferably fresh.

750 g (1 1/2 lb) fresh squid
2 tbsp good olive oil
1 large onion (around 250 g/8 oz), chopped
50 g (2 oz) celery
2 cloves of garlic, minced
a small handful of fresh parsley or coriander, minced
2 tbsp dry white wine or vermouth
juice of 1/2 a small lemon

Clean the squid and dice the tentacles. Heat the oil in a frying pan and sauté the onion, celery and garlic for 3–4 minutes over a medium heat. Season with salt and pepper and add the coriander or parsley, and the tentacles. Stir-fry gently for 30 seconds. Add the wine or vermouth and the lemon juice and cook for another 30 seconds, till around half the liquid has evaporated. Allow to cool, then stuff loosely into the squid sacs. Flatten them out, leaving a 1in gap between the stuffing and the end of the sac. Sew up the ends or thread with small skewers. When the grill is hot, brush the squid with 1–2 tbsp of olive oil or plain vegetable oil and cook for 5–8 minutes per side, turning once. Serve immediately with steamed beans or a salad, and some good bread to mop up the juices.

Scallops

A pan-grilled scallop is a thing of beauty. The fierce heat of the pan 'seizes' the tender scallop and caramelizes the outside while the inside – if you don't overcook – retains its juicy sweetness.

There are two problems with pan-grilling scallops. One is that, like prawns, they are very expensive. Save them for special occasions. The other problem, related to the cost factor, is that the best scallops for grilling are the large ones – and these are the most expensive of all. The smaller 'Queen' scallops are cheaper, but they're harder to cook.

It can be done, however. One method is to cook them individually. This takes a lot of constant attention, as there will be a lot of the little nuggets cooking at one time and they all need to be turned at just the right moment. Cooking time:

2 minutes, turning 3 or 4 times

A better method is to skewer them and cook them *en brochette*. This is the method I use, as a starter for a dinner party or a main course if there are just two diners.

PAN-GRILLED MEALS

In all these enterprises the vegetables should be cooked first – up to a couple of hours in advance – and the meat or fish left till just before serving.

1. *Lamb chops in marinade 2 (see page 89)*
   Aubergine slices
   Courgette slices

2. *Hamburgers*
   Onions
   Red peppers

Cook the onions and peppers whenever you want to, then put them on the burgers and eat with a ketchup or a tomato *salsa* (see page 323).

3. *Salmon or red mullet*
   Fennel
   Potatoes

A Pan-grilled Vegetarian Buffet

This is a perfect meal for a summer lunch. It will take around 45 minutes to cook, but once the main part of the work is finished you have nothing more to do until just before serving; and the final cooking takes only 10–15 minutes. Then you can enjoy yourself.

Up to 6 hours in advance, pan-grill an assortment of vegetables. I suggest:

aubergines
courgettes
fennel
mushrooms
onions

Pile them on a platter and, when cool, cover with aluminium foil. Fifteen or 20 minutes before serving, reheat the grill pan and cook some ¼ in slices of waxy potato. While they're cooking, make a sour cream or yogurt sauce for the potatoes from:

300 ml (10 fl oz) sour cream or Greek yogurt
juice of ½ a lemon
1 clove of garlic, crushed
a small handful of fresh herbs – dill, coriander, parsley
salt and pepper

Make also a vinaigrette for the other vegetables. This, of course, can be done well in advance.

Serve the potatoes in one bowl, the sauce in another, and the vinaigrette on the mixed vegetables. I have never met anyone – vegetarian or carnivore – who didn't enjoy this meal.

BREAD

One item I haven't mentioned for cooking on the miraculous grill pan is bread. It can be done, and it's good. This is a version of *bruschetta*, the Italian version of toast, which has become an eminently trendy food in recent years. The technique is simple: brush slices no more than ½ in thick with a little

extra virgin olive oil

and slap them on to a medium grill pan. Cook, without turning for

30–90 seconds

and then brush the top with oil. Turn and cook for a similar time, and serve immediately. This makes a good accompaniment to any pan-grilled meal – though it's just as good served with anything, including breakfast. If you're not eating it at breakfast time, try rubbing the toasted bread with a cut clove of garlic and/or a cut tomato. This is a version of the Spanish *pan con tomate*, and is well worth making when there are good tomatoes around.

Flash-Roasting

THE PRINCIPLE

You take smallish pieces of fish or meat or vegetables and cook them – with or without preliminary browning – in a very hot oven for a very short time. The aim is to preserve as much of their natural flavour as possible, and to cook them as fast as possible without burning.

THE DETAILS

Flash-roasting, using a very hot oven, is an excellent trick for quick meals. When I'm cooking informally, this is one of the techniques I use regularly.

Flash-roasting applies intense heat very quickly. The normal roasting action – driving the food's moisture inwards while heating it and the surrounding tissue – is intensified and speeded up. Ideally the result should be lightly brown on the outside and moist on the inside, with the relatively brief cooking time preserving as much as possible of the natural moisture of the food.

There's a widespread belief that only large joints of meat are suitable for roasting. This is rubbish. Anything can be roasted, and many foods benefit from it.

Another myth holds that some meats need slow or medium-fast roasting, while others need fast roasting. My experience doesn't bear this out. The more I cook, the more I find myself using the highest setting – 230°C (450°F, Gas 8) – more than any other.

Having said that, I must add that if a joint is very large, high heat may dry out the outside before the inside is cooked. This is another reason to use flash-roasting mostly for smaller cuts. (But even this rule isn't universal – see pages 135, 136)

At the other end of the size spectrum, flash-roasting very thin pieces of meat, fish or poultry will not produce the browning reactions (see page 49) that are essential to the flavour of certain foods. A steak or chop, for instance, must be at least 1 in thick or it won't brown, and even then the browning will not necessarily add enough of that essential ingredient to the flavour of the meat. With thinner pieces, pan-grilling is the answer (see page 81). Or use the grill pan to brown the meat first, before flash-roasting.

IS IT ROASTING OR BAKING?

Some of the dishes in this chapter would, in other cookbooks, be called 'baked' rather than 'roasted'. In fact, though the two processes are thought of as being distinct, they are really the same. Why do we roast beef but bake bread, when both dishes are given precisely the same kind of cooking? The distinction is nothing more than a linguistic convention. Thus, though purists may object to my use of the term 'roasted' for some of the dishes in this chapter, I prefer to call them roasted because the application of heat has as much to do with the way we treat a rib of beef as it does with what un-lazy cooks do when they bake a lump of bread dough.

THE TECHNIQUE

There's nothing to it. First you preheat the oven to

230°C (450°F, Gas 8), or to
240°C (475°F, Gas 9)

if your oven goes up that high. If you're cooking yourself your evening meal, this should be the first thing you do when you walk in the door: preheating an oven to maximum temperature can take a while. But you can use that time to change your clothes, pour yourself a drink, turn on the radio, throw away the junk mail that arrived with the lunchtime post, and get the food ready for cooking. When the oven is up to temperature, you put in whatever you're cooking on the top rack of the oven. Then you just leave it for the times given below.

It's essential to use the top rack of the oven because this is where the heat is at its highest. As the air heats it rises; as it cools on contact with the food, which is at a lower temperature, it sinks again; and more hot air rises to continue the rapid cooking action. NB: if you have one of the new fan-assisted ovens, the distinction between top rack and middle rack becomes somewhat less important. And cooking times in general will be shorter. But since you have one of these fine pieces of equipment and I do not, you already know more about this subject than I do.

Cooking will be even faster the closer the food gets to the ceiling of the oven: the metal stores heat and thus gets even hotter than the ambient temperature of the air. Indeed, flash-roasting with the food less than 2 in from the ceiling of the oven becomes something like a cross between roasting and grilling. You can use this effect to good advantage for browning flash-roasted dishes, if you wish to.

But if you do use it, make sure the food isn't too close to the oven ceiling or it may get unpleasantly charred before the interior of the food has cooked. And needless to say, you must be sure that the food never touches the oven ceiling. Having scraped a few square feet of chicken skin off ovens in my day, I can testify personally that it's no fun.

THE EQUIPMENT

No special equipment is needed for flash-roasting, but I recommend using

a roasting or baking tin

rather than a Pyrex, enamelled, or ceramic dish. The thin metal of a roasting or baking tin gets hotter and speeds up cooking. And if you're cooking the food right in the dish, rather than on a rack, this is an important consideration. A rack may be used for plain poultry or red meat; roasting right in the tin is better for fish and for meat dishes cooked with vegetables or a sauce. In fact, I do most of my flash-roasting right in the tin. The only things I always use a rack for are very fatty cuts of meat. If you like to see the fat dripping away from the food, you should use a rack. The one from your grill, being perfectly flat, is good for this purpose.

Flash-roasting is a good way of cooking for guests, since the work can usually be done well in advance and completed, quickly, when your guests arrive. Very few flash-roasted dishes take more than half an hour to cook, so you can time them from the point when your guests have settled in for a preprandial drink. And if you make full use of the oven space, you will be able to cook two or even three dishes at the same time. Flash-roasting can be combined with

parcel-roasting (see page 180),
braising (see page 162), and
gratins (see page 185)

in a way that's both fuel-efficient and gastronomically satisfying.

But please bear in mind that the more you cook in the oven at any one time, the longer every dish will take to cook. If you're braising a piece of lamb and stick in a *gratin dauphinois* (see page 188), the temperature of the oven will drop suddenly and everything will take a few minutes longer.

When you're cooking for yourself, and in a hurry, dishes can be flash-roasted without further adornment. As long as you have good materials to start out with – a fine piece of fresh fish, a free-range chicken leg – you will be eating well. But naturally, you can also try a wide range of toppings, marinades and sauces. Use any of the basic marinades (see page 89) or a Spicy Yogurt Marinade (see page 94) to make the dish more special. And see the recommendations below.

POULTRY

CHICKEN

A whole chicken needs the special treatment described in Chapter 1. Pieces of chicken – and other birds – respond enthusiastically to flash-roasting. If you're cooking informally, the pieces can just be seasoned and popped in the oven. If you want to make them look better, e.g. for a dinner party, you may brown them first. Marinating too produces a good flavour, and you'll find a list of suitable marinades on page 89. There's also a list of suggested variations following the main instructions here.

PREPARATION

Of the many shortcomings of British butchers, none makes my blood boil faster than the way they 'quarter' a chicken. At a French *boucherie*, the wing is detached from the breast and the breast from most of the underlying bone and connective tissue. The leg is neatly carved off the carcass, taking with it the delectable 'oyster' which may be the best part of any bird. In Britain, by contrast, the bird is just hacked into 4 pieces. This makes the cook's job harder. If you want the quarters to look nice and to lie flat in the pan or roasting dish, you have to do some dissecting yourself. Breast must be detached from wing and from bone – and I suspect that thousands of people just throw them away. Legs must be cut away from the section of backbone that's left sticking to them as a clumsy, useless appendage.

While this makes me nearly apoplectic with rage and frustration, I can't recommend that you go through the dissecting routine on a regular basis. It's kind of therapeutic, if you like that sort of thing. (And I have to admit that I do like it, but I am peculiar.) But for everyday purposes, it is not the sort of thing that lazy cooks go in for. For dinner parties, yes. But not when you're cooking for yourself.

So you will probably, most days, just want to leave the chicken in its bought state. That's fine, with two minor qualifications.

> **Breasts**: Cut the wings off. They won't cook at the same rate as the breast, and in any case they should be saved for a special chicken wing dish (see page 76).
> **Legs**: Cut them in two, at the joint between drumstick and thigh. This makes turning and serving easier.

There's one other poultry preparation that's perfectly suited to flash-roasting, and that is hacking through the bone. This technique originated in Chinese cooking, but I use it to prepare chicken destined for all types of flavouring. The best way to do it is with a heavy Chinese cleaver; an alternative method is provided for cleaver-less cooks. For both methods, you need to start with chicken quarters, legs or breasts. Here's how.

With a cleaver: Holding the chicken on the chopping board with one hand and the cleaver in the other, bring the cleaver to shoulder level and chop down hard. Aim for a section of the chicken which is farthest away from the hand holding the meat on the board. Try to cut pieces that are between 1 and 2 in square, but don't worry too much about size; they'll cook just fine even if some pieces are a little bigger than others. Repeat until the chicken is cut up. And please: be careful about hacking too close to the hand on the chopping board. When the victim is smaller than a few inches in length, don't bother holding it down. Better to have to retrieve a piece of chicken from the floor than to go searching for a severed finger.

With an ordinary cook's knife: Use a large knife with a deep blade. Place the knife at the point where you want to make your cut, and smack the back of the blade with a wooden kitchen mallet (or even just a stout length of scrap wood). You'll quickly see how hard you have to pound, and probably you'll be surprised by how little force is needed. Repeat until the chicken is cut up.

Again, this is too much like hard work for really lazy cooks. But it's also therapeutic, especially if you're feeling furious about something.

BROWNING

Now that you have your chicken pieces ready, you can brown them if you wish. I skip this stage most of the time, as the pieces brown satisfactorily (at least for my taste) in the intense heat of the oven. But if you want to brown, proceed as follows.

Heat 2 tbsp of vegetable oil in a frying pan or grill pan (see page 49) till almost smoking. Put the chicken pieces in, leaving at least a 1 in space between them so the pan doesn't get too crowded. (Crowding produces steam, which inhibits browning.) Cook for 1–3 minutes per side, till golden brown; you may brown either on both sides or on the skin side only. Remove to paper towels and finish the other pieces. Browning can be done well in advance, which is useful for dinner parties. Do the browning in the morning, so you are the only person who gets a lungful of smoke, then leave the meat to cool, cover with a plate or kitchen foil, and refrigerate till needed. Remove from the fridge around 30 minutes before you want to cook, then finish the cooking in the evening. For more detailed information about browning, see page 49.

Chicken can be treated in two different ways for flash-roasting: in joints or in chunks. Here are the timings in an oven preheated to 230°C (450°F, Gas 8):

Breast: 25–30 minutes
Leg: 30–35 minutes
Wings: 20–25 minutes
Chunks: 15–20 minutes

If you cook good chicken in this way with nothing more than salt and pepper as seasonings, you will end up with a very good meal. But of course there are other tricks. Here are a few of them:

To give extra flavour with no extra work, use one of my favourite tricks for flash-roasting. Before you put the chicken in the roasting pan, scatter on the bottom one or more of the following:

1 medium onion, sliced very thin
1–2 cloves of garlic, sliced very thin
2 stalks of celery, sliced very thin
2 small carrots, sliced very thin
1 thin slice of ginger per chicken piece
1 whole bay leaf per chicken piece
whole Indian spices: cumin, fennel, coriander, fenugreek, cardamom
dried herbs: thyme, sage, rosemary, tarragon, herbes de Provence

Then put them in the roasting pan and lay the chicken pieces on top. Actually, you can use any of the combinations suggested for roast and casserole-roasted chicken. The flavourings cook into the chicken without burning, as they're moistened by the bird's juices. And the vegetables will retain quite a lot of crunch after such brief cooking, which is fine by me. Softer results can be obtained by adding dry wine or sherry to the vegetables in the roasting pan; this produces a small quantity of intensely flavoured instant gravy which needs nothing more than degreasing (see page 52). Or you can soften them further, and produce larger quantities of nearly-instant gravy, by proceeding as follows.

Remove the cooked chicken from the roasting tin and turn off the oven. Keep the chicken warm in the turned-off oven. Put the roasting tin, with its vegetables still in place, on a burner over a low heat. When the vegetables start to heat, pour in

225 ml (8 fl oz) chicken, beef or vegetable stock
50–60 ml (2 fl oz) dry white wine or dry sherry

Bring it to a gentle boil and cook, stirring regularly, for 4–5 minutes. Lift out the vegetables with a slotted spoon and keep them for serving with the chicken. Either reduce the gravy further for a stronger flavour, or just skim off the fat and serve as is.

Another flash-roasting trick for chicken is to make it with oil and vinegar, leaving a slightly tart cooking liquid which can then be either deglazed (as in the preceding suggestion) or just served as is. Here's the technique:

   Line the pan with

thinly sliced onions
herbes de Provence (see page 338)
bay leaves

Now sprinkle on top of this

about 1 tbsp wine vinegar

and leave it to sit for a while if you feel like it. In the meantime, mix thoroughly

1 tbsp wine vinegar
3 tbsp extra virgin olive oil
1 tsp dried tarragon, rubbed between the fingers to 'grind' it
plenty of salt and pepper

Put the chicken pieces in the pan and brush the 'vinaigrette' on top, or drizzle it on if you can't be bothered to brush. (Brushing makes for a more uniform coating.) Flash-roast for the times given above, and serve either deglazed or just with the onions and cooking liquid. (You'll have to degrease the liquid first.) This dish is particularly good at room temperature.

For a slightly more complex party dish, here is a combination of flavours that I particularly like with flash-roasted chicken. These ingredients will accompany a jointed 1.5–2 kg (3–4 lb) chicken, or 4 legs or 4 breasts.

Flash-roasted Chicken 'à la Provençale'

Brown the chicken if you wish to. Put in your roasting tin a selection of fresh or dried herbs, such as

fresh: basil, parsley, thyme, marjoram
dried: thyme, marjoram

Put the chicken on top of the herbs, trying to cover them completely with chicken. Now scatter over the top:

125 g (4 oz) green olives, stoned and quartered
2 large ripe tomatoes or 4–6 tinned Italian plum tomatoes, roughly chopped
2 medium cloves of garlic, minced

These ingredients can sit either on the chicken or in the bottom of the pan, or both. Finally pour on around

50–60 ml (2 fl oz) dry white wine
a squeeze of lemon (optional)

Roast in the way described above, and serve with noodles or rice.

Glazes

You can also use glazes on flash-roasted chicken to give flavour and extra colour. These mostly flavour the skin, so some of the effect will be lost to those people who don't eat chicken skin. But there's usually some trickle-down effect from the glaze, and the colour alone makes it worthwhile. If you use a glaze, you don't have to brown the chicken in chunks.

Here are a few easy glazes that I use regularly. Both of them should be brushed on to the chicken skin with a pastry brush for maximum coverage. These quantities will suffice for 4 chicken quarters.

Port and Balsamic Vinegar Glaze

2 tbsp ruby port
1 tbsp balsamic vinegar
1 tbsp honey
1 tsp herbes de Provence

Mix the ingredients thoroughly, whisking energetically to make sure the honey gets completely dissolved in the wine and vinegar. (If the honey is thick, you can make this easier by heating it for a few seconds in the microwave, or over a low heat in a small saucepan.)

Honey-Mustard-Soy Glaze

This is inspired by a coating for roast lamb in Julia Child's *Mastering the Art of French Cooking*. It is just as good – nay, better – on flash-roasted lamb chops.

1 tbsp honey
1 tbsp Dijon mustard
1 tbsp soy sauce
½ tsp powdered ginger

Mix the ingredients thoroughly, making sure the honey is thoroughly blended with the liquid ingredients.

DUCK

A whole duck is a tricky proposition because the legs take much longer to cook than the breast. When the same bird is cut into pieces, it becomes much simpler – and perfect for flash-roasting. Legs may be used this way, but breasts are unquestionably better. If you're buying a whole bird, joint it carefully into 2 boneless breasts and 2 whole legs, and save the legs to make a braise (see page 79). Save the carcass for stock or gravy.

Because of its thick layer of subcutaneous fat, duck breast should be browned before flash-roasting. Getting the timings right here can be very tricky, but the results are so good that it's worth the trouble. After eating a particularly delicious roasted duck breast at Adlard's restaurant in Norwich, I asked chef David Adlard for his technique. Here is my adaptation of his technique.

Heat a frying pan or grill pan till it's very hot and brush the flesh side of the duck lightly with vegetable oil. Slap it on to the pan, flesh side down, and cook for a minute just to brown it lightly. Then turn the pieces over with no extra fat and continue cooking until the skin has turned a deep mahogany colour. This should take anywhere from 3–5 minutes. When the skin has reached the right colour, transfer the pieces to the roasting tin and finish cooking in the oven. The timings after browning:

> **Breast:** 8–12 minutes
> **Leg:** 15–25 minutes

Duck can be seasoned in any of the ways described for chicken, including glazes and dry mixtures. If the meat has been browned, the seasoning should be added afterwards.

GUINEA FOWL

These excellent birds can be treated in exactly the same way as chicken for the purposes of flash-roasting. But because they're somewhat smaller than the average chicken, they will probably take somewhat less time to cook. Figure on

Breast: 20–25 minutes
Leg: 25–30 minutes

Seasoning and finishing are exactly the same as those given for chickens. As the slightly gamey flavour of guinea fowl goes well with sweet things, however, you can add something fruity to the pan. One trick I use is putting in a little fruit juice – apple or orange, by preference – either before or after cooking. You can achieve something of the same effect by sprinkling any flavourings in the pan with one of the following:

ruby port
crème de cassis
dessert wine

and then just cooking the bird in the way described above.

PHEASANT, WILD DUCK, WILD PIGEON

All these excellent birds respond beautifully to flash-roasting, but only if they're cut into joints – 2 boneless breasts and 2 whole legs. In both cases it's the breast that's the star attraction. Pheasant legs are full of tendons and cartilage that make them fiddly to eat, and they never get as succulent as the breast. You might prefer to freeze them and save them for a casserole (see page 80), or to chop them up and turn them into pan-grilled pheasant burgers. Wild pigeon legs are small and incredibly sinewy, but delicious nonetheless. They have slightly less of the chewy material than pheasant. Wild duck is least sinewy of all in the leg, and both joints can be used successfully for flash-roasting. Save the carcass to make either stock or a gravy to serve with the roasted bird; you'll find instructions for lazy stock-making on page 245.

The target timings are somewhat different for the three birds.

Pheasant: 10–12 minutes for breast or leg
Pigeon: 10–12 minutes for breast, 4–5 minutes for leg
Duck: 15–20 minutes for breast or leg

All these game birds go even better with sweet flavours than guinea fowl. Try roasting some apple slices with the bird, or brush the skins with a softened jam or conserve, e.g.

apricot
orange marmalade
plum

But the powerful flavour of these delicious things, just boosted a little with herbs or aromatic vegetables, will make a terrific meal for anyone's palate.

MEAT

Flash-roasting is suitable for chops, steaks, and small (i.e. thin) joints of meat. As a useful rule of thumb, 'thin' in flash-roasting means anything under 3 in. This is a good maximum thickness to aim at, though you can get away with 4 in if necessary. Because browning is so important to the flavour of meat, this first step is essential if you're flash-roasting really thin pieces such as steaks or chops. See the procedure given on page 49, and brown the meat on both sides.

It's hard to give hard-and-fast timings for flash-roasted meat. So much depends on the temperature of the meat, its inherent toughness, and the degree of doneness that you consider right. And this is without considering either the idiosyncrasies of your oven or the precise position in the oven at which you do your roasting. But the guidelines below should set you on the right track. Just keep an eye on things the first couple of times you cook: your oven and mine might be very different creatures.

PORK

Pork can be flash-roasted as small joints, steaks cut from leg or shoulder, or chops. In this as in other methods of cooking pork, I prefer those cuts that have 'red' rather than white meat – in other words, the cheaper cuts like shoulder, hand or 'spare rib chops' rather than the loin. These are easier to keep juicy, and I think they taste better. A thick piece cut from the leg also makes a good flash-roaster.

The drawback of flash-roasting pork is that it's hard to get the skin to become crackling. See the chapter on braising (page 69) for further remarks on this subject. The important point to remember when flash-roasting is that the cuts you're likely to use – small joints and chops – may not have skin on them in the first place. If they do, you will have to do without crackling. I think this is a small price to pay.

Timing flash-roasted pork is simple enough. Figure on:

12–15 minutes for every inch of thickness

The timing for chops and steaks will be considerably lower if you've browned them first and popped them straight into the oven. If you've browned them in advance and allowed them to cool, the reduction in cooking time will not be that great.

Because pork is used so extensively in Chinese cooking, I find that Chinese flavours provide the perfect accent to flash-roasted pork whether in chops, joints or steaks. See the soy sauce marinade on page 89 for a simple suggestion. Or just brush the meat before roasting with the Honey-Mustard-Soy Glaze on page 128. If you like pork with fruit, as many people do, try roasting the pieces on

prunes or dried apricots

well soaked in hot water and a little red wine. Chop the fruit roughly before scattering it in the roasting pan, and serve the pieces with the meat.

BEEF

Oven-fried beefsteak is a great dish, and one of the easiest around. You'll probably need to buy it from a good butcher who cuts meat to order, as the steak must be at least 2 in thick to achieve the best results. Fillet, forerib, rib eye, sirloin and T-bone are all perfect for flash-roasting. Brown them well first so the outside is a crusty brown. If you've got plenty of time, do the browning well in advance so your kitchen will have time to clear of smoke. The timings will vary quite a lot, depending on the temperature of the meat before cooking, the extent of the preliminary browning, and the length of time the beef sits between browning and roasting. Mostly, however, I have found that you can be pretty confident of needing around

10 minutes per inch of thickness

for a well-browned piece of beef.

Having said that you need a thick piece of meat for successful flash-roasting, I should add immediately that thinner cuts too can be cooked this way. Even steaks as thin as ½ in can be flash-roasted, though the results won't be quite as good as a freshly grilled steak. But this is a good way of serving steak to large numbers of people, if you're ever so inclined. The steaks should first be pan-grilled over a ferocious heat (see page 90) for precisely 30 seconds per side. They can then be put straight into the oven or cooled and refrigerated, then brought back to room temperature before cooking.

Then you put them in a roasting or baking dish, put the dish over a gentle heat to get them sizzling, and put them in the oven for

3–4 minutes

The meat in this technique can easily be combined with a sauce of your liking, which transforms the dish immediately. If you have some good stock or gravy left over from another dish, why not try a simple version of the classic English onion gravy? Here's how.

Onion Gravy

2 medium onions
a thick pat of butter
225–300 ml (8–10 fl oz) stock or beef gravy

Slice the onions as thin as you can get them without driving yourself crazy or massacring your fingertips. Melt the butter in a heavy saucepan and cook the onions slowly for 4–5 minutes, just to soften them and colour them lightly. Add the stock or gravy and bring to a boil, then turn down and simmer very gently, partly covered, for 30–40 minutes. The onions should be very tender and very sweet. Spoon this over the cooked meat.

As long as we're talking about steaks, we might as well talk about baked potatoes: the two go together perfectly. You can make a complete meal in the oven for up to 8 guests as follows.

Preheat the oven to 180°C (350°F, Gas 4). Around 3 hours before you plan to eat, prepare a tray of

red peppers with anchovies and garlic (see page 184)

and roast them as in the recipe. While they're cooking, prepare either a

clafoutis (see page 304) or
discs of shortcrust pastry (see page 309)

and bake them in the oven after the peppers have come out. Remove and set aside. If you're making pastry discs, prepare any of the toppings that follow the recipe. Brown the steaks for 1 minute per side, put them on another tray, and set aside. This can all be done well in advance.

One hour before you plan to eat, cook

1 baked potato

per person. At the temperature above, this will take around 50–60 minutes. You can shorten the cooking time by turning the heat up to 230°C (450°F, Gas 8) for the last 10 minutes, and you will need to do this to finish cooking the steaks. While the potatoes are cooking on the middle rack, prepare a green salad; this should be all the vegetable accompaniment you need for this substantial and satisfying meal.

Serve the peppers as a starter, perhaps with bread, or pan-grilled bread, when the potatoes are around 20 minutes from being cooked. When the potatoes are done, or nearly done, turn the oven up to 230°C (450°F, Gas 8). Take out the potatoes if necessary. Put in the steaks and finish cooking as described above, and serve with the potatoes, salad, and perhaps a tomato *salsa* (see page 323). The oven, which will have done heroic service, can now be turned off.

Rib of Beef

If you don't have a lot of people to feed, a large joint of rib of beef is not for you. It takes a long time to cook and is usually done at medium temperature. If you're feeding 2, 3 or 4, however, you can get one or two ribs cut by the butcher, flash-roast, and end up with one of the most splendid meals imaginable. The cut is a cross between a steak and a joint, and the flash-roasting technique – preceded by ample browning – produces results that are every bit as good as the traditional roast. Here's the way I like to do it.

Start with a piece of rib that's around

2–2½ in thick

Preheat the oven and heat a large frying pan (or grill pan) till it's very hot. Sear the beef in the pan for 5 minutes per side, then remove it to a roasting pan that's large enough to hold it easily. Scatter on top a good sprinkling of salt, pepper, and some dried herbs. The top choices are:

rosemary
herbes de Provence (see page 338)

Roast for 20 minutes (rare) or 25–30 minutes for medium-rare. If you happen to have a meat thermometer, the reading should be 120°F for a rare steak. Be sure to give it 15–20 minutes of resting time before carving it, and carve on the bias into thickish slices. (NB: don't try to slice in the usual roast beef manner, i.e. into thin slices running parallel with the side of the beef. It won't work.)

LAMB

Lamb is my other favourite choice among flash-roasted meats. This is partly because I happen to love lamb, and partly because it takes so well to this technique whether in chops, steaks, chunks or small joints. The general rule applies that thinnish pieces (under 1 in) don't do well in flash-roasting, but it can be done for large dinner parties. The timings are closer to those for pork than those for beef, as lamb shouldn't be rare. Figure on

12–15 minutes per inch of thickness

and start testing sooner rather than later. If lamb shouldn't be red inside, neither should it be grey and overcooked.

Good seasonings for flash-roasted lamb include marinades (see page 89), herbes de Provence, or a little tomato sauce (see page 233). To finish the dish off, you can deglaze the roasting pan with wine, stock, or water (at a pinch). Any gratin or potatoes *boulangère* (see page 148) will make a good accompaniment.

Here is a good variant on flash-roasted lamb which I've made very successfully more times than I can count.

Flash-roasted Lamb with Tomato Sauce

2 tbsp olive oil
500 g (1 lb) shoulder or leg of lamb, boned and cut into 1 in cubes
1 large onion
1 clove of garlic (or more, if you're crazy about garlic)
1 tsp thyme
100 ml (7–8 tbsp) tomato sauce
50 ml (3–4 tbsp) dry white or red wine

While the oven is preheating, heat the oil in a frying pan or grill pan and sauté the lamb till lightly browned (around 1 minute per side). Remove to a roasting dish and add the onion, garlic, and thyme. Cook for a couple of minutes, stirring constantly, till the onions are soft and lightly coloured. Pour in the wine and stir vigorously for a few seconds, then scrape the contents of the pan into the roasting pan with the lamb. Spoon over the tomato sauce and cook in the oven for 10–20 minutes, till the lamb is just cooked. Serve with rice or pasta.

There are few dishes more impressive for large dinner parties than a leg of lamb, and few more impressive ways of preparing the leg than to 'butterfly' it. This means boning the leg so that it rolls out in a flat piece of roughly uniform thickness. Butter-flying is easy if you've had some experience at it, but probably you'll want to get the butcher to do it.

And if you do that, try flash-roasting it with an Indian-style marinade. This recipe is inspired by one in Madhur Jaffrey's *Invitation to Indian Cooking*, where the well-marinated leg is cooked on the barbecue. By all means do it that way during the summer months. In colder weather, my flash-roasted recipe is just as distinguished. The same thing could be done with a shoulder of lamb, at a much lower cost. The results won't look quite as elegant, but the flavour will be every bit as good. Making the marinade is much easier with a food processor. Start it the day before so the lamb has 24 hours of marinating time.

Butterflied Leg of Lamb

2 bay leaves	6 thick slices of ginger
2 cloves	4 large cloves of garlic
1 small dried red chili or 1 tsp chili powder	1 medium onion
	juice of 1 lemon
2 tsp whole cumin	2 tbsp vegetable oil
10 green cardamom pods	300 g (10–12 oz) low-fat yogurt
1 tsp turmeric	1 leg of lamb
1 tsp whole coriander	

Process the bay leaves, cloves, chili, cumin, cardamom, turmeric and coriander long enough to turn them into a coarse powder – around 20 seconds. (If you don't have a food processor, grind the spices with a mortar and pestle or a coffee grinder.) Add the ginger, garlic and onion and process till they're coarsely chopped. (If you don't have a food processor, chop them by hand as fine as you can get them.) Add the lemon juice, oil and yogurt and process until you have a smooth, thin paste. (If you don't have a food processor, this will have to be done by hand; use a whisk.)

Trim the lamb of fat, if necessary, and spread the marinade over it with a spoon or spatula. Cover it and leave overnight in the fridge, spooning the marinade over and turning a couple of times (if you remember to).

Remove the meat from the fridge 2 hours before you plan to cook. Preheat the oven and scrape excess marinade off the meat. If you want to brown the meat, use a very large frying pan or grill pan, well preheated over a high flame. Brown the meat just for a couple of minutes, and on the skin side only. Then put it in a large roasting tin with the skin side down and scrape the marinade on top of the meat. Cook for 30–35 minutes, and serve with the browned skin side up. This needs some basmati rice and plain French beans (steamed, boiled or cooked à l'étuvée) to go with it.

Finally, for smaller gatherings, you can flash-roast a rack of lamb: one of the choicest cuts from this choicest of quadrupeds. The rack is made up of the cutlets, small chops from the neck end of the ribcage. There are usually 6–8 cutlets in each rack, and they make a perfect meal for 2 people.

For lazy cooks, the drawback of a rack of lamb is that it needs careful trimming if the result is to look suitably impressive: 3–4 in of meat, fat and gristle must be trimmed from the ends of the bones, which must then be scraped quite clean of soft tissue. I do not want you to do this yourself. If you can get your butcher to do it, however, here's the way to flash-roast this excellent cut:

Preheat the oven to 230°C (450°F, Gas 8). Trim away most of the fat from the top of the rack and brush it lightly with

1–2 tsp extra virgin olive oil

Now sprinkle it lightly with herbes de Provence or other herbs. You will need around 1 tbsp or maybe a little less. Put it in the oven for

15–18 minutes

brushing once with oil if the herb crust on top seems to be getting too dry. Allow it to rest for 10 minutes before carving and serving.

FISH

Flash-roasting has produced some of the best fish I've ever eaten, and it is one of the simplest of all fish cookery techniques. The fish cooks for a short time only, so there's little danger – as long as you watch your timings carefully – of drying out the delicate piscine flesh.

Browning reactions are less important in fish cookery than with meat: you don't expect fish to have that browned flavour. If you want the pleasant contrast between the delicate texture of the fish and something a little crunchier, however, you can produce it by painting or coating the flesh side of a fish steak or fillet with dried herbs or a herb-breadcrumb mixture. You can also combine flash-roasting with pan-grilling or plain frying to produce browning reactions. This works particularly well with thick steaks or fillets of cod or haddock.

Flash-roasting can be used for either fish pieces or whole fish. Happily, the timings are essentially the same whatever form the fish is in. The only variable is thickness, and here you can use the Canadian system, described by Julia Child in *The Way to Cook*, as a guideline:

When cooking fish in the oven, give it 10 minutes per inch of thickness.

While this should be used as a guideline only, it is a very useful one.

It's possible to flash-roast fish without adding fat before cooking, but the judicious addition of oil or butter will (a) keep the underside of the fish from sticking to the pan and (b) keep the surface of the fish from drying out. Since fish is one of the famous 'healthy' foods of the modern diet, many people assume that its healthy properties should be maximized by cooking it in a polyunsaturated vegetable oil. I am all in favour of healthy eating, but there's no reason to confine yourself to cooking according to dietary rules all the time. Fish tastes OK with polyunsaturated vegetable oil. It tastes even better, I think, with animal-derived fats and with extra virgin olive oil. So don't think you have to use safflower oil every time you flash-roast a piece of fish. Butter is better.

You can also use other animal fats for a stronger, more distinctive flavour which never fails to win plaudits. Here are some possibilities:

duck fat
goose fat
bacon fat, from green or smoked bacon
chicken fat

Naturally, I would not suggest that you buy a goose just to get the fat for flash-roasting a piece of cod. But if you happen to have some left over, do try it out. One tablespoon should be more than enough for 500 g (1 lb) of fish as long as you apply it with a pastry brush; and some of it will be left in the tin, so the fat won't add unduly to the caloric content. A dash of vermouth or wine may be mixed in before brushing.

Glazes

You can also glaze fish, and almost any flash-roasted fish will look and taste even more splendid if you give it a good brushful before cooking. The glaze should be clean-tasting rather than overpowering, and you can, if you wish, brush it on in advance so the fish has a chance to marinate. You can also do it at the last minute with equally good results. However you do it, brush the glaze only on to the fish flesh; if brushed on to the skin it will just slide off. Here are two quick glazes that work well for me. Both these quantities will generously glaze 500 g (1 lb) of fish.

Butter–Soy Sauce Glaze

2 thick pats of butter (around 25 g/1 oz)
1 tbsp soy sauce
1 tsp dry sherry

Over a very gentle heat, heat the butter till it just melts. Stir in the soy and sherry, and quickly brush on to the fish before the butter hardens.

Tomato and Balsamic Vinegar Glaze

1 tbsp extra virgin olive oil
1 tsp balsamic vinegar
1 tsp tomato purée

Mix the ingredients well, making sure the purée is fully dispersed in the oil and vinegar. (This is easiest with a wire whisk.) You can make this hours in advance, but whisk again just before brushing it on to the fish.

The next recipe is half-glaze, half-sauce. It is absolutely delicious, and well suited to even the fanciest dinner party. Your guests will think you've done something spectacular, but making the glaze takes all of 3 minutes. These quantities are enough for a couple of pounds of fish, and the recipe is especially good with flat fish.

Cream and Parsley Glaze

a small handful of parsley
1 spring onion
1 large pinch of dried thyme or tarragon
3 tbsp double cream
salt and pepper

Mince the parsley and spring onion and mix with the remaining ingredients. If possible, give it 15 minutes resting time for the flavours to blend. Brush some on to one side of the fish and put the fish in the roasting tin. Then spread the rest on the other side and put the fish in the oven.

FLAT FISH

Flash-roasting works well for whole flat fish – sole, plaice, brill, halibut or small turbot. The skin acts as a natural seal to lock in the juices from the fish, thus keeping the flesh moist. When peeled away, it reveals the flesh cooked simply and delicately (in spite of the fierce heat). Just brush the roasting tin and the fish with whatever oil or glaze you're using. Roast for

> **Sole or plaice:** 8–10 minutes
> **Brill:** 12–14 minutes
> **Small turbot:** 14–18 minutes

and serve immediately.

BROWNING

While it's true that fish doesn't need browning (and never browns in the way that meat does), glazed fish can benefit from a bit of browning *after* the main cooking has been completed. This is a technique that I often use with flat fish. Three or 4 minutes before you expect the cooking to be done, preheat the grill to a blazing heat. Remove the fish from the oven when it's perhaps just a little bit short of fully cooked and stick it under the grill till the skin is bubbling furiously and very slightly browned. This should not take more than

1 minute

if the grill is properly hot. Let it sit for 30 seconds or so, then remove it carefully from the pan and serve it forth. This works especially well with cream-glazed fish (see above).

Fillets of smaller flat fish – plaice, dab, flounder, sole or small brill – are a little trickier than whole fish, as they are so thin that they may cook almost instantly. I would check any of them after

3 minutes

and wouldn't expect them to take much longer than 5 minutes in all. In general, I don't use flash-roasting for these fish. Given all the effort of preheating the oven, it hardly seems worth the trouble just for 3 minutes of fish. Of course, if you're using the oven for other things anyway, flash-roasting thin flat fillets makes sense. And see the section below on a flash-roasting variant for use at dinner parties.

Fillets or even steaks of the larger flat fish – halibut and turbot – are excellent when flash-roasted. Choose fillets if you can: they're easier to manage and serve. Brush the roasting pan with oil/butter and the fish with oil or a glaze, and roast using the Canadian method (see page 139) as a guide. I don't like browning them under the grill, as the unprotected flesh has a tendency to dry out.

Flat Fish Fillets in Layers

When you're cooking food to serve at a party, you can vary the flash-roasted technique to produce a simple but excellent dish that I call Fish Lasagna. There is no pasta in the dish: the layers consist of fish fillets interleaved with vegetables and other stuff. It looks impressive, and it tastes good. And no one will ever know that it's hardly taken you any time to prepare. Here is the basic technique, with a couple of suggestions for different flavourings. Note that you can use a heavier dish – a gratin or baking dish – if you want to make the presentation a little snazzier. These quantities serve 4.

Fish Lasagna

8 fillets of plaice, sole, or flounder
1 medium onion
2 cloves of garlic
2 thick pats of butter
two 300 g (10 oz) packets of frozen chopped spinach
1 large pinch of nutmeg
50 ml (3 generous tbsp) double cream
4 tbsp fresh-grated Parmesan

Wash and dry the fish. Chop the onion and garlic very fine. Melt the butter in a saucepan and gently cook the onions and garlic for 2 minutes, then add the frozen spinach and let it defrost gently, turning and scraping the block every couple of minutes to speed it along. (This will take around 10–15 minutes.) When it's defrosted, turn the heat up slightly and add the nutmeg. Let it cook for a couple of minutes, till the spinach seems almost completely dry. Add the cream and cook again till it seems very dry (3–4 minutes). Stir in 2 tbsp of the cheese and leave to cool.

Butter a gratin or baking dish around 6 × 10 in in size. Line the bottom with 2 fillets, making sure they form something like a single flat layer. Smear on a quarter of the spinach mixture. Season with salt and pepper, and repeat the procedure with the remaining fish and spinach until it is all used up. The top layer should be spinach. Sprinkle on the remaining cheese. Bake in the oven for

30–35 minutes

till the fish is just cooked and the spinach is hot. I have found that a lasagna 2½ in deep takes exactly half an hour.

If your gratin dish is very large, or if you're cooking for 2 instead of 4, you could make this using only 2 layers of fish. The time needed will be around

15–20 minutes

ROUND FISH – FILLETS OR STEAKS

This type of fish – salmon, cod and haddock are my favourites – works even better in the flash-roasting technique. There's something to be said for both steaks and fillets. Steaks make convenient serving portions and look nice on the plate, and they can be cut to any thickness you specify. On the whole, however, I prefer thick fillets. You roast them with the skin side down and can then either serve the skin (which should get a bit crispy from the heat of the roasting pan) or leave it behind.

Whole pieces of a large fillet can be roasted if you like, but it's easier to serve them if you cut them into portion-sized pieces beforehand. Generally speaking, a piece of fillet around 3–4 in square will make a good-sized portion. The timing for any fish cooked in this method should be based on the Canadian method, i.e.

> 10 minutes for a 1 in piece
> 20 minutes for a 2 in piece

If you combine flash-roasting with pan-grilling or plain frying, the cooking time will be somewhat shorter – but not all that much shorter. This combination method is best with very thick cuts of fish, around 1½–2 in. I like doing it with cod fillet, but you can use steaks if fillets aren't available.

Whichever method you use, the technique is the same. First preheat the oven. Then preheat the grill pan or frying pan (which can't be nonstick for this purpose) over a very high heat. Brush the flesh side of the fillet generously with

vegetable oil or
extra virgin olive oil

and season it with salt and pepper. When the pan is really hot, slap the fish on with the flesh side down and cook it for

> 2 minutes

without moving it. Brush the skin, season, and turn the fillet over. You'll have to be careful when turning because the flesh may flake a little, but if you get the edge of the spatula right underneath the fish you should be OK. Cook for another 2 minutes.

You now put the fish into the oven. If your grill pan or frying pan has ovenproof or removable handles, you can use it as a cooking dish. If it doesn't, transfer the fillets to a roasting tin. In either case, the fish will need anything from

5–10 minutes

in the oven, again depending on the temperature of the fish when you began cooking it.

Cod fillets cooked in this way make a very good partner for Beetroot and Chili Salsa (see page 330), but they could also be served with nothing more than lemon wedges.

VEGETABLES

Vegetables too can be flash-roasted, using techniques which are described in the next chapter (see page 180). Either parcel-roasting or open roasting will do, and since the technique works at any temperature, you can easily combine the cooking of the vegetables with whatever main dish you're planning to serve.

Indeed, one of the greatest attractions of flash-roasting is its usefulness as the basis for an entire oven-cooked meal. This is especially useful for last-minute dinner parties. On occasion, everyone has to cook a dinner party at the last minute. When this happens to you, flash-roasting a whole meal, or most of it, may be the best thing you can do.

It's a curious phenomenon that almost any flash-roasted vegetable, in my experience, takes approximately the same time. You can rest easy if you set your timer for

30 minutes

and then settle down to read the paper. Here is a list of vegetables that take well to flash-roasting in an open pan. (For more detail about parcel-roasting, see page 180.)

small new potatoes (see below)
baking potatoes, sliced 1 in thick
aubergines, sliced 1 in thick
fennel, sliced 1 in thick
onions, sliced 1 in thick
peppers, red, yellow or green (in that order of preference)
tomatoes

Just brush them with any of these fats:

extra virgin olive oil
butter, preferably clarified
bacon fat
goose fat
duck fat
plain vegetable oil

Season lightly with salt and pepper, pop them in the oven, and relax. If you wish, you can check them half-way (i.e. after 15 minutes) and spoon some of the oil over them. But they should be fine even if left to get on with cooking undisturbed.

THE BOULANGÈRE VARIATIONS

Potatoes are the first choice for flash-roasting. I am particularly fond of flash-roasted new potatoes, well scrubbed and skins left on. The skin crisps up beautifully while absorbing some (but not too much) of the cooking fat. The insides get creamily tender. And most people, accustomed to eating new potatoes boiled, are terribly impressed.

But main-crop floury potatoes also do well with flash-roasting, and I am crazy about one particular method. There is a famous dish in French bourgeois cuisine called *pommes boulangère* which combines potatoes and onions with a little butter and stock, and cooks them in the oven till the potatoes are just cooked through and the onions soft. The dish usually takes around 45 minutes to cook, which makes it a bit time-consuming for true flash-roasting. But it's so easy, and so delicious, that I feel justified in including it here – especially because it has spawned a wealth of combination dishes in which the spuds are cooked with meat or fish to make a complete main course.

Any dish described as '*à la boulangère*' is perfect for lazy cooks because you start cooking the spuds while you get the other ingredients ready. Then you add them to the potato dish and relax while they finish cooking. Here is the basic recipe – in quantities sufficient to serve 4 people as a side dish – plus variants using meat and fish.

Many of the classic *boulangère* dishes use large chunks of meat which need more cooking than the potatoes. These are of no relevance here. I've concentrated on using smaller pieces which will cook easily in the time between getting home from work and the time at which you're feeling hungry.

Pommes Boulangère

2 large waxy potatoes (around 400 g (14 oz) in weight)
1 medium onion
2 thick pats of butter
175 ml (6 fl oz) chicken or beef stock (optional)

Preheat the oven to 230°C (450°F, Gas 8). While it's preheating, slice the potatoes around ¼ in thick; you can peel them if you're cooking for friends, but for ordinary meals it's fine (and easier) to leave the peel on. Finely chop or slice the onions into pieces or shreds. Smear a baking dish around 8 × 10 in with some of the butter, and put in a layer of potatoes. Now put in a layer of onions, then finish with another of potatoes. Pour in the stock if you're using it, and dot with the remaining butter. Bake at the top of the oven until the spuds are cooked and lightly browned, around 30–35 minutes. If you want to, you can cover the dish lightly with aluminium foil for the first 15–20 minutes of cooking. You can even leave it on throughout, which makes it less likely that the potatoes will dry out. You won't brown the crust if you proceed this way, but *pommes boulangère* is not a gratin (see page 185), so a crust isn't essential. On the other hand, it tastes good.

Once you've mastered this dish – and you'll probably get it right on the first try – you can move on to the variations. Use just about any meat you like. Brown it first if necessary (see page 49). For the first two variations, using thick slices of cooked ham (which always makes a good partnership with potatoes) and a piece of fish fillet, browning is happily superfluous.

Ham Boulangère

ingredients for basic Pommes Boulangère (see above)
4 slices good cooked ham, each ¼–½ in thick
a small handful of parsley

Chop the parsley as fine as you can be bothered. Proceed with cooking the potatoes as described in the master recipe, but be sure to include the stock. Also: when you put in the onion layer, add to it the chopped parsley. Cover with foil and cook for 20 minutes. Now remove and add the ham slices in 1 layer, with a little overlap if necessary. Cover again (so the ham doesn't dry out) and return to the oven for another 15 minutes. The ham just needs to be heated through, as it's already cooked. Serve with mustard and pickles on a cold winter night.

You can also use another humble ingredient: sausages. The sausages cannot be industrial-grade specimens in this dish, as their poor flavour and texture will shine through revoltingly.

Sausages Boulangère

ingredients for basic Pommes Boulangère (see above)
250 g (8 oz) onions
500 g (1 lb) best sausages

Preheat the oven to 180°C (350°F, Gas 4). Wash the potatoes, peeling them if you wish, and cut them in slices around ¼–⅜ in thick. Cut the onions in half lengthwise and then into slices around ¼ in thick. Butter a baking dish and put in a layer of potatoes. Season lightly with salt and pepper, then put in all the onion slices plus another dose of salt and pepper. Finish off with the potatoes, more salt and pepper, and finally the sausages. Cook in the middle of the oven for 35–40 minutes, till the potatoes are cooked and the sausages lightly browned. The juice from the sausages will moisten and flavour the spuds.

The following recipe is a major departure from true *boulangère* cooking, as the fish is flavoured with Indian spices. Use the Spicy Yogurt Marinade (see page 94) or a simpler version using either so-called curry powder or so-called tandoori mix. There are good enough brands of both these preparations, but it's almost as easy – and much tastier – to make your own.

Cod Boulangère à l'Indienne

ingredients for basic Pommes Boulangère (see above)
500 g (1 lb) cod, haddock, or pollack fillet
2 tbsp low-fat yogurt or fromage frais
1 tsp mild curry powder or tandoori mix
1 tsp wine vinegar
juice of ½ a lemon

If the fish skin is scaly, remove the scales or cut off the skin altogether (or get the fishmonger to do this for you). Put in a dish large enough to hold the fish in one layer. Mix the remaining ingredients and smear lavishly all over the fish. Leave to marinate for at least 1 hour, and all day (or overnight) if possible.
   Prepare the potatoes and get them cooking. They will need 25 minutes in the first stage, as the fish needs only 10 minutes in the oven. After 25 minutes, lay the fish pieces on top and cook, uncovered, for another 10–15 minutes. Serve with a green salad.

The third variation is my favourite of all: lamb chops *à la boulangère*. You can use cutlets, loin chops, slices from the leg or shoulder, or chunks or strips of boneless shoulder. Whichever you use, this is one of the best meat dishes imaginable.

Lamb Chops à la Boulangère

ingredients for basic Pommes Boulangère (see above)
4–8 lamb chops, around 500 g (1 lb) in weight
1 tsp dried rosemary, crumbled, or herbes de Provence
50 ml (2 fl oz) dry white wine

Get the potatoes cooking as described above. They will need 20–25 minutes in the first stage of cooking. While they're cooking, brown the lamb for around 1 minute per side – just enough to brown it deeply but not cook it through. Remove the potatoes from the oven and sprinkle on the herbs, then put on the chops in a single layer and drizzle on the wine. Return to the oven for 15–20 minutes more, until the chops are done medium-rare and the potatoes cooked through. Serve immediately.

The basic *boulangère* ingredients – potatoes and onions – can be used together in a much less formal way. You cut them up, strew them in hot fat in a roasting tin, and just stick them in the oven. This is a dish simple enough for an evening alone yet delicious enough to serve to guests. The way forward:

500 g (1 lb) potatoes
250 g (8 oz) onions
2–3 tbsp vegetable oil, bacon fat, or duck fat

Chop the potatoes and onions into chunks or slices no more than around ½ in thick. Heat the oil in a roasting tin or in the preheated oven (for around 5 minutes by the latter method) and put in the vegetables. Stir them to coat with oil, season with salt and pepper, then roast in the oven for 30–35 minutes. The potatoes should be crisp and light-brown on the outside, tender to a sharp knife on the inside.

Needless to say, you can do the same thing with either potatoes on their own or onions on their own. If you add a small handful of fresh herbs, either before or after cooking, you'll be treating your guests to a memorable experience.

Vegetables of
Distinction

Vegetables have suffered from an excess of good press. They are good for us, low in calories and rich in vitamins, fibre and minerals; and most people, we know, eat too little of them. If they ate more vegetables, their health would probably improve.

Why is all this good press a problem? Because it has given rise to a new orthodoxy about the culinary treatment of the basic material. Having acquired a reputation for being 'healthy', vegetables are supposed to be cooked lightly or not at all – preferably by steaming or stir-frying.

Healthy eating is a fine thing, but sometimes you need a break. And lazy cooks can have one if they use some lesser-known methods which produce delicious results with a minimum of trouble. Like most of the methods in this book, these are relatively leisurely affairs. Split-second timing is much less important here than in steaming or stir-frying.

KNOW YOUR MATERIALS

If you've ever shopped at a UK greengrocer, you've probably experienced something like the following scenario. You walk in and see a box of picture-perfect mushrooms – unblemished, pearly white, caps tightly closed. So you ask for mushrooms and the person serving you turns his or her back to take them from a different box and put them in a bag. When you get home you find that these are yesterday's mushrooms, or last week's: dry, brown, wrinkled and disgusting.

If this happens to you, you have two choices. One is to shop at supermarkets. And ardently though I support the idea of shopping locally at specialist suppliers, I can see why so many people prefer supermarkets. You can pick precisely what you want, without enduring the scowls when you squeeze a melon or ask for five ounces of carrots if that's all you need. And if you buy a cauliflower that turns out to be inedible, you have only yourself to blame.

The other choice is to be persistent and *insist* on picking out everything yourself at your local greengrocer. You can do this in a way that's both firm and polite. Pick the melons up and sniff them to see if they're ripe. (If they smell strongly and sweetly of melon, they're ripe.) Point to the tray of mushrooms and say, 'Please take them from there.' Squeeze the courgettes to make sure they haven't gone soft. If the proprietors object, make it clear that you will not shop there unless they let you pick things out yourself. If they still object, leave. (Saying something rude is optional. Personally, I find that it's a useful catharsis – though the desirability of achieving catharsis bears an inverse relationship to the size of the person serving me.)

In my experience, however, even reluctant greengrocers eventually give in to intelligently picky shoppers. Once it becomes clear that this is the way you shop, they'll put up with it if they want your custom. You'll have become a regular customer, and retailers love regular customers. It's as simple as that. And if the greengrocer is a good one, he or she will come to value the attention of a careful shopper. Ask questions – the person serving you may be an expert – and learn from the answers.

Of course, if you shop at supermarkets then all these complaints are irrelevant. In any event, this is all a long-winded way of saying that you have to be careful when you're choosing vegetables. I can't give detailed instructions on what to look for in each vegetable, but a few basic principles apply.

1. Vegetables should be firm to the touch, not soft or flexible or wrinkly. Give them a good squeeze – at both ends and in the middle – to test for firmness. With long, thin vegetables such as carrots and courgettes, try bending them. If they bend, reject them.

2. Any hint of brown is a sign that the vegetable has passed its peak of freshness and is declining into senescence.

3. Big is not necessarily better. As vegetables grow, they can often become (a) too starchy, (b) too fibrous or 'woody', or (c) too watery. Items (a) and (c) affect taste. Item (b) affects texture. All three are undesirable. Small is beautiful in all of the following: carrots, courgettes, aubergines, turnips, parsnips. If you're boiling or steaming them with the skins on, potatoes will cook better if fairly small.

VEGETABLES
À L'ÉTUVÉE

In French, *étuve* can mean a steam bath, an incubator, or a damp, warm cellar used for ripening cheese. In the kitchen, cooking something *à l'étuvée* means heating it slowly in a covered pan. The food cooks by a combination of heat from the pan and steam released by the vegetables. This technique is perfect for many vegetables, and it's especially welcome for lazy cooks because the vegetables can be left to their own devices while you get on with other things. Here is the basic technique.

Chop the vegetables (see table below) and prepare any flavourings you want to use. Get out a heavy frying pan or shallow casserole. For every 500 g (1 lb) or so of vegetables, heat in the pan around 1 tbsp of one of the following:

extra virgin olive oil
butter
duck or chicken fat (highly recommended)
plain oil

The fat or oil should not be too hot: the lowest setting on your hob should do the trick. Put in the vegetables and flavourings. Toss the contents till they are well coated with oil, then put on the cover and leave the pan alone. In theory, you should check it and give it a stir every 5–10 minutes. In practice, this isn't always necessary.

BROWNING

Vegetables, like meat, can sometimes be browned. Combining this technique with cooking *à l'étuvée* can be delicious, but it works best with certain vegetables – onions, carrots, potatoes are the three biggies in this category. To brown first, proceed as follows:

Put the oil in the pan over a high heat – not the hottest, but something just below the hottest. Add the vegetables in a single layer, taking care not to crowd them too much. Let them cook that way for a couple of minutes, then pick one piece up and check it out: if it hasn't coloured, put it back to cook for another minute or two. When it's turned a light caramel colour, turn all the pieces so the browned side faces up. You can proceed this way almost indefinitely, trying to brown every single square millimetre of surface area, but in practice this is tiresome and difficult. A few browned patches are usually enough to give both flavour and colour.

Here are some detailed instructions for two vegetables that work particularly well when cooked à l'étuvée, followed by a list of approximate timings for other vegetables.

The nutritionally-minded will note that cooking à l'étuvée flies in the face of the quick cooking which preserves the nutritional content of vegetables. I have nothing to say to them except that these dishes taste delicious – and the vitamin C content can be beefed up by adding lemon juice at the end. (This is usually a delicious addition in any case.)

Cabbage à l'Étuvée

One of the best vegetables for this technique, easy, cheap and delicious. Green-leafed cabbages are best (e.g. Savoy), though the white stuff will do fine.

Take a whole head of cabbage and cut it in half lengthwise. Using a small, sharp knife, cut out the hard, woody core and then slice it around ⅜ in thick. Heat some oil medium-hot in a casserole and stir-fry the cabbage for a few minutes, turning down the heat if it's browning more than you want it to. Season heavily with salt and pepper. When it's well mixed with the oil, add spices. I like using around 1 heaped tsp of each of the following whole Indian spices:

cumin	*fennel seeds*
coriander	*cardamom*
fenugreek	

Mix well and cook for another couple of minutes. Add a little bit of stock or water and bring to the boil, then cover, turn the heat down, and cook slowly for anything in the vicinity of

45–90 minutes

If that sounds vague, it's because the exact cooking time will depend on the amount being cooked, the size and thickness of your pan, and the degree of crunch you like in your cabbage. But since cabbage is equally good at the chewy and the melting stages, you don't need to worry too much. Stir it every 10 minutes or so, and add more liquid if needed.

You can also turn out a quick and easy one-dish meal by cooking large chunks of meat in the cabbage. Lamb and especially pork give the best results. Cut the meat in 1–2 in pieces. Browning is optional (see page 49). Put the meat in, making sure it's well buried within the mess of cabbage. It will be done when the cabbage is done.

Potatoes à l'Étuvée

Potatoes cooked *à l'étuvée* are best left unpeeled, so they retain their shape and don't release starch from the insides. For this reason the technique works best with small new potatoes, each a maximum of around 2 in in diameter; the ideal size is 1½ in. Try to make sure the potatoes are around the same size, so they're done at the same time.

500 g (1 lb) new potatoes, each around 1½ in in diameter
2 sprigs of fresh rosemary
6 cloves of garlic
2 tbsp extra virgin olive oil or chicken, duck, or goose fat

Heat the oil over a moderate heat in a frying pan that has a lid. Add all the ingredients and stir to coat, then cover the pan and turn the heat right down to its lowest setting. Set a timer for 30 minutes and leave the potatoes to cook, shaking the pan *without taking the lid off* every 5 minutes or so. They should be done in 30 minutes, but test one by sticking a very small, sharp knife into the centre. If the knife goes in smoothly right to the centre, the spuds are cooked.

If the potatoes are cooked before the other dishes they can be left quite happily, covered and with the heat off, for up to an hour. If they've sat that long, reheat them over a very gentle heat for 2–3 minutes. Eat them with chicken or lamb chops, or even with scrambled eggs. Everyone loves this dish.

VARIATION

Use sage instead of rosemary, and substitute for the garlic

1 medium onion, sliced as thin as possible

Add the potatoes and sage on their own and set the timer for 15 minutes. Cook, covered, shaking the pan occasionally. After 15 minutes add the onions and stir them around. Set the timer for another 15 minutes and cook, shaking occasionally. By 30 minutes the onions will be soft, sweet, and very lightly browned. They will be ridiculously delicious. Eat immediately or let them sit for a while, then reheat quickly just before serving.

Other Vegetables *à l'Étuvée*

This should give you the basic idea. Once you've cooked by this method a couple of times, you can use it for any vegetable. Here are a few of my favourites, with approximate cooking times and a few suggestions for extra flavourings.

French beans: Leave them whole or cut in half. After coating with the oil, leave them to cook for 10–15 minutes. A sliced clove of garlic, added first, makes a nice companion for beans. So do sliced mushrooms, which should be added around half-way through.

Broccoli: Cut them into smallish pieces so they have a better chance of cooking evenly. Cook for 15–20 minutes, and flavour at the end with soy sauce and Chinese oyster sauce, or with lemon or lime juice plus a minced spring onion.

Carrots: Slice ⅛–¼ in thick and cook for 15–20 minutes. I like the sweetness of cooked carrots all on its own, but you can add a little minced ginger or a pinch of caraway seeds at the beginning of cooking. Fresh herbs at the end, especially dill, are also a good bet.

Courgettes: Slice ¼–½ in thick and cook for 10–15 minutes. They won't need any more than that because courgettes are watery and delicate. Garlic is a good accompaniment, or garlic, ginger and spring onion (see page 332).

Vegetables Steeped in Stock

If you have some really serious chicken stock lying around – or liquid left over from braising some other vegetables or a meat dish – use it for steeping vegetables. This is a variation on braising, designed for cooking in a saucepan on top of the stove. The resulting dish is a cross between a vegetable dish and a soup, and it makes a good accompaniment to a roast or steak. Here is an example.

Steeped Courgettes

500 g (1 lb) small courgettes
285 ml (10 fl oz) truly delicious chicken stock or braising liquid, strained

Trim the courgettes and cut them into 1 in pieces. Bring the liquid to a boil and put in the courgettes. Stir them around for a minute or so, then put the cover on half-way and simmer for another 2 minutes. Turn off the heat and leave, half covered, for 20–30 minutes. Serve with the liquid if it's sufficiently well flavoured, or save it (refrigerated) for recycling in another dish.

Attention-free Vegetables

Cooking *à l'étuvée* is easy, but here's a technique that's even easier. You cut up the veg, put them in a heavy pan with a little bit of liquid (stock or water), and just let them simmer over the gentlest heat – stirring only when you remember to – for anything up to 40 minutes. Broccoli, onions, beans and carrots are particularly good when treated in this way. Take

500 g (1 lb) vegetables

and cut them in small pieces. Take a heavy pan that has a lid and, if you wish, heat in it

1 tbsp extra virgin olive oil or a thick pat of butter (1–2 tbsp)

Now put in the vegetables along with around

60 ml (4 tbsp) stock, braising liquid, or water

Season with salt and pepper, stir well, and put the lid on. Turn the heat down to its very lowest point and let the vegetables cook gently, stirring every 5 minutes or when you remember to. Cooked by this method, broccoli (a good choice) will take around 25–30 minutes to reach the perfect *al dente* soft-crunch result. When cooked, the vegetables can easily be left for up to an hour with the lid on; if you will be leaving them, however, it's usually worth undercooking slightly.

BRAISED VEGETABLES

Braised vegetables are delicious. The cooking is very gentle, and the flavour can either be simple – the vegetable itself with just stock – or as complicated as you care to get. You can use any vegetable you want, but the more delicate ones – courgettes, for example – have a tendency to soften to the point of major mushiness.

The time to braise vegetables is when you're using the oven anyway – for roasting or braising a meat dish. This makes maximum use of oven space, and most braised vegetables go well with most red meat dishes. Since you'll be cooking the vegetables while another dish is in the oven, cooking times and temperatures will be determined by the main dish.

Happily, this is not a problem. Braising is always a relatively temperature-insensitive method, and braised vegetables are no exception. As long as you adjust the cooking times accordingly, you'll get good results at any temperature you happen to use. Here are some guide times and temperatures which should cover most cooking situations. They are all based on using the middle shelf of the oven; using a lower or higher rack will lengthen or shorten the cooking time by around 20 per cent. Remember also that the more you're cooking in the oven, the lower the effective temperature will be.

> 180°C (350°F, Gas 4): 1–1½ hours
> 200°C (400°F, Gas 6): 50 minutes–1¼ hours
> 230°C (450°F, Gas 8): 30–45 minutes

Classic braised vegetable recipes usually call for the use of ample quantities of butter. I am all in favour on this point, as the butter adds flavour and richness to the finished product. But braising without butter works equally well from the technical point of view – i.e. there is no danger of sticking unless the dish gets seriously overcooked – and it makes a major saving in the calories department. Let your conscience be your guide.

Most classic recipes call also for browning the vegetables. This too is optional, though it lends the inimitable browned flavour to the dish and is therefore a Good Thing on culinary grounds. I've included instructions for this, so you can do it if you're feeling particularly energetic. If you don't brown, the flavour will still be excellent.

My favourite braised vegetables are celery, carrots, chicory (Belgian endive), and cabbage. The first three are treated identically, while cabbage is somewhat different because it has to be chopped or sliced. Here are the basic recipes, followed by some variations. Remember, the flavourings possibilities are infinite. You can use the unadorned vegetable (which is perfectly good, incidentally), or you can add your own selection.

Braised Celery

First get the right dish: Pyrex or enamelled cast iron, and of a size that will hold the vegetables snugly but easily in a single layer. Thin metal baking dishes are inappropriate, as they will conduct heat too rapidly and may lead to overcooking.

Cut the base from the head of celery and wash the stalks. Top and tail them, and cut into pieces around 3–4 in in length.

If you wish to brown the vegetables first, use

1 thick pat of butter (1–2 tbsp), or more if you're not worried about calories

and melt it in the gratin dish (or in a frying pan if you don't want to use Pyrex on the hob). When it starts to sizzle, put in the celery and cook for a few minutes, turning steadily, until the pieces are lightly browned. I usually skip this stage, even though some writers consider it to be essential.

Now put the celery in the gratin dish (if you haven't done the browning in it) and pour on

200–800 ml (7–28 fl oz) stock or other liquid

The stock should be as good as you've got, and the home-made variety is obviously preferred. But a cube will do fine if it's all you have. I've specified a wide range of quantities because it will depend on how much you're cooking and the size of your gratin dish. The important thing to remember:

the stock should three-quarters cover the vegetables

As long as you follow this rule, the celery will be cooked properly. Now you can add salt and pepper if desired. Pepper is always a good thing, just a light, uniform sprinkling over the surface. If you're using stock from a cube, salt may not be needed – stock cubes tend to be pretty salty to begin with.

Finally you can take, if you wish,

a thick pat of butter (1–2 tbsp)

Break it into little pieces and dot it over the surface. This is strictly optional, though it does lend a smoothness and richness which I hate to do without.

The dish is now ready for braising. Cover it loosely with aluminium foil, which slows the evaporation of the cooking liquid and protects the vegetables from the fierce oven heat, and put the dish in the oven – preferably on the middle shelf. Again, 180°C (350°F, Gas 4) for 60–90 minutes is the target timing. But if you're using a different temperature for another dish, you can easily adjust the cooking time. Check the dish every 20 minutes or so to monitor its progress.

Braised Carrots

Carrots are braised by exactly the same method as the one used for celery. They should be topped and tailed, and peeled or washed as you prefer; if they are large, cut them into pieces around 3–4 in in length. Then braise as in the celery recipe.

Braised Chicory

This will need nothing more than a trimming of the bottom (taking care not to cut off too much, as leaves will fall away if you do) and removal of any brown leaves. It's important with chicory to fit the heads snugly into the gratin dish, as the leaves tend to fall apart if the heads have too much space in which to flop about. Some people tie them with thread or string, but a snug fit makes this unnecessary. Braise as in the celery recipe.

Braised Cabbage

Eating braised cabbage makes cabbage-haters change their minds. I cook this dish regularly, especially in winter, and it always gets a rave review.

My favourite flavourings for braised cabbage are Indian spices, large quantities of garlic and rosemary, and tomatoes. Whichever you use, the procedure is the same. Prepare the cabbage as for Cabbage *à l'Étuvée* (see page 158) and sauté it for 5–10 minutes in one of the following:

butter
extra virgin olive oil
duck or bacon fat

If you're using butter, make sure you do the initial cooking over a very low heat or the butter will burn. Now put in the flavourings. Here are some ideas:

Indian spices (see page 158)
4–5 large cloves of garlic, peeled and cut in half, plus a large sprig of fresh
   rosemary or 1 tsp dried
a 400 g (14 oz) tin of Italian plum tomatoes, well drained and de-seeded if you
   have the energy

Put in the stock, bring to the boil, then cook in the oven or on the hob. This dish benefits from really long cooking.

A Dinner Party Trick

Lazy cooks normally eschew the elaborate presentation found in fancy French-type restaurants. But if you have some really well-cooked braised cabbage, here's a trick I learned from my old friend Dorothy Pace – the best cook I know – which will knock your friends' socks off with hardly any effort. All you need is a set of ramekins or other small, ovenproof dishes. It helps to have cabbage that's very thinly sliced for this dish, but it's not essential.

Boil a kettle of water. When the cabbage is very soft, put it in the ramekins using a slotted spoon. Pack it down well, then squeeze out most of the liquid. (This is easiest if you press the bottom of one ramekin on to the surface of the cabbage in the others.) Now pour on to each filled ramekin

1 tbsp single cream

Give it a minute to sink into the cabbage. Place the ramekins in a baking tin and pour in the boiled water till it comes at least three-quarters of the way up the sides of the dishes. Now place the baking tin in the oven and cook for a while. Approximate cooking times:

180°C (350°F, Gas 4): 45 minutes
200°C (400°F, Gas 6): 35 minutes
230°C (450°F, Gas 8): 25 minutes

When the cabbage on top of the ramekins is slightly browned and the centres are hot, the dish is done. They can now be unmoulded on to the dinner plates, producing a neat, disc-shaped mound which looks ridiculously impressive. Dorothy omits the cream, tops her cabbage mounds with a quickly-fried slice of *foie gras*, and serves them as a starter. They are just as good as a vegetable accompaniment to any braised or roasted meat dish. If you want to serve them as a starter and you feel comfortable poaching eggs, the poached eggs would make an excellent topping. Just plop one egg on to each unmoulded mound of cabbage.

CHARRING

Charring takes cooking *à l'étuvée* one step further. When you cook vegetables long enough over a sufficiently high heat, with little or no liquid, browning reactions take place at the surface. This produces a delicious contrast of flavours between the slightly 'burnt' outside and the moist interior.

Charring is also related to stir-frying but it differs in that you don't keep the food in constant motion. And the aim is not, as in true stir-frying, to cook all the pieces of food to exactly the same degree. Indeed, this technique aims precisely to *avoid* uniformity in the final result.

The cooking vessel must be fairly large so the vegetables don't steam rather than fry. If using an ordinary pan, use plenty of oil so the vegetables don't stick. Less oil is needed in a nonstick pan. If you're cooking a large quantity of vegetables, an enamelled cast-iron casserole might be best.

The technique is more or less identical for all charred vegetables:

Clean the vegetables and slice them as suggested in the list below. For every 500 g (1 lb) or so of vegetables, heat around

1 tbsp of plain oil or extra virgin olive oil

Don't use butter, as it will burn over the intense heat of the pan. When the oil is hot, put in the vegetables. Season well with salt and pepper, then stir well to mix the oil in. Turn the heat up a bit higher, and cook for the time given for each individual vegetable below. Stir every few minutes, or when you remember to.

Some vegetables will benefit from being cooked initially with the cover on, so they get a chance to soften right through to the centre. With a little experimentation you will soon see which technique you like. But if you do use this one, remember to take the cover off for the last couple of minutes or the vegetables won't char.

The finished dish will contain some pieces that are well browned, some that are lightly browned, and some that are not browned at all. Similarly, some pieces may be on the soft side while others are lightly cooked. This does not matter. Charring aims to produce a contrast of flavours and textures, so the lack of uniformity is an advantage rather than a disadvantage. Needless to say, this is a blessing for lazy cooks.

Some charred vegetable dishes are well known – the American hash brown potatoes are a good example. The same principle can be applied to a wide range of green vegetables and to other starchy types too. Here are a few of the best.

Beans, French

This is the first vegetable to experiment with, as it is easy and the results are delicious. Just prepare the beans in the usual way (washing, topping and tailing), then cook as described above.

Cooking may take anywhere from 5–15 minutes depending on the size of the pan, the quantity of beans being cooked, and the heat of the pan. They are every bit as good served at room temperature. A spectacular rendition of charred beans appears in Chinese cuisine under the name of 'Dry-fried Beans'. The best recipe for this dish, as for so many Chinese dishes, appears in *Yan-Kit's Classic Chinese Cookbook*, by Yan-Kit So.

Broccoli

Separate the stalks from the florets, leaving around 1 in of stalk attached to the florets. Peel the stalks if you're feeling energetic; otherwise, cut them in halves or quarters depending on their thickness, and then into 2 in lengths. Now, using a small, sharp knife, cut the florets into small pieces no more than 1½ in at their thickest. If you've peeled the stalks, they may be cooked with the florets. If you haven't, proceed as follows:

Heat around 1 tbsp of oil over a medium-high heat in a frying pan large enough to hold the broccoli in one layer. When it is very hot, put in the stalks. Stir to coat with oil, then cover and leave for 1 minute. Add the florets, stir to mix well, and cover again for another minute. Stir again and leave for another minute. Now turn the heat off and leave the pan covered. Before you do this, further flavourings may be added. I suggest:

garlic
thinly sliced mushrooms
shredded spring onions
thinly sliced onions

You may also add a few tablespoons of flavouring liquid, such as

balsamic vinegar
stock
soy sauce
Chinese oyster sauce
lemon juice

Regardless of whether you add further flavourings, leave the pan covered for at least 5 minutes. The broccoli will now be done. If you wish to leave it longer, serving the broccoli at room temperature, remove the lid of the pan.

Brussels Sprouts

Even people who don't like Brussels sprouts will like charred Brussels sprouts. Because they're round and very dense they need somewhat different treatment from other vegetables. Cut the ends off and wash the sprouts, discarding any leaves that come away in washing. Heat the oil very hot, preferably in a pan large enough to hold the sprouts in one layer, and put them in. Shake or toss to coat well with oil, then cover tightly and cook for

   8–10 minutes

depending on the size of the sprouts. Toss them well several times during cooking. Test after 8 minutes, and when they seem done just turn the heat off and leave them with the pan partly covered. They will stay hot, without overcooking, for a good 10 minutes. If you wish, you can reheat them just before serving with flavourings. See the possibilities listed under Broccoli for some ideas, or try

1 tsp minced garlic or ginger

Cabbage

Charred cabbage is a really stunning dish, one that never fails to win oohs and ahs when I serve it to friends. Use Savoy or another green-leafed cabbage by preference; but the white-leaved type will do just fine. Slice it fairly thin and cook for around

   10–20 minutes

depending on how crunchy you like your cabbage. Again, I love cabbage flavoured with Indian spices (see page 158) and often serve it this way. A few tablespoons of braising liquid or good stock are also a surefire winner, as are soy sauce and oyster sauce.

There is a more unusual way of charring cabbage which is somewhat trickier but a very good party piece for small groups. Take a whole head of white cabbage, trim it and cut it in half lengthwise. Cut the round ends off each half. Remove the hard core and, using a very sharp, thin-bladed knife, slice lengthwise right through each hemisphere to make whole slices around 1 in thick. Keep the slices together so the leaves stay in place: this takes careful treatment. Heat the oil in your pan to a high heat and put in the slices, again keeping them intact. Now turn down the heat and cook the slices for around

10 minutes per side

taking care when turning to keep the slices intact. This isn't exactly easy, because the layers of cabbage have a tendency to fall away, but it looks and tastes splendid. If you're not serving it immediately, it can happily be cooked in advance and reheated, in the pan or in the oven, for 10–15 minutes before serving. Dribble each slice with a little balsamic vinegar, lemon juice, soy sauce or Chinese oyster sauce just before presenting the dish to your guests.

Celery

Celery can take a while to char because it contains so much water, but the excellent results are worth the wait. This is also a particularly forgiving vegetable: equally good whether soft or crunchy, it can happily sit for a couple of hours and bears up well to a final reheat. The following is one of the best charred vegetable dishes I've ever made.
Clean

1 large head or 2 small heads of celery

and slice on the bias around ¼–½ in thick. Heat the oil in the pan till medium-hot and put in the celery. Stir to coat with oil, then just leave it for 2 minutes and toss. Leave for another 2 minutes and toss again. Figure on repeating this 3–4 times, for a total initial cooking time of

10–12 minutes

While it's cooking, chop

4 thin slices of ginger, peeled
1 clove of garlic
1 large spring onion

Now turn the heat up to high so the celery can char. Cook this way for

4–5 minutes

stirring every minute or so. When the celery is flecked through-out with deep mahogany-coloured charring marks (it probably won't get really black), add the ginger/garlic/spring onion mixture. Turn the heat off, and pour in

2 tbsp stock or water
1 tbsp soy sauce

Cover immediately and leave the pan alone for at least 5 minutes (and up to several hours). The stock/soy mixture will reduce, flavouring the celery in the meantime, and the residual heat will take just the right amount of crunch out of the celery. This is a really delicious accompaniment to any grilled or roasted meat or poultry.

Courgettes

Courgettes, like celery, have a lot of water. Unlike celery, they have a delicate structure that doesn't allow a lot of latitude in timing. So charring them can be a little tricky.

But it's simple as long as you do remember two points: (a) use a very high heat from start to finish, and (b) aim to cook them as quickly as possible. The very large courgettes, which have an even higher water content and a spongy texture, are not suitable for charring. (Most of the time they are not really suitable for anything except stuffing, but that's another matter altogether, and no concern of lazy cooks.) Use the small, rock-hard versions instead. Slice them ¼–½ in thick and aim to cook for

3–4 minutes, or less if you're cooking a very small amount

Mange-touts

Hard to char because they take so little time to cook. But you can get a charred result by starting them (and continuing) over a ferociously high heat. Figure on a maximum of 3 minutes, stirring every 30 seconds or so.

1 large pat of butter (about 15 g/½ oz), or 1–2 tbsp extra virgin olive oil
500 g (1 lb) mange-touts, washed, topped and tailed

Melt the butter or oil in a heavy frying pan that has a lid. When the butter starts to sizzle and bubble, put in the mange-touts and stir-fry them for 2 minutes. (If using butter, you will need to moderate the heat somewhat to prevent burning.) Put on the lid and cook for 1 more minute, then turn off the heat. They can now sit quite happily for an hour or more. When you're just about ready to serve, turn the heat on to medium-high and remove the lid. Let them cook for another 1–2 minutes, stirring a few times, until they're done the way you like them.

Onions

Ah, the versatility of the onion. It's delicious when you cook it slowly and gently for a long time, and equally delicious – but totally different in character – when charred quickly over a sadistically high heat. This method leaves quite a lot of strong onion flavour, as the vegetables will be barely cooked in parts. Do not use a nonstick pan: the high heat will damage it.

Cut the onions in half lengthwise and then into shreds that are as close as possible to ⅜ in thick; don't tear your hair out if they end up a bit thinner or thicker. Heat the oil really hot in a large pan. Add the onions plus some salt and pepper. Let them sit undisturbed for a minute, then stir and toss well. Repeat this procedure every minute or so for around

5 minutes in all

Test one after that time to see whether they're done the way you like them. If they are, you can now either eat them immediately or leave them for a while, serving hot (reheated) or at room temperature.

Parsnips

If you want to char parsnips, or to cook them in any variation of stir-frying, you have to choose small ones: the large ones can be as tough and dense as the heartwood of a cherry tree. Slice in the way described and remove the cores if they are very thick. Then cook them for quite a long time, perhaps as much as 30 minutes. Or begin the cooking over a low heat, pan covered, and with a little stock or braising liquid to help soften them. Then, when they've softened a little, turn the heat up and start charring. This way it shouldn't take more than

10–15 minutes

Potatoes

These are the star of the charred vegetables. But they need careful treatment, especially if you're using a 'floury' potato such as King Edwards. And don't make them if you're watching your calories, since potatoes need much more oil than other vegetables. Here's the way I do them:

Cut the potatoes in chunks or fat finger-shaped slices which are no more than ½ in thick. Peeling is optional. Choose an ordinary frying pan (i.e. not a nonstick pan). Heat at least 3 tbsp of oil very hot in the pan. Put in the potatoes and stand back to avoid splattering oil. Shake the pan but don't stir for a couple of minutes. Season with salt and pepper. Now, using a stout, sharp spatula, scrape and lift the potatoes and turn them over as best you can. Don't worry if some of it sticks to the pan. Turn the heat down to medium and let the potatoes cook on their own for a few more minutes, then scrape, turn, and toss them again. Continue doing this for 10–20 minutes more – a total cooking time of

20–25 minutes

What you will end up with is a panful of potatoes that combine (a) soft white centres, (b) brown exteriors, and (c) randomly scattered blackened bits. This is just as it should be. Whatever you call them, charred potatoes are one of the most delicious things in the world. Eat with roast chicken, braised meat, or just a couple of fried or scrambled eggs.

If you have some medium-sized new potatoes (around 3 in on the long side), like the ones that come from Egypt, here's another good way of cooking them. Because they end up being thicker than the potatoes in the preceding method, they will probably turn a light mahogany colour rather than getting properly charred. But they are no less delicious, and the technique is virtually (a) foolproof and (b) attention-free. I do it in a nonstick pan so less oil is needed.

Wash the potatoes and leave the skins on. Cut each potato in half, lengthwise, then cut each half into quarters. You will now have 8 pieces per potato, each piece with 3 cut sides and a rounded piece of skin. In a large nonstick pan which is large enough to hold the potatoes in one comfortable layer, heat

2–3 tbsp vegetable oil, extra virgin olive oil, duck fat, or bacon fat

over a low heat. Put in the potato pieces with one of the cut sides down. Set the timer for 10 minutes and turn each piece on to another cut side when it goes off. Repeat this process once more, turning each time so that the cut side faces down. After 30 minutes the potatoes should be nearly done. Turn them all with skin side down for a couple of minutes more, and remove them when a small sharp knife easily pierces the skin. They can happily wait in the pan for 10–20 minutes after the cooking is completed.

CONFITS

Sometimes you can transform a simple meal not by doing something to the main dish itself but by serving something special to accompany it. *Salsas* (see page 323) are one good example of this trick. Vegetable *confits* are another.

The term *confit* comes from the French and is used for dishes originally prepared with the purpose of preserving. Usually it is applied to a piece of meat or poultry that has been cooked in its own fat. The technique was originally used to preserve meats in the days before refrigerators and freezers existed; now it's used because a *confit* of duck, goose, or pork is one of the greatest things humans ever laid their teeth into.

Confits of vegetables are a modern invention, and the term usually describes the slow cooking of garlic, shallots, or other members of the *Allium* family in oil with aromatic ingredients. They take a long time to cook but no time to prepare, and once they're cooking they look after themselves. That's why they're a godsend for lazy cooks.

Confits are true all-purpose concoctions, generally suitable for serving with just about any meat, fish, vegetable or starchy dish. Always make more than you think you need, especially if you're serving them to guests. They're intensely flavoured but long, slow cooking reduces them considerably in volume. For example, the half-pound of leeks in the Confit of Leeks with Dubonnet and Tarragon Vinegar (see below) is barely enough to fill 2 small ramekins. So people tend to take more than they really need, unless you avoid this problem by spooning out the *confit* yourself. But then your guests will simply ask for more, because the stuff is so delicious.

Leftovers, if there are any, can be kept for a week or two. They will liven up any meal to which they're added. I sometimes make them into a sandwich, on their own or with a slice of ham or cheese. They make excellent pasta sauces (see page 236), and can just as happily be stirred into rice or lentils.

The following recipe is one of the granddaddies of *confit* cookery, based on a recipe in Michel Guérard's vastly influential *Cuisine Minceur* and re-used (sometimes with modifications) endlessly since then.

Onions Braised in Sherry Vinegar

675 g (1½ lb) onions
1 tsp extra virgin olive oil
2 tsp sugar
1 tsp salt
⅛ tsp pepper
3 tbsp sherry vinegar

Peel and quarter the onions, and slice them very thin – around ⅛ in should be your target. Heat the oil in a large saucepan and add the onions, sugar, salt and pepper. Cook, covered, for 35 minutes, letting the onions colour slightly and stirring as needed. Add the vinegar and cook for another 35 minutes, still covered and stirring occasionally. Should any liquid remain when the cooking is finished, cook the onions uncovered for a few minutes to evaporate it. Serve warm.

If the vegetables are cooked in more liquid but for a shorter time they will retain more of their crunch – and a lot more of their powerful flavour. This is no bad thing. It means that the *confit* is less like a relish and more like a vegetable dish, suitable for serving instead of potatoes with any meat or poultry dish. The following dish, similar to one that I first wrote about in the *Guardian*, is a good example of this approach. When you've finished the shallots, use the remaining liquid as a salad dressing or marinade.

Confit *of Whole Shallots*

500 g (1 lb) small shallots
100 ml (4 fl oz) extra virgin olive oil
100 ml (4 fl oz) red wine or sherry vinegar
100 ml (4 fl oz) dry wine, red or white
4 peppercorns
4 whole coriander seeds
a large pinch of dried thyme

Peel and trim the shallots. Put them in a saucepan with the remaining ingredients and simmer, partly covered, for 45 minutes. If the shallots are not completely covered with liquid, you'll need to stir them once in a while. Turn off the heat and leave in the pot. Reheat the *confit* gently (or serve at room temperature) when you're ready to eat.

The next *confit* also uses whole pieces – of garlic rather than shallots – but makes life even easier for lazy cooks by letting them get away without peeling the miserable things. Long cooking subdues the lethal pong of the garlic, but beware: this still packs a fairly powerful wallop. Serve it as a side dish to plain roasted, sautéed, or pan-grilled meats; or roast chicken; or a braised shoulder of lamb. You can even serve it as a starter on its own, with good bread and maybe a cute little green salad.

Confit *of Garlic and Bay Leaves*

2 heads of garlic (around 20 cloves)
2 tbsp extra virgin olive oil
200 ml (scant 8 fl oz) red wine or sherry vinegar
200 ml (scant 8 fl oz) chicken or vegetable stock
4 peppercorns
6 bay leaves
1 large pinch of dried tarragon
100 ml (scant 4 fl oz) fruity white wine (e.g. Riesling)

Peel the papery husks of the garlic away but otherwise leave the cloves just as they are. Combine the remaining ingredients in a saucepan and bring to the boil, then add the garlic and simmer very gently, partly covered, till the liquid is nearly evaporated (40–50 minutes). Stir them once in a while. Turn off the heat and leave them in the pot, and reheat the *confit* gently (or serve at room temperature) when you're ready to eat. This can be eaten with the hands, each diner squeezing out the garlic from the skin for him- or herself. A clove or two added to a puréed soup (see page 243) would be nice. Use the remaining liquid as a salad dressing or marinade.

The next recipe, an Asian spin-off from European ideas, was inspired by a recipe in *Ken Hom's Cuisine: East Meets West*. Where he uses ordinary onions I substitute spring onions. You could use leeks instead. Delicious with chicken or barbecued lamb.

Confit *of Spring Onions, Ginger and Garlic*

2 bunches of spring onions (around 200 g/7–8 oz)
2 cloves of garlic
6 slices of ginger, 1/8 in thick
1 tbsp peanut or vegetable oil
4 black peppercorns
1/8 tsp Chinese five-spice powder or 2 Sichuan peppercorns (optional)
60 ml (4 tbsp) dry sherry or Chinese rice wine
1 tsp soy sauce
100 ml (scant 4 fl oz) chicken or vegetable stock
1 tsp sesame oil

Slice the spring onions into discs 1/8–1/4 in thick, using both white and green sections. Peel the garlic and ginger and cut in paper-thin slices. Heat the oil in a saucepan and put in the spring onions, garlic, ginger and spices. Add the sherry or wine, soy sauce and stock, and bring gently to the boil, then turn the heat right down. Cover the pan partway and cook for 40–50 minutes, stirring occasionally, until the garlic is very soft. Take off the lid, turn the heat up to medium, and boil until the liquid is evaporated. Remove the peppercorns, stir in the sesame oil, and serve hot or at room temperature.

Leeks are also a member of the *Allium* family, and they too make a good *confit*. Try to use small ones, which are more tender and milder in flavour. Use ruby port if you don't buy Dubonnet – or if you haven't been given an unwelcome bottle for Christmas.

Confit *of Leeks with Dubonnet and Tarragon Vinegar*

4 small leeks, white parts only (around 200 g/7–8 oz)
2 tbsp Dubonnet
50 ml (just over 3 tbsp) tarragon vinegar, or plain red wine vinegar
200 ml (scant 8 fl oz) chicken stock
1 tsp sugar
1 whole clove
4 black peppercorns

Trim the leeks and slice into discs ⅛–¼ in thick. Put them in a saucepan with the other ingredients and cook, covered, over a very gentle heat until they're good and soft. Remove the lid and boil over medium heat until the liquid is almost entirely evaporated. The caramelized sugar gives this a beautiful mahogany colour. Serve with lamb or a game dish, such as pan-grilled pheasant (see page 101).

ROASTING VEGETABLES

PARCEL-ROASTED VEGETABLES

I had always thought that roasting vegetables in sealed containers must be an excellent method for lazy cooking. But I never got round to it – that's laziness for you – until I first read Nico Ladenis's *My Gastronomy*. Mr Ladenis writes about the technique with great enthusiasm in his wonderful book, and takes the technique to elaborate, carefully orchestrated lengths. This is to be expected, since he is the very antithesis of lazy cooking. I have adapted it, naturally, for use in a much more casual fashion.

The idea is very simple: you wrap the vegetables in foil, with or without seasoning, and then throw them in the oven. (Mr Ladenis uses the aluminium containers found in Chinese and Indian takeaways, but I think that home cooks can skip this extra expense.) They cook through the combined action of the direct heat from the oven and the steam generated in the tightly sealed parcel. Indeed, this technique could just as easily be called parcel-steaming, rather than parcel-roasting. Some vegetables, especially the starchy varieties, end with a bit of crust on the exterior and a tender interior; others are just tender. Either way, they are exceedingly delicious.

Parcel-roasting is also a fuel-efficient technique if you're cooking something else in the oven as well. Indeed, roasting vegetables on their own is so fuel-*in*efficient that I can't really recommend it. On the other hand, you could easily make a vegetarian meal by roasting 6 or 7 different vegetables at the same time. In any event, here is the basic technique:

Cut the vegetables into smallish chunks – 1 in is perfect. Pour or smear a small amount (around 1 tsp) of butter or extra virgin olive oil on a sheet of aluminium foil and put on the vegetables. There should not be too much on any one sheet: you will need to wrap them up fairly loosely so steam can circulate around the contents. And leave plenty of foil to make an airtight seal. Now put on any seasonings you want. I like using:

salt and pepper
fresh herbs
ginger, garlic, and spring onion (see page 332)
a few drops of vinegar
a few drops of soy sauce (green vegetables only)

You can also add more butter or oil if you're not worried about calories.

Bring the corners of the foil together to form a bag-like shape, or fold the foil to make a roughly oblong parcel. Whichever method you use, make sure the parcel forms a tight seal. Now just toss the parcels on to the top shelf of the oven and bake with whatever else you're cooking that evening. The vegetables should be soft but not squishy.

This technique is good with a wide range of vegetables. Here is a list of the ones that I like best:

aubergines	*fennel*
broccoli	*garlic*
cauliflower	*onions*
chicory (Belgian endive)	*peppers*
courgettes	*small parsnips*
celery	*potatoes*

It's hard to get precise about timings, since you're likely to be cooking the vegetables as an accompaniment to something else. So the timing for the vegetables will be determined (and slightly complicated) by several factors: the temperature at which you're cooking your *plat principal*; the position of the vegetables in the oven; and the total amount of food being cooked in the oven at any one time. Remember, the more food you have in the oven, the longer it will take to cook everything. And see the notes on oven position on page 186.

Sounds complicated? Don't worry, that's the bad news. The good news is that (a) you can parcel-roast vegetables at any temperature you feel like and (b) there's a lot of latitude in determining doneness. An extra 5 or 10 minutes won't make a lot of difference, whatever vegetables you're using. Moreover, in my experience most vegetables need around the same amount of cooking time. So here is a table of parcel-roasting times for *all* vegetables, prepared as above, at a range of temperatures you're likely to be using.

180°C (350°F, Gas 4): 1 hour
200°C (400°F, Gas 6): 45 minutes
230°C (450°F, Gas 8): 30–40 minutes

Just to give you the idea, here is a sample recipe for parcel-roasted broccoli, flavoured Chinese-style.

Parcel-roasted Broccoli with Oyster Sauce

500 g (1 lb) fresh broccoli
1 large clove of garlic
4 thin slices of ginger, peeled
4 spring onions

1 tbsp peanut oil
½ tbsp (approx.) soy sauce
1 tbsp oyster sauce

Wash and trim the broccoli, and cut it into pieces around 1 in long. If the florets are very large, cut them in half lengthwise. Divide the broccoli between 4 squares of foil as described above. Mince the garlic and ginger, and cut the spring onions into shreds or discs. Divide these ingredients between the 4 parcels. Sprinkle the remaining ingredients on each one, aiming to use just 4–5 drops of soy. Grind on some black pepper and wrap up the parcels. Pop in the oven and let them cook. I've had best results cooking this dish in the middle of a 200°C (400°F, Gas 6) oven for around 45 minutes.

PAN-ROASTED VEGETABLES

Parcel-roasting isn't needed for certain vegetables: those with a thick, tough skin can be roasted on their own, smeared with oil (optional) and just left to get on with it in a baking pan. See page 228 for suggestions on using roasted vegetables in pasta sauces.

Here are the main choices:

aubergines
onions
peppers
potatoes

For all these items the procedure is the same. Use the vegetable in its unpeeled form. Wash if necessary and smear with extra virgin olive oil if you want to. Then put in a baking tin that's large enough to hold everything in one layer. Put in the oven with your principal dish and cook till needed. The roasting times given above (see page 182) will be a useful guideline. And that's it, apart from the following notes.

> **Aubergines**: If roasted at a high temperature and towards the top of the oven, the skin may blacken and char. No problem. Scrape off the skin before serving, or use to make an aubergine purée (the so-called 'Poor Man's Caviar') with extra virgin olive oil, lemon juice, garlic and parsley. If serving as a side dish, try to use smallish aubergines which will form a single portion.

You can also roast aubergines in slices around 1 in thick. Brush them on both sides with olive oil, and insert (if you feel like it) a sliver of garlic, sun-dried tomato, or anchovy fillet in each one.

Onions: These can be large or small; simply adjust the cooking time. When a sharp knife goes in easily, the onions are done. And the skins do not need to be oiled before cooking. Roast onions are indescribably delicious; fragrant and sweet, they hardly taste like onions. To serve, put the whole onion(s) on each diner's plate and let them do the unpeeling. This is messy – provide a bowl for the skin – but no-one will mind. Serve with optional butter and maybe a small bowl of minced fresh herbs for your guests to sprinkle on top.

Peppers: Roasted peppers have become insufferably fashionable in recent years, but don't let that put you off. They are fashionable because they're delicious. If you're dining informally, give each diner a whole pepper and let them deal with it themselves. If you want to be a little more elegant (read: energetic), cut the peppers in half and remove the seeds, then smear with extra virgin olive oil and add any or all of the following:

a few snippets of tinned anchovy
½ a clove of garlic
a sprinkling of herbs
a handful of green olives, coarsely chopped
a couple of sun-dried tomatoes (see page 341), minced

If you roast the peppers in halves, the cooking time will be somewhat shorter. Around 25–30 minutes at the very top of a 200°C (400°F, Gas 6) oven is a good way forward, especially if you're cooking other dishes at this temperature. But a lower or higher one really will do fine, if that's what you're using anyway.

Potatoes: Use small ones, unpeeled, either waxy or floury type. Shake the pan or turn them every 20 minutes or so. You won't get the crispy crust, but what you do get will be delicious. And the skin will do some crisping up of its own, so the experience is not a million miles away from ordinary peeled potatoes roasted in pints of oil.

Roast vegetables are so delicious that they need little help in the way of extra flavouring. But they will certainly not suffer if they get it. Here is a flavoured butter I like using with any of the vegetables listed above:

Garlic Butter for Roasted Vegetables

50 g (2 oz) unsalted butter
a small handful of parsley
3 shallots or 2 small spring onions
1 large clove of garlic

Soften the butter by leaving it at room temperature for 30 minutes or so. Chop the remaining ingredients as fine as you can get them, then mix with the butter and a little bit of salt and pepper. This quantity will suffice for a pound or two of vegetables.

Incidentally, I don't want you to think that I'm unaware of classic roast potatoes – the most famous roasted vegetable of all. It's just that they don't quite fall into the category of lazy cooking. Though one of the simplest dishes as far as results and ingredients are concerned, they call for a fair bit of attention if you're going to achieve the right combination of crisp crust and perfectly-cooked interior. Besides, pan-roasted new potatoes are better – and a lot less fattening.

GRATINS

Gratins are everybody's favourite vegetable dish. Soft inside and with a browned, crunchy crust on top, they never fail to please. You can serve them as a starter, a light (or not so light) main course, or a side dish. And however you serve them, the only problem they present is that there's never enough. People can eat as much of a well made gratin as you set in front of them.

Gratins are good for lazy cooks for two reasons, apart from their splendid flavour. First, they take little time to prepare – rarely more than 20 minutes of active cooking. Second, like braised and roasted vegetables, they are temperature-insensitive: they can be cooked satisfactorily in a low, a medium, or a high oven. So if you're braising a shoulder of lamb (a dish for which gratins might have been invented), you can put in the gratin and it will cook just right, as long as you co-ordinate things properly. The target temperature plus timing for all the gratins below is

180°C (350°F, Gas 4): 40–60 minutes

assuming the dish is on the middle rack of an otherwise empty oven. If you're cooking other dishes at the same time, these timings will need to be adjusted by anything from 10–25 per cent. And if you use either of the other basic settings, adjust the cooking times accordingly. Here are the approximate numbers.

200°C (400°F, Gas 6): 35–50 minutes
230°C (450°F, Gas 8): 30–40 minutes

But again, please note that cooking times will need adjusting if you cook the dish on a lower or higher rack, or if you're cooking other dishes at the same time.

POTATO GRATINS

The most famous gratin dishes in French cuisine are made with potatoes, and they take several different forms. The main distinction is the liquid used to cook the basic ingredient. *Gratin dauphinois*, the most famous dish, uses cream. *Gratin savoyard* uses stock. Apart from that, the two dishes are fundamentally identical as far as procedure is concerned. I've given here a basic *gratin dauphinois* recipe which can serve as a model for all others, whatever vegetable is used.

I've read a few dozen recipes for *gratin dauphinois* and learned that no two are alike. This is good news for lazy cooks, who naturally gravitate towards dishes whose preparation allows for a good deal of latitude.

One step that's usually advised is to wash the sliced potatoes in water and then dry them well. The idea is to remove excess surface starch and thus produce cleaner, less sticky results. Absolutely right – it works. But it is by no means essential for lazy cooks, or cooks who happen to be in a hurry. And while washing the slices is quick and easy, drying them is a major pain in the neck. Skip it if you want to. Otherwise use clean tea-towels for the drying: paper towels will disintegrate with the brisk rubbing that's needed.

Another common feature is to specify cream as the principal cooking liquid. Cream is terrific but milk will do, though obviously giving a much lighter result. I generally use a combination of milk and cream. You can make the dish with single cream alone, but this is *very* rich. Try a combination of milk and double cream, in proportions of anything from 5:1 to 2:1.

A third gratin technique, by no means universal, calls for covering the dish with aluminium foil for the first part of cooking, so that the potatoes don't dry out. This also has the effect of speeding up the cooking, as the trapped steam is hotter than the ambient oven temperature. I don't normally use it myself, but I do sometimes. It's worth trying, especially if you're in a hurry. Just remember two rules:

1. Place the foil on with the *shiny side down*. If you don't, the foil will deflect heat away from the top of the dish and slow down cooking.

2. Remove the foil at least 20 minutes before cooking is done, so the top has a chance to brown.

If the dish hasn't browned enough by the time the spuds are cooked, you can put it under a fiercely hot grill for a couple of minutes.

A fourth step that you see a lot of in *dauphinois* recipes is rubbing the gratin dish with a cut clove of garlic. In my experience, this produces a level of garlickiness that's barely perceptible to the average palate. If that's the way you like garlic, fine. If you like more of it, mince the clove and put it in the dish with the potatoes.

Gratin Dauphinois

500 g (1 lb) floury potatoes
1 clove of garlic
around 250 ml (9 fl oz) milk, single cream, or a combination
½ tsp grated nutmeg
2 tbsp or so grated Gruyère or Parmesan cheese (optional)

Preheat the oven to 180°C (350°F, Gas 4). Peel the potatoes and slice them as thin as you can manage – around ⅛ in is ideal, or even thinner if you have a mandoline or a food processor with an adjustable slicing disc. If you want to, wash the slices in cold water and dry them well.

Now wipe your gratin dish with softened butter and put the potatoes in, trying to create overlapping layers like the scales of a fish. If you're making more than one layer, you can season each layer with salt, pepper and nutmeg; you can also wait till all the potatoes are in before seasoning, and no one will notice the difference. Pour on the milk and/or cream and sprinkle on the cheese, if you're using it. Finally, dot the whole thing with

2 thick pats of butter

broken up into little pieces, and bake in the oven, using the guide times above.

NB: I can't stress too often the need to adjust your cooking times if (a) you're not using the middle shelf and/or (b) you're cooking other dishes at the same time. You will also need to adjust timings if you use foil for part of the cooking. Making these adjustments gets very easy once you've done it once or twice. Use your digital timer to remind you when to check on the progress of the dish(es).

VARIATIONS

1. Use sour cream or *crème fraîche* instead of some or all of the ordinary cream.

2. Chop a small onion very fine and use it instead of (or in addition to) the garlic.

3. Add fresh herbs to the potatoes – parsley, dill, thyme, rosemary.

4. Cut a couple of rashers of bacon into thin shreds, then fry till medium-crisp and sprinkle on the bottom of the pan before the potatoes go in.

5. Use another cheese on top instead of grated Parmesan or Gruyère. Emmenthal, Cheddar, and Caerphilly are all good bets. If you use a good blue cheese, especially Stilton or Roquefort, you have a dish swanky enough to serve as a main course.

Gratin Savoyard

This is essentially the same dish but using stock instead of dairy products. Obviously, good home-made stock will make a big difference here. But don't worry if stock cubes are all you've got: the dish will still be good. Use chicken or beef cubes.

Or get fancier in your choice of liquids. Leftover braising liquid, especially from beef, is an excellent cooking medium for potatoes. If there are bits of meat and vegetables floating around in it, all the better. Stock-based gratins don't have quite the knockout visual effect of a creamy-white *dauphinois*, but no-one will mind.

Cookery writers, myself included, tend blithely to assume that everyone has the equipment needed to make potato slices that are all exactly ⅛ or 1/16 in thick. It *is* easy if you have the right equipment. It is well-nigh impossible if you don't. Here is a recipe that does away with the need for careful slicing. The potatoes are chopped rather than sliced, and combined with onions, and cooked in the usual way. This is best made with waxy (e.g. Cyprus) potatoes, and it's almost as good as an ordinary sliced gratin. What's more, it's much easier.

Chunky Potato Gratin

500 g (1 lb) Cyprus potatoes
250 g (8 oz) onion
100 ml (around 4 fl oz) single cream
150 ml (around 6 fl oz) milk
2–3 tbsp grated Parmesan or Gruyère

Wash the potatoes and cut them in chunks around ¼–½ in square. Peel the onions and cut them in chunks around the same size. Butter the gratin dish and scatter the onion all over the bottom. Put on the potato chunks and season with salt and pepper. Mix the cream and milk and pour it over, then sprinkle on the cheese and dot with butter. Cook as described above for around 40 minutes in a 180°C (350°F, Gas 4) oven.

OTHER VEGETABLE GRATINS

Potatoes are such a good gratin vegetable, it's arguable that we don't need to use any other. But they are not the only one – and some of the best gratins can be made with parsnips, aubergines, fennel and even Brussels sprouts, among others. Indeed, once you've got the knack you can use just about anything you fancy in gratins. This is a good field for the experimentally inclined.

But there are complications when you leave the realm of starchy vegetables and move into the more watery types. If precautions are not taken to drain away most of the water content, the vegetables are liable to overcook before they brown on top. And an overcooked, waterlogged gratin is disgusting. You wonder why the cook has bothered. Here are a few recipes in which the waterlogged problem never arises.

Parsnip Gratin

If you love parsnips as much as I do, you'll go nuts about parsnip gratin. The parsnip flavour is very sweet, so I like jazzing it up with the sharp flavour of curry powder.

(My inspiration here is the parsnip soup in *Jane Grigson's Vegetable Book*.) Because parsnips can take a long time to cook, I normally use the foil technique when I cook them *en gratin*.

500 g (1 lb) smallish parsnips
250 ml (8–9 fl oz) whole milk, or half milk and half cream
1–2 tsp mild curry powder

Preheat the oven to 230°C (450°F, Gas 8). Peel and trim the parsnips as needed, then slice them around ¼ in thick. Butter a gratin dish and put in the vegetables, arranging them neatly in overlapping layers if you can be bothered. Mix the milk/cream with the curry powder and pour on, then cover with foil and bake in the oven for 50 minutes. Remove the foil and cook for another 10–15 minutes. Actually, the parsnips may well be done after 50 minutes; the foil-less baking is intended mainly to brown them. You can brown more quickly under a hot grill, which will only take around 5 minutes. Do not skip the browning: the crust it produces is the high point of the dish.

Brussels Sprout Gratin

Like charred sprouts, this is a dish that wins over even the most passionate sprout-hater. It calls for one additional step in cooking, but it's worth the few extra minutes of work.

500 g (1 lb) large Brussels sprouts
200 ml (7 fl oz) stock or braising liquid
1 thick pat of butter (1–2 tbsp)
3–4 tbsp grated Parmesan or Gruyère

Preheat the oven to 230°C (450°F, Gas 8). Wash the sprouts but do not trim them in any way. (The idea of cutting a cross in the base of each sprout has always struck me as a waste of time.) Bring at least 1.5 litres (3 pints) of water to a rapid boil and put in a generous tbsp of salt. Dump in the sprouts and boil them for 5 minutes exactly, then remove and drain well. When cool enough to handle, cut off the bottoms of the sprouts, discarding any leaves that come away, and cut each one in half lengthwise. Put them in a gratin dish that will hold them in one layer and pour on the liquid. Dot with butter and with the optional cheese, and cook for slightly less than the guide times given above (page 186).

This recipe is easily adaptable to higher or lower oven temperatures than the standard 180° (350°F, Gas 4). For example, I got perfect results after 25 minutes using the top shelf of the oven at

230°C (450°F, Gas 8)

and could just as easily have used a lower temperature plus longer cooking time. How's that for flexibility?

Aubergines

Aubergines too need preliminary cooking, but in a frying pan rather than boiling water. This takes extra time, and lazy cooks will not happily part with that commodity. But aubergine gratins are so delicious that they're worth making for friends, if not for everyday meals. The preliminary procedures can be carried out well in advance. And – the major bonus – aubergine gratin is one of the few vegetable gratins that can be served cold or at room temperature.

This recipe is based on the classic Parmigiana idea, combining the aubergines with tomato sauce and mozzarella. But it is much simpler because you don't have to interleave the vegetables with alternating layers of sauce and cheese. Try to use smaller aubergines, which have better flavour and texture than the big ones.

Lazy Parmigiana

2 medium aubergines (around 600 g/1 ½ lb in weight)
50–100 ml (2–4 fl oz) extra virgin olive oil
1 mozzarella cheese, sliced or chopped
50–75 g (2–3 oz) black or green olives, sliced (optional)
1 small clove of garlic, minced

1 generous tsp herbes de Provence or a small handful of fresh herbs: basil, thyme,
   parsley
a 400 g/14 oz tin Italian plum tomatoes, or chopped tomatoes, or passato
3–4 tbsp grated Parmesan

Preheat the oven to 230°C (450°F, Gas 8). Slice the aubergines around ½ in thick, sprinkle them with salt, leave them for 30 minutes, then dry them. (I find increasingly that this step is unnecessary.) Then heat around 30ml (1 fl oz) of the olive oil in a heavy frying pan and fry the slices very quickly for around

   5 minutes per side

till the slices are browned and soft all the way through. I can't really specify the amount of oil because this will depend on the amount of aubergine you're making. Try to use as little as possible, however: aubergines soak up oil the way a sponge soaks up water. You'll be aided in this enterprise if you brush the oil on, as described in the chapter on pan-grilling, and you can certainly use the grill pan – over a *lowish* heat – instead of an ordinary frying pan. You can also make the pre-cooking virtually oil-free by grilling the slices, or by cooking them with very little oil in a nonstick frying pan. The results aren't nearly as luxurious that way, but they're still pretty good – and they save on calories. Everyone can eat twice as much with a clear conscience.

Once the slices are fried or grilled, lightly oil the gratin dish (unless you've used ample oil in pre-cooking) and put in a layer of aubergine slices. Top that layer with the olives, half the mozzarella, the garlic and the herbes de Provence or fresh herbs. Put in the remaining aubergine slices. Now chop the tomatoes roughly if they're whole, and spread them out as evenly as possible over the dish. Top with the remaining mozzarella, and sprinkle on the grated Parmesan as evenly as possible.

Cook till the cheese is brown and the whole dish is bubbling merrily. This should not take very long, as the aubergines have been pre-cooked. Start testing after 40 minutes in a 180°C (350°F, Gas 4) oven. I find that 25–30 minutes in a 230°C (450°F, Gas 8) oven works very well.

Fennel

Fennel makes one of the best gratins. Try to use smaller bulbs: the larger, older ones may be tough and stringy. No seasoning apart from salt and pepper is needed, as fennel is so fragrant and delicious.

Fennel Gratin

500 g (1 lb) fennel
150 ml (around 5 fl oz) single cream
200 ml (around 7 fl oz) milk
1–2 thick pats of butter
2–3 tbsp grated Parmesan or Gruyère

Trim the fennel, reserving the feathery leaves if you wish to add them to the dish (or use them as a garnish for an assembled salad). Slice across the grain into pieces around ¼ in thick. Butter the gratin dish and put in the fennel pieces, doing your best to make the surface as level as possible. (This is useful for looks and for even cooking.) Mix the cream and milk and pour them on. Dot with butter, season with salt and pepper, and sprinkle on the cheese. Bake for around 40–45 minutes at 180°C (350°F, Gas 4). The top should be nicely browned and the fennel very tender. This can easily sit in the turned-off oven for 10 minutes before serving, and it goes particularly well with fish or chicken.

Fennel is a fairly watery vegetable, so there may be too much liquid left in the pan after cooking. Simply remove it to a bowl with a spoon or bulb baster; allow it to cool for 30 seconds or so; then drink it surreptitiously before you take the dish out to your guests. It's delicious stuff.

Spinach

The last vegetable gratin, made with spinach, is different from the others in that the raw material is a homogeneous mass rather than slices or chunks. It is also one of the few dishes in this book for which I positively recommend using frozen food.

Spinach takes well to freezing, and it is a labour-saving item of which lazy cooks should take advantage whenever they can. The first stage of cooking is quick and simple, and after that's done you can set the dish aside for hours until you're ready to cook. Note that there is no milk in this one, just cream and seasonings. The inside remains creamy while the top gets a nicely delicate crust. This is a very good party dish, especially when served with braised (see page 53) or pan-grilled (see page 93) lamb. These quantities serve 4.

Spinach Gratin

1 medium onion
1 large clove of garlic
2 large pats of butter (around 50 g)
two 300 g (10 oz) packets chopped frozen spinach
1 large pinch nutmeg
90 ml (6 tbsp) double cream
4–5 tbsp grated Parmesan

Chop the onion and garlic very fine. Melt the butter in a saucepan and gently cook the onions and garlic for 2 minutes, then add the frozen spinach and let it defrost gently, turning and scraping the block every couple of minutes to speed it along. (This will take around 10–15 minutes.) When it's defrosted, turn the heat up slightly and add the nutmeg. Let it cook for a couple of minutes or even longer, till the spinach seems almost completely dry. Add the cream and cook for another couple of minutes, again letting the spinach dry out substantially. Mix in half the Parmesan, season well with salt and pepper, and set aside, if you want to, till you're ready to cook.

When you're ready to cook, preheat the oven to 180°C (350°F, Gas 4). Butter a gratin dish and spoon in the spinach, flattening the top with the back of the spoon. Sprinkle on the remaining cheese, dot with butter, and bake at the middle of the oven for

30–40 minutes

till the spinach is bubbling inside and slightly crisp on top. This is a truly delicious dish.

PASTA GRATINS

These should really come into the chapter on pasta. But the technique makes them more akin to other vegetable gratin dishes, so here they are.

The most famous pasta gratins are humble dishes – so humble, in fact, that self-styled sophisticates turn up their noses at them. I'm talking about the lowly macaroni cheese, or tuna noodle casserole in my native USA. But anyone who dismisses such delicacies suffers from self-defeating snobbery. Good-quality Italian dried pasta, cooked extremely *al dente* and then baked with a flavourful creamy sauce, is excellent stuff – cheap, filling, and perfect for a cold winter's night. At its very simplest, the dish can be made with just pasta, milk, eggs, and cheese. The essential formula to master is:

225 ml (8 fl oz) of liquid will cook 125 g (4 oz) of pasta

Once you've mastered the basic recipe, you can start varying endlessly. I won't even begin to try to list all the possibilities. Here is a basic recipe, followed by a quick stroll down Variations Boulevard.

Baked Macaroni

125 g (4 oz) short pasta – penne, fusilli, rigatoni, conchiglie (shells)
2–3 thick pats of butter
4–5 tbsp freshly grated Parmesan
1 egg
225 ml (8 fl oz) milk

Preheat the oven to 180°C (350°F, Gas 4). Cook the pasta till it's just *al dente*. Drain well and mix with the butter and around half the cheese; season with salt and pepper. Pour into a gratin dish, then beat the egg with the milk and pour it on. Sprinkle on the remaining cheese and bake at the centre of the oven for 40–50 minutes, till the interior is bubbling and the top crispy and brown.

That's around 10 minutes of active cooking time. With hardly any more effort, you can make this much more exciting and substantial. Here are 5 easy options.

1. Use half milk and half either single or double cream.

2. Use *crème fraîche* or sour cream instead of ordinary cream. (This is particularly delicious.)

3. Mix some leftover liquid from braised meats or vegetables into the milk.

4. Add nutmeg, paprika, or cayenne pepper to the milk mixture.

5. Add a chopped clove of garlic or chopped onion, as in Gratin Dauphinois.

Once you've got the basics down, you can vary this dish to your heart's content. Here are a few ideas for additions to make macaroni gratin more substantial, exotic, or just plain good.

smoked cod or haddock, soaked in hot milk for 5 minutes, then skinned, boned and flaked
smoked chicken, cut off the bone in ½ in chunks or slices
3–4 slices of ham, cut into shreds or fingers
dried mushrooms – Chinese black or porcini – reconstituted and briefly sautéed in butter or olive oil
ginger, garlic, and spring onion (see page 332)
a 250 g (8 oz) tin of tuna or salmon
2–3 sun-dried tomatoes (see page 341)
a lavish handful of fresh herbs

This list could go on and on – just use your imagination and the tastiest ingredients you have lying around. For the record, here are two of my favourite variations on the macaroni theme.

Macaroni Cheese with Mozzarella and Sun-dried Tomatoes

250 g (8 oz) short pasta – penne, fusilli, rigatoni, conchiglie (shells)
2 tbsp extra virgin olive oil
2 sun-dried tomatoes
1 mozzarella cheese (250 g/8 oz)
a few leaves of fresh basil (optional)
4–5 tbsp freshly grated Parmesan

Cook the pasta, drain it, and mix it well in a bowl with half the oil. Chop the tomatoes, cheese, and basil (if using), and mix them in too. Put the mixture in a baking dish and sprinkle on the Parmesan. Dribble on the remaining oil or dot with butter, and bake in the oven for 30–35 minutes. This is a fairly dry gratin; if you want it wetter, add 4–5 tbsp of milk or single cream to the pasta mixture before baking.

Macaroni Cheese with Bacon and Gorgonzola

This is a really classy gratin, suitable for dinner parties as a starter or even as a main course. I've doubled the quantities here, as this is the sort of dish that no one can stop eating. If you're serving this dish as a main course, baking at the centre of the oven, roast some peppers (see page 184) as a perfect light starter.

125–200 g (4–6 oz) streaky bacon, rinds removed
250 g (8 oz) button mushrooms
250 g (8 oz) short pasta – penne, fusilli, rigatoni
1–2 pats of butter (optional)
4–5 tbsp freshly grated Parmesan
2 eggs
450 ml (16 fl oz) milk
200 g (6 oz) Gorgonzola cheese

Cut the bacon into thin shreds and fry *without extra fat* in a small pan (preferably nonstick) till lightly crisp (around 2 minutes). Remove and drain on paper towels. Slice the mushrooms around ⅛ in thick and fry them in the remaining bacon fat, then add to the bacon. Preheat oven to 180°C (350°F, Gas 4). Cook the pasta till it's just *al dente*, then drain well; mix with the butter and around half the Parmesan, and season with salt and pepper. Beat the eggs and mix with the milk. Break the Gorgonzola into small pieces and add to the milk. Mix the bacon and mushrooms with the pasta and pour into a gratin dish. Then pour on the egg/milk/cheese mixture and sprinkle on the remaining Parmesan. Cook as in the master Baked Macaroni recipe.

Some Modest Proposals for Pasta

In Peter Bogdanovich's movie *Targets*, a director played by Bogdanovich himself says that his chosen career is futile. 'The good movies have all been made,' he complains. I sometimes feel the same way about pasta recipes. The best have all been written; anything else is just a variation on old themes.

But it's still worth thinking about ideas for pasta, even if the great discoveries have been made by other people. It is one of the many virtues of this wonderful food that you needn't think of it as being in any way 'special'. If you like the stuff – and most people do – you can mix it with just about anything and it will inevitably turn into a satisfying meal.

And pasta is particularly suitable for lazy cooking because you don't have to do much to make a delicious sauce. Given a packet of pasta and a well stocked cupboard, you can get home at 8 and be sitting down to a delicious dinner by 8.30 – and most of that time will be spent waiting for the water to boil. This chapter aims to give some suggestions about how to go about doing just that.

In saying that there are no new pasta ideas, I don't mean to deny the achievements of first-rate Italian cookery writers like Marcella Hazan and Anna Del Conte, who experiment tirelessly and produce recipes that are truly worth following. But even though I love pasta, I don't regard myself as being in that league. So I am going to do something different in this chapter. I am going to give my personal view of pasta and its sauces from first principles, and to proceed from there to give some ideas for sauces you can invent yourself. Think of it as an opportunity to experiment with no rules whatsoever and you've got the right idea. Invention and improvisation are the essence of making pasta sauce.

PORTION SIZES (OR: HOW LONG IS A PIECE OF STRING?)

All the sauce recipes in this chapter are designed for use with 500 g (just over 1 lb) of dried pasta. If this were a normal cookbook, I would now tell you how many people that serves. But this is not a normal cookbook.

The received wisdom holds that 500 g (1 lb) of dried pasta

serves 6–8 people as a starter, 3–4 as a main course. I am not so confident as to make such predictions. There are a lot of variables in pasta cookery, notably hunger, greed (not the same thing as hunger), the type and quantity of sauce, and the number and size of the other courses you're serving. Another variable is the appetite (and personality) of each diner. For those who are as fanatical about pasta as I am, the concept of serving size is irrelevant. I've been to numerous dinners where the cook has followed someone else's guidance as to how much pasta to make, and where everyone (including the host) has ended up indecorously scraping the serving bowl with their fingers.

You should also account for the usefulness of pasta leftovers when deciding how much to make. I have yet to meet a pasta sauce that didn't taste good, either hot or cold, the following day. Whenever I make the stuff, I make too much. Sometimes there is pasta left over, sometimes there is not.

The proverbial bottom line here is that you should follow your own counsel. But if you're worried about making an error, err on the side of excess. Remember the popularity of pasta; remember the awfulness of not having enough; remember the leftover angle.

FRESH v. DRIED

All these recipes are for dried pasta rather than fresh. Lazy cooks don't have time to make fresh pasta. It's great fun if you like that sort of work, and high-quality home-made pasta is unquestionably a wonderful thing. But if you're not making it yourself then you probably shouldn't use it. One irrefutable exception here: the fresh pasta made by first-rate Italian delicatessens *is* worth buying, and I urge you to do so. Just remember that the fresh stuff contains far more water than dried, and slightly more will be needed per portion.

But if you have access only to factory-made fresh pasta, don't bother buying it. In my experience, this stuff is far too expensive for what you're getting. Fine Italian dried pasta, as Marcella Hazan points out, is a superb product – and cheaper than the fresh varieties sold in supermarkets.

THE THREE TYPES OF PASTA SAUCE

Lazy cooks need to know how long something takes to cook, and with pasta sauce there are three subdivisions on this crucial point:

1. Instant sauces
2. Fast sauces
3. Long, slow sauces

Instant sauces are made by chopping ingredients, cooking them while the pasta cooks, and pouring them straight from the cooking pan on to the cooked pasta. If the sauce ingredients need no cooking, the sauce qualifies for the title 'instanter'.

Fast sauces need a little more preparation and cooking than instant types – perhaps as much as 30–45 minutes in all.

Long, slow sauces are the ones on which folklore (read: TV advertisements) is based – a cheerful Italian mama with ample bosom, leaning over a simmering cauldron of tomato-ey goop and tasting incessantly with a wooden spoon. Behind the haze of TV sentiment lies the reality: long, slow sauces need long, slow cooking. And they often need long, slow preparation as well, since they typically combine a lot of ingredients which, when simmered at length, blend together to form a seamless, harmonious whole.

All three types of sauce are suitable for lazy cooks. Even long, slow sauces can meet your needs as long as they don't take a lot of active cooking time. Your choice of type will depend on your circumstances (e.g. are you about to faint from hunger?) and your preference of the moment.

WHAT MAKES A PASTA SAUCE GOOD?

Before moving on to look at the three types of sauce in detail, let's pause to consider the qualities that go into making a successful pasta sauce. Some of the tastes you need are:

1. Sweetness
2. Salt – including seasonings
3. Smoke
4. Acid
5. Fat
6. Sharpness, spiciness, heat
7. Freshness
8. Body
9. Liquid
10. Cheese

As a general rule, every good pasta sauce will have at least two of these qualities. And most combine three, four or more. To take one example from the 'instant' category, Spaghetti Aglio e Oglio (olive oil and garlic): here you find a predominance of qualities 5, 6 and 7. In a well-made *ragù* (the classic meat sauce of Bologna), you find all the qualities coming through from the ten or more ingredients used in that great dish. When you're improvising your own pasta sauces – and this chapter aims to help you improvise – try to think in terms of these categories. Combining them creates balance and complexity, even in very simple dishes.

And how do you get the qualities into your pasta? It's easy: there is almost nothing that won't taste good in a pasta sauce – as long as it's all used in the right way. Here is my list of ten basic ingredients for pasta sauce.

TEN BASIC PASTA SAUCE INGREDIENTS

1. Tomatoes – fresh, tinned, sun-dried, purée

These serve a variety of purposes in a pasta sauce; which purpose will depend on the form in which the tomatoes are used, and on the way they're used.

On the whole, I use tinned Italian plum tomatoes rather than fresh ones. This is not a decision I make willingly, I hasten to add, as there is nothing better than a vine-ripened tomato from the sunny fields of Italy or Provence. The problem is that good tomatoes are harder to find than an honest man, and that the specimens we usually get – especially those from Jersey and

Holland – are flavourless abominations. Wherever I specify tomatoes, therefore, what I mean is either Italian plums or *good* fresh ones. In practice, this will usually mean the tinned type. And don't be ashamed of using them.

2. Olive oil or butter

These give flavour, body, and fat. They are quite distinct and will give completely different results. A good tip for lazy cooks is to use both in a single sauce. This adds complexity to the sauce without effort.

Where I specify extra virgin olive oil, I mean just that. Especially in the simplest 'instant' sauces, the flavour of the oil will be an important component of the flavour. The better the oil, the better the sauce.

3. Mushrooms: fresh or dried, wild or cultivated

These too serve a variety of purposes, depending on the type of mushroom used and the way they're cooked. Cultivated mushrooms do not have a strong flavour of their own but it deepens with long cooking and also adds body. Wild mushrooms, either dried or fresh, have an incomparable flavour which will be one of the dominating aspects of any dish they're used in. Dried Italian *porcini* (*ceps* in French) are delicious and widely available from good delicatessens. Morels are also excellent, though even more expensive (by a heart-stopping margin) than *porcini*. Any fresh wild mushroom – *porcini*, *chanterelles*, even field mushrooms – should be treated gently and reverently.

4. Anchovies: the little tins in oil, or large tins in salt

These indispensable larder standbys give sharpness and salti-ness to whatever they're used in. Deploy them sparingly, especially in tomato-based sauces, but always have at least one tin on hand. They never go off, and they're delicious.

5. Herbs, spices, and chilis: fresh or dried

These are used in small quantities, but they give maximum oomph per ounce. They are what makes the difference between a good pasta sauce and a merely ordinary one. And they are ridiculously easy to deploy. Only chilis take any preparation.

Herbs can be anything you like, either dried or fresh. Just remember that dried herbs have a more concentrated flavour than fresh, and that some herbs are not worth using in their dried form. Basil and parsley are two examples. But dried thyme, rosemary and marjoram are excellent things, and tarragon – though admittedly much better when fresh – is also good dried.

Spices are not used enough in pasta sauces. Nutmeg appears in many classic Italian dishes, as do the usual run of herbs. But the spices that hail from non-European countries are splendid in pasta sauce. Think of: coriander, cumin, fenugreek, cardamom. These can be delicious when well used, and are so surprising that your guests won't know what's hit them – till they've cleaned their plates.

Chilis are the bee's knees when it comes to pasta sauce. Indeed, I can think of few ingredients more guaranteed to raise the level of excitement of a simple sauce than a judicious addition of dried or fresh chilis, or of chili sauce. If using either dried or fresh, remove the seeds and white membrane from the interior. If using chili sauce, add it drop by drop. Both these suggestions should be ignored if you like really fiery food.

6. Cream and related substances
Cream or something with a creamy texture add body, fat, and smoothness to a pasta sauce. They add texture as well, plus their own sharp flavour if the cream is cultured (e.g. Greek yogurt, sour cream, *crème fraîche*). Of course, they also add calories. They are not for everyday pasta-making if you eat the stuff three or four times a week. But they also produce some of the quickest pasta sauces of all.

7. Smoked things
There's something about the combination of smoke and pasta that sends most people wild with delight. And smokiness can be imparted by a wide variety of ingredients: bacon, ham, and other pork products; fish, including salmon, eel, mackerel, cod or haddock; grilled or roasted vegetables, cooked at a sufficiently high heat so the skin gets charred. Just remember that many smoked foods are hot-smoked, i.e. smoked *and* fully cooked. This means that long cooking at the sauce-making

stage may dry them out. All fish (especially salmon) should be cooked as briefly as possible, just to heat it through. Bacon can take more cooking, especially in a lot of liquid, while ham should be treated gently. The smokiness of charred vegetables comes from full cooking, so here too the aim should be quick reheating and nothing more.

8. Olives: green or black
Olives are another of the great pasta companions, adding both oiliness and an inimitable sharpness. The green ones usually have a sharper flavour, while the black variety tends to be sweeter and blander. If they're sold in a herb or garlic marinade, all the better.

9. Cheese
Parmesan is the first cheese that comes to mind for pasta sauce. Used sparingly, it adds nothing more than an accent of sharpness plus its distinctive nutty flavour. Not all sauces need it, but for those that do it is indispensable. I hope I don't need to say that Parmesan should be bought in hunks, preferably from a good Italian delicatessen where they break the cheese into irregular pieces rather than slicing it. The grated stuff sold in little tubs is worse than useless: buy a sharp, mature Cheddar rather than this insipid junk.

But Parmesan isn't the only cheese that has a place in pasta. Creamy cheeses such as Gorgonzola, Bel Paese and Roquefort have a different kind of sharpness which may also throw in saltiness and fat. Melted and tossed, mozzarella creates a tangled web which can make serving a little messy: but its smooth flavour is delicious when combined with Parmesan. And goat's cheese, whether young or mature, creates a pasta dish on its own. Crumble it on top with some fresh herbs for an instant meal of distinction.

10. Aromatic vegetables
The best in this category are the *Allium* family – onions, garlic, shallots, spring onions, and leeks. Carrots and celery may also be used, but only if they're very well cooked. These add sharpness and sometimes (in the case of carrots) sweetness.

One item missing from these lists is uncured (i.e. fresh) meat. This isn't because meat has no place in pasta sauce. On the contrary, it's essential in the classic Bolognese sauce (*ragù*), which uses no fewer than three different meats. But most meat sauces are, like *ragù*, of the long-cooked variety. And lazy cooks have least time for this type of dish. Do note, however, the Stir-fried Chicken recipe on page 228.

LEFTOVERS

One of the best ways of cooking lazy pasta is to sauce it using leftovers. That's one reason that lazy cooks always make 'too much' of everything. As long as you're not fussy about such outmoded concepts as 'authentic' and 'proper', leftover sauces are a doddle and a godsend. Some leftovers are good enough to use on their own, with nothing more than grated Parmesan to complete the dish, while others need a little extra, either for lubrication or bulk, to complete the sauce. In either case, the imaginative use of leftovers with pasta will provide some of the best meals you've ever had. There's only one rule to remember:

> when re-using cooked meat, fish, or vegetables, do not let it overcook

This rule is a simple matter of common sense. Since the food has been cooked once, you don't want to heat it so thoroughly the second time round as to let it dry out or (in the case of vegetables) go unappetizingly mushy. And in fact this is a good thing for lazy cooks, because it means that the reheated sauce will need minimal attention and cooking the second time round.

PASTA SHAPES

In some of the recipes here I specify a particular type of pasta. Please do not regard my specifications as fixed and immutable. Many writers on Italian cookery – including some whose opinions I respect to the point of cowering reverence – say that certain types of sauce are best suited to certain pasta shapes. I do not exactly disagree with them, but I personally have never complained (or heard complaints) about a mismatch between sauce and pasta shape. If you like rigatoni more than spaghetti, use it for making Spaghetti Carbonara or Spaghetti with Fresh Herb Sauce. When the sauce is right, no one will notice if you're using the 'wrong' shape.

INSTANT SAUCES

There aren't that many truly instant pasta sauces, apart from the ones you get out of a jar. Lazy cooks can't do it any faster than that. They can, however, do a lot better.

But they can only do better if they have quality ingredients. These are always important, but never more compellingly important than with instant sauces. When you cook something for only an instant or two, the quality of the ingredients will shine through very clearly. If the quality is low, that will be all too apparent. If the quality is high, everyone will cheer and ask for seconds.

The instantest of instant sauces are those that need no cooking at all, and lazy cooks, for obvious reasons, should take to these sauces the way a pig takes to truffles. Uncooked sauces are made by chopping up some stuff while the pasta is cooking, then mixing it with the cooked pasta and eating without further ado. This is less a matter of cooking than of mixing. And I am therefore going to resist the temptation of giving recipes for uncooked sauces. Mine would not be any better than yours, and this is truly an area where improvisation is essential. The recipe, such as it is, is as follows:

1. Go to a good delicatessen with the words UNCOOKED SAUCE imprinted in your mind.
2. Look at what's there, taking the following list as a starting point.

sun-dried tomatoes (in oil only)
vegetables in jars – peppers, artichoke hearts, mushrooms, mixed vegetables
olives, green and black
soft cheese – young goat's, ricotta, Gorgonzola, Brie, etc.

hard cheese – Parmesan, Pecorino Romano, etc.
salami
prosciutto *(or another 'raw' ham)*
mortadella

3. Take them home and get your pasta cooking.
4. While it's cooking, chop your assorted goodies into bite-sized pieces and put them in a bowl. Add 3–5 tbsp of extra virgin olive oil and toss.
5. When the pasta is cooked, drain it and put in a bowl, then pour on the mixture and toss very well. Serve immediately.

That's all there is to it.

NB: the sauce ingredients will be at room temperature and will therefore lower the temperature of the pasta. If you're worried about this, take the pasta out when it is *just* this side of fully cooked. Drain it, then return it to the cooking pot and toss with the sauce ingredients for a minute or so over a very low flame. This will finish the cooking and bring everything up to a suitably high heat. The work involved takes little more time and effort, and should not put off even the laziest cook. (Any easier than this and you might as well open a tin.)

Here is an example of an instant sauce. Though usually found on pizza or risotto, it works equally well with pasta. The idea, in essence, is to combine cheeses with different flavours for maximum complexity of flavour. Since all you do to it is melt the cheese, you're basically allowing expert cheese-makers to do your cooking for you. That's all the more reason to buy good cheeses. Seek out the best source in your area and buy from them with a vengeance: if you buy, they'll stay in business.

Incidentally, though the sauce calls in theory for four cheeses, you can use fewer if you like. If I'm only using one cheese, I like it best with Gorgonzola.

Quattro Formaggi (Four Cheeses)

100–125 g (4–5 oz) Italian cheese, preferably 2 or more of the following:
  Gorgonzola, Mozzarella, Bel Paese, Fontina, ricotta
500 g (1 lb) pasta
2 thick pats of butter (around 25 g/1 oz)
2–3 tbsp single or double cream (optional)
a small handful of fresh herbs (optional)
3–4 tbsp freshly grated Parmesan

Cut the cheese(s) into small dice, around ¼–½ in. Boil the pasta till it is just short of fully cooked, and return it to the pan with the cheese, butter and optional cream. Over a very low heat, stir it steadily till the cheese is melted and hot. This can take as long as 3–4 minutes, depending on the type and quantity of cheese. Stir in the herbs and a little of the Parmesan and serve the pasta immediately, with the rest of the Parmesan passed separately.

Here's another instant sauce, this one based on cream and smoked cod or haddock. You should try to use undyed fish if possible, but dyed will do if you can't get the other stuff.

Smoked Fish Sauce

375 g (12 oz) smoked cod or haddock
4 spring onions or 1 small onion
a small handful of parsley
2 thick pats of butter (around 25 g/1 oz)
170–225 ml (6–8 fl oz) single cream

Skin the fish and take out any bones lurking within. Slice it thin. Slice the spring onions into thin discs and mince the parsley. While the pasta is cooking, heat the butter over a low heat and add the spring onion or onion. Stir it for a minute or so, then add the fish and cream and turn the heat up slightly. Let the mixture heat through *without boiling*, mix in the parsley, and pour the sauce on to the cooked pasta. Parmesan is optional; grated Gruyère would be a good match with the fish.

Those are two examples of the very fastest sauce. Now for a selection of those that take only slightly more time. All can be prepared in advance if you wish, but they can also be prepared while the pasta is cooking. Do it whichever way suits you.

THE CARBONARA VARIATIONS

Spaghetti Carbonara, made with bacon and eggs, is one of the simplest of pasta dishes and one of the best. At one point in my life I used to eat it every night – and sometimes I wish I still did. The only thing that takes time here is cutting the rind off the bacon. Buying rindless bacon will cut down on the preparation time, and so will buying *prosciutto* or *pancetta*, the Italian version of bacon. If using *prosciutto*, just add it to the pan so it can heat through.

The Carbonara procedure, which calls for beating the eggs and 'cooking' them by pouring them on to the pasta in the bowl, can be adapted in a variety of ways. And it is perfect for lazy cooks because the base of the sauce – the eggs – is ready before you start cooking. Here is the basic recipe plus a series of variations.

Spaghetti Carbonara

200–250 g (6–8 oz) streaky or back bacon, green or smoked
1 thick pat of butter (optional)
3 eggs
2 tbsp freshly grated Parmesan (plus extra for the table)
500 g (1 lb) dried spaghetti

While the water is heating up, de-rind the bacon (if necessary) and cut it into thin shreds – anything from ⅛–¼ in will do. Heat the butter if using – a nonstick pan eliminates the need for it, and saves on calories – and gently fry the bacon till it's cooked the way you like it. I like it slightly crispy but never crunchy. At a low heat, this may take as long as 15 minutes; a higher heat will reduce the cooking time to 5–6 minutes, but I use a gentle heat because it eliminates both the danger of overcooking and the need for close attention. This can be done well in advance and then left off the heat for several hours.

In the meantime, beat the eggs in a small bowl and mix in the cheese. When the pasta is cooked, drain it into a big bowl and scrape the bacon on to it, leaving behind as much of the bacon fat as you like. (The fat adds flavour and body but plenty of calories as well.) Pour on the egg/cheese mixture. Serve immediately with extra grated cheese.

This dish is complete in itself and needs no further elaboration. You can, however, add creaminess to the sauce by using only 2 eggs and substituting

2 tbsp double cream, sour cream, or crème fraîche

You can make Carbonara even more filling and satisfying by adding other ingredients to the basic bacon-and-egg mix. Two of those that I like best are onions and mushrooms. Here's the procedure. It follows the basic recipe and takes only a minute or two of extra preparation.

Carbonara with Onions or Mushrooms

Chop around ¼ in thick either

200 g (7–8 oz) onion or
200 g (7–8 oz) pearly-white button mushrooms

Proceed with the basic recipe up to the point at which you start cooking the bacon. If you're using onions, add them to the pan after 2–3 minutes (to make the onions really soft) or 4–5 minutes (if you want them crunchier and stronger-tasting). It's entirely up to you and your taste buds.

If using mushrooms, add them when the bacon is around 2–4 minutes from being cooked. They should be cooked very quickly or they will start to disintegrate, give up too much of their water, and turn an unappetizing greyish-black colour. Again, this can be done well in advance and then left off the heat for up to half an hour. In the meantime, beat the eggs in a small bowl. When the pasta is cooked, scrape the bacon/ mushroom on to it and mix in the egg/cheese mixture. Dig in.

Some recipes for Spaghetti Carbonara tell you to use *prosciutto*. This is a splendid idea, but I don't agree with the recipes that call for cooking the ham as you would cook plain old bacon. This is because *prosciutto* has already been 'cooked' in the long salt-cure that gives it its characteristic flavour and texture. If you subject it to further heat, it will dry out. Here's a better way of proceeding with *prosciutto*, and even easier because the ham is not cooked. Bear in mind that you can also use French *jambon cru* or Spanish *jamón serrano*, both of which are similar to *prosciutto* – and sometimes just as good.

Carbonara with Prosciutto

Follow the basic recipe for Spaghetti Carbonara but substitute

200 g (6 oz) prosciutto

for the bacon. Do not cook it. As soon as the pasta is cooked, mix in the shredded ham and pour on the eggs. This may not need extra salt if the ham is very salty.

People who don't eat meat are sadly excluded from the ranks of the Carbonarists; my heart goes out to them. But they can eat this variation, which uses squid, scallops or prawns instead of the ham. Inauthentic, perhaps, but delicious.

Carbonara with Seafood

200–250 g (6–8 oz) squid, scallops or shelled prawns
1 shallot or 1 spring onion
1 thick pat of butter
1 tbsp dry white wine or dry vermouth
2 eggs

2 tbsp single or double cream
2 tbsp freshly grated Parmesan (plus extra for the table)
500 g (1 lb) dried spaghetti

NB: If using squid, the cleaned weight should come to at least 200 g (6 oz). The prawns may (and probably will be) frozen, but they must be raw rather than precooked.

   Prepare the seafoody stuff by cutting into thin rings (squid), thin discs (scallops), or hefty chunks (prawns). Mince the shallot or spring onion. Heat the butter in a frying pan and gently fry the onion for 1 minute, then add the wine and the seafoody stuff and continue cooking gently for no more than 2–3 minutes, till the fish is barely opaque and firm to the touch. (It will continue to cook when it's mixed with the pasta, so you mustn't overcook at this stage.) Beat the eggs with the cream. When the pasta is cooked, mix in the seafood in the usual way along with the egg/cream mixture and the cheese. This will probably be a wetter sauce than the standard Carbonara, so supply a spoon with it.

OIL AND GARLIC

If you have nothing in the house except pasta, extra virgin olive oil and garlic, you can dine like a prince. These ingredients were made for each other: the olive oil and garlic form what Marcella Hazan calls one of the 'mother' sauces of pasta cookery. On its own, this is delicious. Embellished and elaborated, it is even more delicious. And it takes around 2 minutes to prepare.

Pasta all'Aglio e Oglio

For 500 g (1 lb) of pasta take

3–6 cloves of garlic
100–125 ml (around 4–5 fl oz) extra virgin olive oil

Get the pasta cooking. Peel the garlic and chop it very fine, then heat it gently in the oil. If you want a strong taste of raw garlic, heat it for only 2–3 minutes. Longer cooking will still leave a powerful blast of garlic, but with less rawness. Some people say you should never brown garlic, but others like it that way. See how you like it. This can be done in advance if you like, but it takes so little time that there's little point in advance cooking.

When the pasta is finished, you can either (a) pour the oil and garlic over it, or (b) strain the oil on. This will depend on how much you love garlic and what you think your guests can tolerate. Certainly there is nothing like the powerful blast of garlic that comes with serving the chopped bits. But you decide.

VARIATIONS

Add to the oil any of the following, or a combination of 2.

a small handful of parsley or another fresh herb, chopped; mint is a goody
a chopped dried red chili
a chopped fresh chili, red or green
4–6 chopped anchovy fillets
a chopped sun-dried tomato
a chopped spring onion

If you're garlic-shy, you can dispense with it and make an instant sauce of oil and fresh herbs.

Fragrant Herb Sauce

This is another of the simplest pasta sauces. As long as the herbs are good, it will be delicious as a starter, a side dish, or – if you're as crazy about pasta as I am – a main course. If you have a herb garden with plenty of variety, you can experiment endlessly with different combinations.

a large handful of 3 or more of the following fresh herbs: basil, tarragon, dill,
  chives, thyme, coriander, sage, rosemary, mint, marjoram
75–100 ml (5–7 tbsp) extra virgin olive oil
½ a fresh green chili (optional)

Get the pasta cooking. Chop or tear the herbs into coarse shreds and mince the chili if you're using it. Warm the oil in a small saucepan and, if using the chili, cook it in the oil for a minute or two. Put the herbs in the oil, let them heat up for 1 minute, then pour over the cooked pasta. This doesn't really need Parmesan, but you can use it if you like.

CREAM SAUCES

Cream makes an exceedingly delicious partner to pasta all on its own, just with grated Parmesan and salt and pepper. You will know this if you've ever eaten any Italian pasta dish *alla panna fresca* – with fresh cream – or its elegant relation called Fettuccine all'Alfredo. Better still, the cream can be combined with a variety of ingredients to make some of the best instant pasta sauces imaginable. We've already seen one of them, a sauce based on cream and smoked cod or haddock (page 213). Here are some more.

NB: Ignore the following recipes if you are determined not to eat anything that's very high in calories. Cream is one of the most calorie-intensive foods around. But bear in mind that if the portions are small, even a cream-rich sauce will not be all that fattening, and that everyone deserves a treat now and again. I am certainly not suggesting that you eat a creamy pasta dish every day, or every week.

Like all the recipes in this chapter, these cream sauces are intended for use with 500 g (1 lb) of dried pasta. But I must give a qualification to this general rule. Some people like creamy pasta dishes to be on the light side, for reasons of health or gastronomic pleasure. Others like them to be fairly swimming in cream. I tend towards the former approach, though my motives have more to do with gluttony than with health: the less cream I put in the sauce, the more pasta I can eat. So the measurements for cream may be too low for your taste.

On the other hand, if you follow my example and use less cream, the dish may be somewhat dry for your taste. This can be counteracted by using the Italian trick of reserving a jug of the pasta water when cooking is finished. If, on tossing, the dish seems too dry, pour on a little of the water. This will moisten the proceedings considerably.

While the recipes below give single cream among the alternatives, it makes more sense (though not from the caloric point of view) to use double cream or even *crème fraîche*. The heavier creams take less time to reduce than single cream, and they are more likely to give perfect results.

These dishes can be eaten for your own everyday suppers or served to guests at dinner parties. In the latter situation, try serving them as a starter where the main course will be something fairly small and/or light. Here's a perfect menu of this variety: Pasta with Cream Sauce (or Variants), Flash-Roasted Salmon (see page 145), Charred French Beans (see page 168).

Instant Cream Sauce

While the pasta is cooking, heat

225 ml (8 fl oz) single cream or
200 ml (7 fl oz) double cream or
200 ml (7 fl oz) sour cream or crème fraîche

over a medium heat till it starts bubbling and steaming. You can now cook it for several minutes, to reduce and concentrate the cream, or just long enough to get it really hot. It will be good either way.

NB: Some books tell you not to boil the cream hard for fear of curdling, but I personally have never encountered this problem. Neither has Marcella Hazan, who firmly recommends (in *Marcella's Italian Kitchen*) a really vigorous boiling to reduce cream. Incidentally, she (and many other Italian cookery experts) would add an ounce or two of butter to the basic cream sauce. I have never found this to be strictly necessary, but it does make the sauce richer and more lustrous.

When the pasta is cooked and drained, pour the cream on and toss well, then sprinkle *generously* with Parmesan and serve. Or, in line with the standard Fettuccine all'Alfredo routine, you can add the pasta to the cream in the pan and continue cooking it over a low heat. If doing it this way, undercook the pasta very slightly. Many recipes for Fettuccine all'Alfredo ask you to heat only half the cream initially, and to add the remainder to the pot after the pasta has gone in. This makes for a somewhat whiter sauce, but I am unconvinced of the need for it.

VARIATIONS

If you think this is too simple even for a committed lazy cook, try combining the cream with something else. In all the suggestions below, heat

1 thick pat of butter

in a heavy saucepan and gently cook the added ingredient(s) for the time indicated. Then pour in the cream and continue cooking till the cream is cooked.

> **cooked ham**, shredded: 1–2 minutes
> *prosciutto*, shredded: 10 seconds
> **frozen green peas**: 4–5 minutes (till barely cooked)
> **raw prawns**, thawed if necessary and diced: 1 minute
> **raw red pepper**, diced: 4–5 minutes
> **roasted red pepper**, diced: 1 minute

These are nothing more than suggestions. Just about any flavourful ingredient, raw or cooked, can be combined with cream in this way. Here are three of the simple sauces that I like best.

The first one, which I am crazy about, is inspired by a sauce that Nico Ladenis serves with roast lamb. It doesn't really come under the instant category, but if you do the preliminary cooking in advance (and that's certainly easy enough to do, even for lazy cooks), the last-minute preparation takes no time. Long cooking greatly tempers the strength of the garlic, but be warned: this is a dish for garlic-lovers only, and preferably for those who don't have to travel to work the next day on a crowded train. NB: You could also make this sauce with roasted garlic (see page 182).

Garlic Cream Sauce

1 large or 2 small heads of garlic
cream as in the basic Instant Cream Sauce recipe above
1 tbsp fresh tarragon, thyme or parsley, minced
grated Parmesan

Separate the garlic cloves but do not peel them, and put them in a small saucepan. Boil a kettle of water. Pour in water just to cover the garlic and boil for 2 minutes. Drain, cover again with water, and boil again for 2 minutes. Drain again, then pour in the rest of the water, bring to the boil, and simmer for 30 minutes. Now drain the garlic and slip the cloves out of the husks; they should slide out easily. Put through a sieve (this is easy because the garlic is so soft) and return to the saucepan. Add the cream and herbs, mix well, and simmer gently for 2–3 minutes. Pour the sauce over the cooked pasta, toss, and serve the cheese separately.

Cream and mushrooms, in my view, are one of the great combinations. Here is an easy sauce that exploits their synergy to the full.

Cream and Mushroom Sauce

250 g (8 oz) pearly-white button mushrooms
a small handful of parsley
2 thick pats of butter (around 25 g/1 oz)
cream as in the basic Instant Cream Sauce recipe above
plenty of salt and pepper

Clean the mushrooms while you're getting the water boiling. Slice them thin, around ⅛ in, and mince the parsley. Melt the butter in a frying pan or saucepan and gently cook the mushrooms for a few minutes. When they're just soft and starting to throw off a bit of liquid, add the parsley and the cream. Let the mixture come up to a good heat and season with salt and pepper. It can sit like this for 15 minutes or so, but is better if you pour it straight on to the pasta.

This final variation is made with dried mushrooms rather than fresh. Dried mushrooms have a more concentrated flavour, so very little is needed. And that's just as well, since they're wickedly expensive. Use Chinese dried black mushrooms, Italian *porcini* (French *ceps*), or morels (French *morilles*). Because all these items are so costly, I have dignified the sauce by giving it a fancy French name. You could make this a more substantial dish by combining fresh and dried mushrooms, but I think it's swankier to have the expensive morsels on their own. Minced fresh herbs, especially basil and parsley, can be added just before serving. But even without them, this is a really delicious sauce. Make it only for people you really like. You could also serve it over rice or fish.

Crème de Champignons Secs

25–50 g (1–2 oz) dried mushrooms
2–3 large spring onions, or a comparable slice of ordinary onion
a hefty pat of butter
cream as in the basic Instant Cream Sauce recipe above
25 g (1 oz) grated Gruyère (optional)
grated Parmesan

Soak the mushrooms in 100 ml (4 fl oz) of hot water just until soft (around 15 minutes). Gently squeeze out the grit and pat dry. If you wish, strain the soaking water and boil it in a small saucepan to reduce by half. In the meantime, get the pasta water boiling. Cut the stems off the mushrooms and mince them; trim the spring onions and mince. Heat the butter in a small frying pan and cook the onion for 3–4 minutes, long enough to soften it and make it smell really great. Add the mushrooms and cook for a minute or two, turning steadily to coat well with butter. If using the soaking water, add it to the frying pan and cook over a brisk heat till the liquid is nearly evaporated. Get the pasta cooking and add the cream to the frying pan. Turn the heat down to its lowest point and cook for 4–5 minutes. (If the sauce is done before the pasta, turn the heat off and let it sit uncovered.) When the pasta is done, toss it with the sauce, stir in the cheese(s), and serve. This sauce does benefit from being tossed with the pasta in the frying pan.

ALMOST-INSTANT SAUCES

THE STIR-FRY VARIATIONS

Stir-fried sauces rank among the easiest and most versatile in the pasta-maker's repertoire. While the water is boiling, you chop some vegetables, plus maybe some meat or some bacon. You add some seasonings, either solid or liquid, and stir-fry them for a few minutes. When they're done, you turn off the heat and let them sit while the pasta cooks. Just before the pasta is done, you turn the heat back on under the frying pan. Then you put the drained pasta in a bowl, pour the contents of the frying pan on top, and eat. Or you can return the drained pasta to the pasta pot, dump in the stir-fry, and heat it all together over a gentle heat.

Vegetables

The beauty of stir-fried sauces is that you can – and should – use whatever is looking swell in the markets and/or in your larder. On the whole, however, you will want some nice fresh vegetables in it. Stir-fried vegetable sauces are a good choice when vegetarians are coming to dinner. They are also one of the best dinner options when you're dining alone and don't want to go to a lot of fuss, since they create one-dish meals that take a lot of beating. When I'm dining alone, I eat these with delight.

The only fixed rule about the vegetables is that they must be in small pieces, which is the essential rule about stir-frying generally. Thick pieces won't cook fast enough. More important, they will make a difficult mouthful. Ideally the pieces of vegetable should be of the same approximate stature as the pieces of pasta, so you can combine the two in a single rapturous mouthful. Here are some possibilities.

asparagus, sliced on the bias in 1–2 in sections
aubergines, sliced in 2–3 in shreds around the thickness of your index finger
broccoli, cut into small florets
celery, sliced on the bias around ¼ in thick

courgettes, sliced into ¼ in thick discs
fennel, quartered and thinly sliced
leeks, young, sliced around ¼ in thick
mushrooms, fresh or dry, sliced around ¼ in thick
onions, white or red, quartered and thinly sliced
peppers (red, yellow, green, in that order of preference), quartered and thinly sliced
spring onions, sliced on the bias in 1–2 in sections
fresh tomatoes (de-seeded and jelly removed), diced or shredded

Meat (or Fish)

If you're not constrained by the need for a meatless dish, consider adding one of the following. All quantities are for 500 g (1 lb) of pasta.

50–100 g (2–4 oz) ham or bacon
50–100 g (2–4 oz) duck breast, skinned and shredded
50–100 g (2–4 oz) smoked chicken, skinned and shredded

These should cook in the same time needed for the vegetables.

FLAVOURINGS

In flavourings as in vegetables, you are spoiled for choice. Here are a few of the biggies:

garlic
fresh herbs
sun-dried tomatoes
chilis – dried or fresh
chili sauce
lemon or lime juice
balsamic vinegar (see page 344)
sesame seeds (for an Oriental touch)
soy sauce (for an Oriental touch)

Any solid flavouring should be chopped very fine and cooked with the vegetables; the liquids can be added at the beginning of cooking or at the end, depending on how sharp you want them to taste.

TOMATO SAUCE

While stir-fried vegetables make an excellent pasta sauce on their own, they can also be combined with a simple tomato sauce (see page 233). For this approach use around

225 ml (8 fl oz) sauce per 500 g (1 lb) of pasta

You can either heat it up separately a couple of minutes before serving and then pour it over the chopped vegetables, or mix it in with the vegetables before the final blast of reheating.

The idea of giving recipes for this kind of sauce is particularly silly. The stir-fried sauce is an improvised, back-of-an-envelope affair. If you've ever stir-fried anything, you know how to make one of these sauces.

Nonetheless, here are three samples of the kind of stir-fried sauce I like to make. They are intended to give nothing more than a general picture of the technique, and of the range of possibilities from ultra-simple to somewhat more complex. The first is the sort of thing you could make for yourself when you're dining alone in front of the television or a good book.

Pasta with Stir-fried Broccoli

1 small head of broccoli (around 250 g/8 oz)
1 small dried red chili
1 small clove of garlic
3 tbsp extra virgin olive oil
1 tsp or so of lemon or lime juice

Trim the broccoli and cut it into very small florets. If you want to shorten the cooking time, you can blanch it in rapidly boiling salted water for 2 minutes. Otherwise, just remove the seeds from the chili and chop it, with the garlic, as fine as you can get it. Heat the oil in a heavy frying pan over a very high heat, and put in the broccoli. Stir-fry for 2 minutes or so, season with salt and pepper, and put in the garlic and chili. Lower the heat and continue frying until the broccoli is done. You can speed this along by adding a tablespoon or so of water or stock, covering the pan, and leaving the broccoli to cook for a couple of minutes. When the pasta is cooked, return it to the pan and toss in the broccoli. Stir well, and add the lemon juice just before you sit down to eat. This goes well with grated Parmesan.

The next one is a party dish, either a starter or a main course. Using three kinds of peppers gives a very impressive combination of colours and – much more important – of flavours. You could, of course, use just one type of pepper. But then the dish wouldn't look like something in a glossy colour photograph. Quantities are for 500 g (1 lb) of pasta.

Sweet Pepper Sauce

2 red peppers
2 green peppers
2 yellow peppers
60 ml (4 tbsp) extra virgin olive oil
1 tbsp tomato purée
60 ml (4 tbsp) cream or crème fraîche *(optional)*
a few sprigs of fresh basil or thyme

Cut out the cores and de-seed the peppers. Slice them ¼ in thick, and cut the strips in half if the peppers are very long. Heat the oil in a large frying pan and stir-fry the peppers with the tomato purée for 4–5 minutes, until they're soft but with just a hint of bite. Add the cream or *crème fraîche*, and the herbs, and mix well. (May be cooked until this point well in advance.) Cook the pasta. When it's almost done, turn the heat on under the peppers and reheat gently. When the pasta is done, drain it and mix with the sauce. Serve immediately, with grated Parmesan.

Finally, here is one of the few sauces in this chapter using fresh meat. Normally I am opposed to any pasta sauce containing fresh chicken, but since this one has an Oriental accent it is OK by me. If you can, use the dried Chinese egg noodles which are widely available in supermarkets or the fresh noodles sold by Oriental shops. Otherwise, use spaghetti. And substitute chunky peanut butter for the tahini if you can't find it. No one will mind.

Stir-fried Chicken Sauce with Sesame Paste

5–6 thin slices of ginger
1 large spring onion or a small handful of chives
1 large clove of garlic
2 tbsp sesame paste (tahini) or peanut butter
2 tbsp soy sauce
1 tbsp oyster sauce (optional)
1 tbsp sesame oil
2 tbsp peanut oil
1 large or 2 small chicken pieces, breast or whole leg

Mince the ginger, spring onion or chives, and garlic. Mix them with the sesame paste, soy sauce, oyster sauce, sesame oil and 1 tbsp of the peanut oil; whisk thoroughly till well blended.

Bone the chicken pieces if necessary and remove the skins if you wish to. Using a very sharp knife, cut the chicken into thin shreds or small dice – a maximum thickness of ⅛ in should be your target. Heat the remaining peanut oil blazingly hot in a wok or frying pan and stir-fry the chicken until it is just cooked. (This may take as little as 1 minute, and you can do it well in advance if you wish. Just scrape the chicken into a clean bowl and leave it till it's needed.)

When the pasta is cooked, dump the sauce and the chicken on top and stir everything vigorously. The sauce, though relatively dry, will pack a good wallop of flavour. Or, to quote what Spencer Tracy said of Katharine Hepburn, 'There isn't much of her, but what there is is choice.'

THE ROASTED VARIATIONS

If you have time on your hands earlier in the day and don't want any last-minute fuss before dinnertime, try making an almost-instant sauce based on roasted vegetables. (You can also do this the night before, if you happen to be using the oven for something else.) All you do is roast some vegetables, let them cool, chop them up, and reheat them at the last minute with some extra virgin olive oil. The slightly smoky flavour that comes with roasting is delicious on pasta, and you can heighten the flavour in all sorts of ways. Figure on using around

325 g (12 oz) of vegetables per 500 g (1 lb) of pasta

Here are some top choices of vegetable for roasting and serving with pasta, with suggestions for preparation:

aubergines, left whole
courgettes, left whole
fennel, bottom and leaves trimmed, and cut in half lengthwise
onions, white or red, topped and tailed, and cut in half or quartered lengthwise;
*   leave the skins on, peel when cooked*
peppers, red, yellow, green (in that order of preference), left whole; peel when
*   cooked, and remove the seeds*
spring onions, ends trimmed off, but left whole
fresh tomatoes, cut in half, cores removed, and de-seeded

Whichever you're using, the procedure is the same:

Cut the vegetables into pieces that should be no more than around 2 in thick at their thickest point. Brush them liberally with extra virgin olive oil and roast them on a baking sheet or roasting dish – with the cut side down – till they're just done, or even a little on the crunchy side. (The exception to this rule is the aubergine, which must be well softened right through or it will be disgusting.) Some may need more time than others: check after around 20 minutes to see how they're getting on. See page 180 for more information about roasting vegetables, but note:

> a low to medium oven will give you fairly un-browned results,
> a hot oven will produce browning and a bit of charring

Both ways are good; they are just different. A low oven will take longer, and tends to produce vegetables that are creamily soft from the outside to the centre. Obviously the hot oven will cook faster, but it may also produce charred bits on the outside of the vegetables. Cut off any carbonized crunchy layers from the outside while trying to retain the pleasantly smoky flavour.

When the vegetables are cooked, remove them and let them cool. If you're making the sauce immediately, you can skip the cooling (but handle with care so you don't burn your hands). Peppers and onions will have to be peeled, of course. Cut the vegetables into pieces that suit the pasta you're serving – they can be small dice, large dice, hefty chunks, or strips. Put them in a bowl or saucepan with more extra virgin olive oil. Figure on

around 2–3 tbsp per 500 g (1 lb) of vegetables

or more if you want a really luxuriant, fattening sauce. When you're ready to eat, you can reheat the vegetables gently on the stove or in the microwave if you have one. (The microwave is perfect for this job.) You can also skip the reheating altogether, if you're feeling really lazy or if the vegetables are still hot. When the pasta is cooked, toss it well with the vegetables, sprinkle on the grated Parmesan, and you're there.

TOMATO SAUCE

Like stir-fried sauces, the roasted ones too can be combined with a simple tomato sauce (see page 233). Use around

225 ml (8 fl oz) sauce per 500 g (1 lb) of pasta

Heat it up a couple of minutes before serving and then mix in with the chopped vegetables.

A TOUCH OF CHILI

Finely chop a fresh green chili and heat it gently in the olive oil before mixing with the vegetables and dumping on to the pasta.

UTILIZING LEFTOVERS

Do you have some braising liquid in the fridge or freezer, perhaps with a few scraps of the meat itself? Heat it up for a couple of minutes before serving and mix in with the chopped vegetables. Don't use more than around

225 ml (8 fl oz) per 500 g (1 lb) of pasta

or the sauce will be too liquid. If you have a lot of liquid, reducing it will produce a more concentrated flavour.

A Creamy Sauce

If you're not worried about calories, any type of cream – single, double, *crème fraîche* or sour cream – makes an excellent liaison for the vegetables. Substitute

1 thick pat of butter (1--2 tbsp)

for the olive oil and use the cream in something like the following quantities:

single cream: 110 ml (4 fl oz)
double, crème fraîche, *sour cream: 50 ml (2 fl oz)*

You may use more if you want a very creamy sauce. Put the cream in a saucepan or frying pan and add the vegetables. Heat fairly gently for a couple of minutes before serving. You can get away without heating it, especially if the vegetables are still hot, but the temperature of the sauce will go down.

For the record, here are a couple of dishes made with roasted vegetables. My inspiration for the first comes from a recipe in *Marcella's Italian Kitchen*, by Marcella Hazan. She uses tomatoes only, while I have combined them with other good things. The combination is almost arbitrary, though it is good. Don't regard this as a recipe – it's really just an extended hint. Make your own combinations and you'll be much better off.

Pasta with Roasted Onions, Peppers, and Tomatoes

5–6 small onions, around 2 in in diameter
2 red peppers
2 ripe beef tomatoes (around 500 g/1 lb in weight)
60–75 ml (4–5 tbsp) extra virgin olive oil

½ a dried red chili, crumbled
500 g (1 lb) dried pasta
2 tbsp balsamic vinegar
fresh herbs of your choice

Prepare the onions, peppers and tomatoes as described above and put them on a lightly oiled baking tray. Bake till they're all cooked: you'll need to play the timing by ear, though I find that they all take around 30 minutes. Remove the skins from all of them. This should be a simple matter of just pulling them off, though the pepper skin may need a little more effort if it's blackened to a charred, flaky crust. Also, if the tomato skin hasn't toughened up in roasting it will not need to be removed. Remove the seeds from the pepper and chop everything coarsely with a chef's knife or in the food processor.

While the pasta is cooking, gently heat all the vegetables in a saucepan with the olive oil and chili. Just before serving, stir in the vinegar and herbs (if using). Pour on to the cooked pasta. Serve with grated Parmesan.

This next recipe is even simpler. It uses just 2 principal ingredients, aubergines and sun-dried tomatoes. The aubergine can be cooked the day before if necessary, but it should not be peeled and mashed until just before serving.

Fusilli with Roasted Aubergines and Sun-dried Tomatoes

2 medium aubergines (around 750 g/1 ½ lb)
3–4 sun-dried tomatoes
1 clove of garlic
1 sprig of fresh rosemary, or 1 tsp dried
75 ml (5 tbsp) extra virgin olive oil
a dash of chili sauce (optional)

Roast the aubergine in a 230°C (450°F, Gas 8) oven, as this is the surest and fastest way of getting the skin to char. (You don't actually eat the skin, but some of the toasty flavour migrates to the flesh and thence to the sauce.) When it's soft all the way through, remove the skin and chop the flesh. Leave the flesh to drain in a sieve for a few minutes so some of its oil will drain away. Shred or mince the tomatoes and chop the garlic and rosemary. Heat the oil in a small saucepan, add the garlic, tomatoes and rosemary, and cook gently for a few minutes. Add the aubergine and the optional chili sauce, and continue heating for a couple of minutes while the pasta is cooking. Pour the sauce over the cooked pasta, and serve with grated Parmesan.

THE TOMATO SAUCE VARIATIONS

Contrary to popular belief, tomato sauce does not need to be cooked gently for hours. You can make a very good one in less than 20 minutes. The flavours will not develop and mingle as they do in a slow-cooked sauce, but they'll still be pretty good. You'll be able to sit down to eat a lot sooner. And you can vary the recipe in many different ways.

It's also worth noting that even slow-cooked tomato sauce is an incredibly easy thing to make. Once you've chopped, measured, fried and poured, the sauce cooks on its own. All it needs is the occasional stir and slurp to make sure it's going all right. A slower procedure is given below.

And when you view it this way, you see that a good tomato sauce is one of the lazy cook's best friends. As long as you have a food processor, it's just as easy to make in large quantities as in small. And what you don't use on the day of making can be packed away into the freezer for future reference. Store it in containers of different sizes, from a yogurt pot to a great jug of the stuff. That way you can defrost only what you need for any occasion, whether it's dinner on your own or a supper party for six.

What I've done, then, is to provide two tomato sauces – one quick and simple, one of the more traditional variety. Make the quick one when you just want to eat as soon as possible and can't be bothered to mess around with endless ingredients. The complicated one is for weekends, when you've got more time and feel like stocking the freezer. Both are delicious.

Almost-instant Tomato Sauce

Since this is something you should make in large quantities – with the freezer in mind – I've given a recipe that will sauce at least 1.5–2 kg (3–4 lb) of pasta. Please note that this is an ultra-simple version of tomato sauce, and that it can be jazzed up *ad infinitum, ad gloriam*. Suggestions follow below

1 large onion
4 cloves of garlic
120 ml (4 fl oz) extra virgin olive oil
2 tbsp herbes de Provence (see page 338)
four 400 g (14 oz) tins of Italian plum tomatoes
1 tbsp sugar (optional)
4–5 leaves of basil (optional)

Mince the onion and garlic, and heat 1 tbsp of the oil in a saucepan. Fry the onion and garlic briskly for around 1 minute, till they're smelling great. Add the herbs, tomatoes and sugar (optional) to the pot, roughly chopping the tomatoes with a wooden spoon, and turn the heat up. When the sauce boils, turn the heat down slightly and cook briskly for 15–20 minutes, till it's reduced in volume by around one quarter. Stir in the chopped or torn basil at the last minute, if using.

Slow-cooked Tomato Sauce

In essence this is the same sauce as the instant variety, but long cooking deepens the flavour. Since it will have more time over the heat, you can add extra vegetables for further complexity. For the quantities given above I suggest

1 medium carrot, minced
1 stalk of celery, minced

Proceed as in the instant recipe, but fry the onions and garlic with the carrot and celery for around 2 minutes. Add the herbs and tomatoes to the pot, roughly chopping the tomatoes with a wooden spoon, and turn the heat up. When the sauce boils, turn the heat down very low and simmer gently for 40 minutes–1½ hours, stirring when you remember to. Make sure the sauce isn't 'catching' (i.e. sticking) on the bottom of the pan, and add a little water or turn the heat down more if it is. When the sauce is reduced in volume by around one quarter, it is done. Stir in the basil at the last minute, if using.

EXTRA FLAVOURINGS FOR TOMATO SAUCE

Which ones to use? The question should be: which ones *not* to use? Here is a partial list of ingredients. These should go in with the herbs and sauce.

2–3 dried red chilis, flaked or finely chopped (if you don't like a very hot sauce, remove the seeds first)
2–3 fresh red or green chilis, finely chopped (if you don't like a very hot sauce, remove the seeds first)
a dash of chili sauce
a few shreds of lemon or orange zest, finely chopped
a few slices of peeled ginger, finely chopped
2–3 sun-dried tomatoes, finely chopped
a hefty squirt of tomato paste or purée
1–2 bay leaves (remove before eating)

You can also add a small handful of aromatic fresh herbs just before serving. Here are a few possibilities.

basil	*fennel*
chervil	*parsley*
coriander	*tarragon*
dill	*thyme*

Omit the fresh herbs if you're making sauce for the freezer, adding them just before serving.

A Creamy Tomato Sauce

Cream is delicious in a tomato sauce, adding silken texture and neutralizing some of the acidity of the tomatoes (which you will notice much more with the quick-cooked variety). For each 500 g (1 lb) of pasta add one of the following:

single cream: 50–75 ml (2–3 fl oz)
double cream, crème fraîche, *sour cream: 25–50 ml (1–2 fl oz)*

Tomato Sauce with Leftovers

An instant success if you've got the right leftovers, which can be meat, vegetables, or even fish. Whatever you've got, chop it into small pieces (around ¼ in should be the target) and add it to the sauce about 30 seconds before serving. You don't want to do more than reheat it at this stage or it will dry out.

Here are a few examples of recipes from elsewhere in this book that would liven up a leftover pasta sauce.

braised oxtail (see page 63)
braised beef (see page 58)
braised vegetables (see page 162)
pan-grilled vegetables (see page 103)
charred vegetables (see page 167)
vegetables à l'étuvée *(see page 157)*

Serve as for ordinary tomato sauce.

Tomato Sauce with Mushrooms

One of the all-time great combinations, and hardly any trouble. For 500 g (1 lb) of pasta, slice

125–250 g (4–8 oz) very fresh white mushrooms

as thin as you can be bothered ($\frac{1}{16}$–$\frac{1}{8}$ in should be the target). Four or 5 minutes before serving, add them to the sauce. They should retain quite a bit of crunch while feeling 'cooked' all the way through – and very hot, of course. Serve as for ordinary tomato sauce.

Tomato Sauce with Ham

Another of the great pasta partnerships. The ideal here would be *prosciutto* or its equivalent, but even ordinary cooked ham will do. Use

125–200 g (4–6 oz) prosciutto
225 ml (8 fl oz) tomato sauce

Cut the ham into skinny little shreds (assuming it's already sliced quite thin). Heat the sauce in a saucepan and add the ham a minute or two before serving.

Tomato Sauce with Anchovies or Olives (or both)

Yet again, a classic combination. Both these ingredients are on the pungent side, so you don't want to add them in large quantities. Anchovies should be added to the sauce when you put in the herbs and tomatoes, while olives can go in either then or around 3–4 minutes before serving. Approximate quantities to use for 500 g (1 lb) of pasta:

3–4 anchovy fillets, drained and chopped into tiny bits
6–8 olives, stoned and chopped into little bits
225 ml (8 fl oz) tomato sauce

Tomato Sauce with Mussels

Nothing involving mussels can ever qualify as true-blue lazy cooking. These delicious bivalves, 'the poor man's oyster', are a pain in the neck to prepare. Even the new farmed mussels need to be dumped into a sinkful of water and have their grimly tenacious 'beards' yanked out. But if you don't mind the extra 5–10 minutes of work, this is a delicious recipe which will sauce 500 g (1 lb) of pasta.

1 bag of mussels (usually 1 kg/2 lb)
1 clove of garlic
2 thick pats of butter
60 ml (4 tbsp) single cream
a small handful of fresh coriander
225 ml (8 fl oz) tomato sauce

Clean the mussels in cold water, discarding any that are open. Mince the garlic and melt the butter over low heat in a pot big enough to hold the mussels. Get the pasta cooking at this point. Cook the garlic gently for a minute or so, then add the mussels, toss well, and cook, covered, for 4–5 minutes or so. Stir at least twice to make sure the mussels are well distributed in the pot. Add the cream, coriander and tomato sauce, and cook for another minute, without letting the liquid boil. (The sauce can happily sit for a few minutes while the pasta finishes cooking.) When the pasta is done, put it into large bowls and ladle the mussels and sauce on top. This is a mess to eat, which is half the fun. Provide another large bowl for the mussel shells.

The next recipe is adapted from a recipe in Marcella Hazan's *Second Italian Classic Cookbook*. It is ultra-simple and amazingly delicious.

Onion and Chilis with Tomato Sauce

1 Spanish onion (around 250 g/8 oz)
1 large green chili
4 tbsp extra virgin olive oil
100–150 ml (4–6 fl oz) tomato sauce

Cut the onion in half lengthwise and slice it as thin as you can get it. De-seed the chili and chop finely. Heat the oil in a saucepan and add the onions and chili, stirring to distribute the oil. When the onion is just starting to sizzle, turn the heat down to the lowest possible heat and cook, covered, for 30–40 minutes, until the onions have caramelized (turned brown and sweet). Pour in the tomato sauce and cook just long enough to heat through. Tip the contents of the pan on to the cooked pasta and toss with the sauce; cheese is optional, and not necessary in my view.

ACCIDENTAL PLEASURES

I can't end this chapter without reiterating my belief that the best pasta sauces are often made with whatever ingredients happen to be lying around the kitchen. Leftovers and the larder are the pasta-maker's most valuable fallbacks. As long as you have (a) a reasonably full fridge with a piece of Parmesan among its contents; (b) a well-stocked larder (with a packet of pasta lurking within); and (c) a freewheeling imagination, you can eat good pasta.

To prove the point, here is a pasta dish I recently made when my wife was ill and unable to eat anything for dinner. I had to put the children to bed, look after my ailing wife, and finish dinner in time to watch the 9 o'clock news. (For the record, this event took place during the 1992 General Election.) I was tired, hungry, and disinclined to spend more time cooking than was absolutely necessary. I got the water boiling, poured myself a drink, and then rummaged around in the fridge to look for something to put on the pasta.

The resulting sauce did not make the greatest pasta dish of all time. It was not something you would want to eat in a restaurant or serve to your friends. You might not even want to eat it at all, because on the surface the ingredients sound like a wild mishmash. If I weren't so lazy, I would try to improve on it in search of further refinements.

But it was delicious, at least at the time of eating, and it illustrates the kind of serendipitous pleasure that can leap from the fridge if only you allow it to. Here is the recipe, reproduced exactly as I made it. Use it as an inspiration rather than a set of instructions. You are unlikely ever to have precisely these ingredients lying around in your own fridge. On the other hand, you are sure to have *something* lying around which will make a sauce that's every bit as good as this one.

An Accidental Pasta Dish

sliced onions from a roast chicken – enough to fill a measuring cup to the 100 ml
  mark (around 3–4 fl oz)
a small handful of fresh coriander
a few sprigs of fresh rosemary
4 anchovy fillets
1 sun-dried tomato
1 tbsp capers
125 g (4–5 oz) penne
juice of ⅓ of a lemon
1½ tbsp double cream
3–4 tbsp fresh grated Parmesan

Put the onions in a bowl. Chop the coriander, rosemary, anchovies, sun-dried tomatoes and capers. Cook the pasta till it is *just* done, drain it, and return to the cooking pot. Put in all the sauce ingredients and heat gently for a minute or so. Dump everything into a large bowl and eat immediately with the grated cheese.

Puréed Soups

Puréed Soups

THE PRINCIPLE

You chop vegetables, cook them lightly in butter, then pour in stock and let them simmer till soft. Once they're soft you purée them, add more liquid (if needed) to thin the soup out, correct the seasoning and – *voilà* – your soup is ready.

THE DETAILS

There are few easier ways to impress your friends – or just cheer yourself up on a miserable winter night – than serving a puréed soup. When the lazy cook entertains, this should always be one of the first choices for a starter. The technique is simplicity itself, and the whole operation can take as little as 10 minutes of active cooking. The result is a fine-textured blend, thickened only by the vegetables themselves, which can taste purely of the main ingredient or present a complex layering of several different flavours.

Before I go any further, I need to acknowledge a debt to John Tovey, writer, broadcaster, and patron of the famous Miller Howe hotel and restaurant in Windermere. Mr Tovey's *Miller Howe Cookbook* (1987) contains a chapter on soups which works on a somewhat similar principle to mine. In detail, my approach differs considerably from his; he and I do not make puréed soups in the same way, and I have not taken any recipes from him. But he first got me thinking systematically about the basics of puréed soup, and he also persuaded me of the value of making them with dry sherry. I am grateful to him on both counts.

If you've ever had a fine, creamy soup in a good French restaurant, you may be surprised by the first puréed soup you make. A puréed soup is different from the classic *velouté* soup of French cuisine. *Velouté* soups are based on a *roux*, an emulsion of cream, egg yolk and flour. They are wonderful things when made properly, but they are not for lazy cooks. (Nor for weight-watching cooks, as the *roux* is stiff with calories.) A puréed soup has the same uniform texture (or nearly uniform), but what creaminess it possesses does not come from the use of liberal quantities of cream. Indeed, it may contain no dairy products at all.

So your first attempt at a puréed soup will not taste or feel like a classic French *velouté* soup. It will, however, taste delicious. And you will get it right the very first time you make one.

THE INGREDIENTS

Puréed soups have three main constituents:

liquid
a thickener (optional)
one or more vegetables and/or fruits to give the soup its predominant
   ('background') flavour

In addition to these there may be a fourth constituent:

one or more ingredients to give the soup a 'highlight' flavour

Let's take them one by one.

LIQUID

The primary liquid for puréed soups is stock, combined if desired with an optional dose of white wine or dry sherry. Stock provides a cooking medium for the vegetables and flavour of its own. Wine provides flavour, and while the quantities are small, the contribution to the total effect is large.

Water can be used instead, but stock is indisputably the superior option. I've made these soups with water several times, and while they're perfectly edible, they're never truly distinguished. The stock adds something indefinable which I can only describe as depth of flavour.

It is a cardinal kitchen rule that the better your stock, the better the dish. The rule applies in soup-making no less than in sauce- or stew-making. Indeed, in clear soups – those where pieces of vegetable or fish or meat are left floating in the stock – it is truer than ever.

Making stock takes time, and lazy cooks don't like to spend a lot of time doing anything in the kitchen, except maybe reading the paper. That's why we generally have to steer clear of clear soups. If you do get stricken by the stock-making bug (and I have to admit that I love doing it myself), here are instructions that are tailor-made for lazy cooks. Try it at least once, and use the result to make a clear soup: the fruits of your uncharacteristic kitchen energy will shine forth in their full glory.

One thing you'll notice if you've read other stock recipes is that I don't add the aromatic vegetables at the beginning of the simmering process. There are two reasons for this. One comes from Shaun Hill, chef at the Gidleigh Park Hotel and restaurant, and author of the *Gidleigh Park Cookery Book*. Chef Hill points out that vegetables give up their flavour fairly quickly, and therefore don't need hours of cooking. Ever since I read his advice I have heeded it, and have found that he's absolutely right. And this leads to the second reason, which plays right into the hands of lazy cooks. Skimming stock is much more difficult when there are bits of onion and carrot floating around in it. If you do most of your skimming *before* the vegetables go in, the whole process will be much easier.

Lazy Stock

The more meat there is on the bones, the better the stock will be. If your bone supply is notably light on meat, add a few chicken pieces (for chicken stock) or beef pieces (for beef stock). Belly of pork, the cheapest cut of all, makes a delicious addition to chicken-and-pork stock, which is an idea taken from Chinese cooking. After you've cooked the pork for an hour or so, you can use it for Pan-grilled Belly of Pork (see page 95).

*1.5 kg (3 lb) chicken pieces, bones, and scraps; or the same weight of beef bones; or
   the same weight of chicken and pork bones combined*
2 small carrots
1 large onion or medium leek
2 cloves of garlic
1 bay leaf
1 tbsp herbes de Provence (see page 338)
1 handful of parsley

Put the bones in a large pot. If you wish to, you can brown them first for a richer flavour and colour. To do this, heat 2 tbsp of plain vegetable oil in the pot and add the bones. Cook over a medium heat for 10–15 minutes, stirring every few minutes, until the pieces are pretty well browned. (Or until you get tired of stirring.) Now add cold water to cover the bones by an inch or so. Put over a high heat and bring to the boil; this will take around 10–15 minutes. Watch the pot carefully at this stage, and skim off the scum that will start rising after 5–10 minutes. In the meantime, chop the vegetables. They don't need to be particularly fine.

When the pot comes to a boil, immediately turn the heat down to its lowest setting and simmer for 1 hour. Give it a final skim, add the remaining ingredients, and leave the pot alone for a minimum of 1 hour or more. An extra hour or even 2 hours will be fine. You should barely notice any bubbles rising to the surface. A gentle shimmy should be the only apparent movement. As long as the stock doesn't boil hard, it will come to no harm – though you might check it after 2 hours just to make sure the water is still high enough to cover most of the contents of the pot.

When you think you've had enough, turn off the heat and let the stock sit for an hour or so. Then lift the bones etc. out with a slotted spoon or kitchen tongs, being careful not to stir up the stock too much. Leave it for another 30 minutes and, using a ladle, transfer the stock to a clean saucepan by pouring it through a fine sieve. Do not spoon out the stock at the bottom of the pot, which will be cloudy and grainy.

OK, I admit it: this is more trouble than most lazy cooks are willing to put up with. But the flavour really will be noticeably better. What the hell, you can't be lazy *all* the time.

Fortunately, you can usually get away with an instant substitute when making puréed soups. Had we but world enough and time, we would all save up scraps of chicken, beg bones and other leavings from the butcher, and make our own stock. Since we don't, most of us are going to end up using cubes. And in puréed soup you can get away with it. Chicken stock cubes are your best bet; tinned broth can also be good, if somewhat more expensive; the fresh chicken stock sold by some supermarkets can be very good, but for puréed soup, in my opinion, the extra cost is unnecessary.

Whatever the source of your stock, try to stick with chicken.

The others all have something against them. Lamb is strongly and distinctively flavoured, and tends to dominate any dish except one made with lamb. Fish is suitable only for fish soups. And some stock cubes are positively disgusting. I have never tasted a good stock made from pork stock cubes, and most fish cubes are also pretty revolting. Stick to chicken, with vegetable stock the second choice. (Or only choice if you're vegetarian; but if you're reading this book you probably eat meat.)

For the record: by far the best brand of stock cube, in my opinion, is Just Bouillon. And even an ordinary chicken stock cube is better than water.

ALCOHOL

John Tovey puts dry sherry in all his puréed soups, and the more I make the things the more I am convinced he's right. Sherry is a much-underrated drink in this country, and just as underrated when it comes to cooking. Because some people like the distinctive sherry flavour and some do not, you may want to use less than I specify. Even if you think you don't like it, do try it at least once. You can use white wine instead but it won't be as good. I strongly recommend that you keep a bottle of the dry stuff (*fino*) on hand at all times. Store it in the fridge and try not to keep it too long; enjoy it as an aperitif instead of the clichéd white wine. It's much better, especially for drinking without food.

Incidentally, white wine does not have to be ultra-dry. I've used Alsace wines (Gewürztraminer and Riesling) as well as Australian and French wines based on the Semillon grape. These have a fuller, fruitier, slightly fatter taste than bone-dry whites, and they are great in soup.

THE TWO STAGES OF ADDING LIQUIDS

There are two stages of adding liquid to a soup. After you've cooked the vegetables lightly in butter for a couple of minutes, you pour in stock that will complete the cooking through gentle simmering. After you've puréed the soup and put it back in the saucepan, you then add more liquid to thin the soup out.

Since this book is about lazy cooking, the truly lazy cook will be asking why I add the liquid in two stages. Surely it's easier and faster to add all the liquid at the simmering stage. Well, you can do this. But the wily lazy cook will prefer to do it in two stages. If you add it all at once, you run the risk of putting in too much. And there is little or nothing you can do with a soup that's too thin. Boiling it down to reduce it is a pain, and it affects the flavour. Two-step addition of liquid eliminates the need to measure precisely at the first stage.

The second-stage liquid can be either extra stock or dairy products – milk, some form of cream, yogurt, or a combination of two or more. You have to decide which you want.

Some puréed soups don't need any dairy products. Especially if they've been made with an ample amount of thickener (more on that in a moment), they will be rich and thick enough to eat without milk or cream. If this is the case, extra stock will be fine. Around half the soups I make are made with stock alone as liquid.

But milk, cream and yogurt do something distinctive, and mostly it has to do with texture. Using them brings the soup up to something that resembles the silken creaminess of a *velouté* soup. It also, in the case of cultured products like yogurt, *crème fraîche*, or *fromage frais*, adds a slightly sour 'tang' to the flavour. Here are the main choices of dairy products for use in soups:

double cream	*Greek yogurt*
single cream	*low-fat yogurt*
sour cream	fromage frais
crème fraîche	*plain old milk*

Needless to say, these have to be used in different amounts for any given quantity of soup. More on quantities follows shortly.

In adding the creamy stuff to soup you have two options: mix it in completely or dribble/swirl/dot it on top. Personally I prefer the latter, at least on soups with a fairly deep colour. It looks nice, even if it is something of a cliché, and you can create patterns which look pretty nifty on top of the soup.

My favourite technique, by no means original, is this: dip a spoon in the creamy stuff and let most of it drip back into the carton or tub. Working very quickly, twirl the spoon around over the serving bowls to form roughly circular ribbons of white on top of the soup. If you're using minced herbs as an additional flavouring/decoration, put them on after the cream.

THICKENERS

In the classic *velouté* soups of French cuisine, the soup is thickened using flour. This is not the way lazy cooks do it, however. Lazy cooks should thicken the soup using starch in the form of a starchy vegetable or a grain. The main choices are:

Vegetables: *potatoes or parsnips*
Grains: *rice or pulses (lentils, dried beans)*

Only one of these is needed, though potatoes and parsnips make a good combination on grounds of flavour.

Thickness is determined by two factors: the ratio of starch to main vegetable and the ratio of total vegetable matter to liquid. By varying these two things, you can make a soup with whatever consistency you like. It can be thin, thick, or anywhere in between.

This decision is entirely up to you. As a general rule, however, the ratio of starchy stuff to the main vegetable(s) should range from

1:3 to 1:10

and the soup will still have everything it's supposed to have. And whatever your preference in the thickness department, don't worry if the soup looks too thick after the first stage of cooking. This can be corrected in the final stage by adding more stock or milk to thin it out.

THE BACKGROUND FLAVOUR

A puréed soup can taste of anything that's capable of being puréed. The choice of vegetables is a wide one, and more detail will follow shortly. In principle, you have to make one important decision: what is the main flavour or combination of flavours you want in your soup. The basic principle here is to look for a good balance of flavours. Parsnip soup made only with parsnips is usually cloying: this delicious vegetable is far too sweet on its own. Parsnip and carrot soup is little better because carrots too are a very sweet vegetable. On the other hand, parsnip and potato *and leek* is delicious; so is carrot and celery and potato. If one vegetable has a particular flavour which you think would be too much on its own, mix it with something else that has a complementary or counterbalancing flavour. Remember also that the strong background flavour in a single vegetable can be counterbalanced by use of a contrasting 'highlight' flavour (see below).

In any event, the choice of background flavour will not always lie in your hands. There's an old saying that you don't plan your menu and then go shopping; you go shopping and then plan your menu. This applies perfectly to puréed soups, which are always the creation of market availability. See what looks good on the day you're planning to cook. Buy it. And create the 'recipe' for your soup on the basis of what you've been able to lay your hands on. The best puréed soups almost always happen by accident, or at least with an element of accidentalness.

THE CHOICE OF VEGETABLES

This is a real pleasure to write about, and a boon for lazy cooks. The simple answer to the big question – what vegetables can I use? – is that you can use just about anything you want. Here is a list of my favourite predominant soup vegetables. Most can be used on their own, with nothing more than thickener and liquid. But many benefit from being used in combinations, with a sharp-tasting 'highlight' flavour to liven them up.

broccoli	*onions*
carrots	*red peppers*
cauliflower	*tomatoes*
courgettes	*turnip tops*
cucumbers	*Savoy cabbage*
green peppers	*sorrel*
kohlrabi	*spring greens*
leeks	*turnips*
lettuce	*watercress*

Again, the decision about which to use will depend on what kind of soup you feel like having and what vegetables are looking good on the day.

PREPARING THE VEGETABLES

Most soup recipes tell you to slice the vegetables thin before putting them in the pot for the initial cooking. You can do this and it will work, but there are alternatives. Most vegetables will work perfectly well if they're chopped into chunks, which is easier. Easier still is to put them in a food processor and process till everything's coarsely chopped. This has the advantage of lowering cooking times, and it also makes the mixture more compact. (Which is an advantage if you're making a lot of soup in a smallish pot.) Remember that everything will be puréed anyway, so you don't need to worry about the appearance of the vegetables.

The only vegetables that need special treatment are 'stringy' vegetables such as celery, French beans, or cabbage. These should be sliced very thin across the strings; otherwise they will be hard to turn into a fine purée. But if you do slice them thin, across the strings, you will get a good purée without the additional step of sieving them (which some other books recommend). I find that a good sharp knife works better for these vegetables than the high-tech food processor.

HIGHLIGHT FLAVOURINGS – SPICES, HERBS, AROMATIC VEGETABLES

You can make excellent puréed soups from nothing more than vegetables, stock, and salt and pepper. Often, however, the careful addition of a 'highlight' flavouring spells the difference between a good soup and a great soup.

A highlight flavouring is hard to describe in the abstract but you probably know what I mean. Even though it might constitute 1 per cent or even less of the total volume of the dish, somehow it seems to transform and exalt the whole operation. Prime examples of highlight flavouring are the fresh lemon you squeeze on a piece of grilled fish; the freshly-grated Parmesan on a plate of pasta with tomato sauce; the paper-thin discs of spring onion floating in a bowl of Japanese *miso* soup. In all cases, the dish would be edible without the highlight flavour; in all cases, it would not be anything like as good. (I might say, parenthetically, that lazy cooking can largely be defined as the use of highlight flavourings to make ordinary dishes delicious without going to a lot of extra trouble.)

Some highlight flavourings should be cooked along with the rest of the soup, usually added with the vegetables. Others can be added at the last moment. And I usually make a lot of highlight decisions when the soup is cooked, puréed, and returned to the saucepan. I stick a spoon in, correct the amount of salt and pepper, and then scratch my head and ask myself: 'What else does this soup need?'

Here is a list of soupy highlights. Those marked * should be added at the beginning of cooking. Those marked ** should be added only at the last moment, just before serving. The others can be added either at the beginning or as a last-minute afterthought.

dried herbs: mixed (e.g. herbes de Provence), tarragon, thyme, rosemary, sage
fresh herbs: just about any of them, but especially dill, coriander, *tarragon,
    chives, parsley, basil
*mild curry powder
*garlic
*ginger (particularly good)
*shallots or spring onion
*lemon grass

ginger, garlic and spring onion (see page 332)
**citrus juice: lemon and lime (best bets) or orange*
citrus zest: lemon, lime, orange
mixed Indian spices (see page 158)
dried or fresh chili (in cautious moderation)
chili sauce
sun-dried tomato (see page 341)
**vinegar: wine, sherry, cider, balsamic*
dry sherry
Thai fish sauce

THE TEXTURE OF PURÉED SOUPS

People have different views about what a puréed soup should feel like in their mouth. Some want a uniform texture, akin to that of baby food, with not a trace of solid material lurking anywhere in sight. I am one of the baby-food contingent. With me there are deep, dark, psychological motivations at work, some of them having to do with the aura of 'professionalism' that hovers above a bowl of perfectly smooth vegetable soup. ('This is the kind of texture you get in a restaurant,' I say to myself. 'It must be good.')

Other people prefer some texture, and I can't say I blame them. They aren't as easily fooled as I am. More important, they like the food they eat to retain some hint of the materials from which it's made; and there is something rustically satisfying about the odd bit of crunch in an otherwise smooth preparation.

But there's texture and there's texture. When you're making puréed soup, remember that the dominant effect of the finished dish must be one of uniformity, evenness, and more or less total mingling of all the elements of the soup. There is room within that effect for a few bits and pieces, here and there, of material that hasn't been definitively pulverized. But the soup should *not* have too many bits like that or it will be less satisfying – and less impressive. You've got to decide whether you're aiming for the puréed effect. If you are, purée decisively. An excessive number of bits will merely suggest that you've been careless.

HOW TO PURÉE VEGETABLES

The most perfectly smooth, even texture in a puréed soup is obtained by puréeing it and then forcing the whole thing through a sieve. This is the procedure recommended by John Tovey in his book, and far be it from me to quibble with a master soup-maker. But if you were willing to do this two-stage puréeing, you wouldn't be reading a book called *The Lazy Cook*. A one-stage process is what you'll be looking for, and the fastest and easiest way to do it is with a machine. (You could also do it by using the sieve, but for lazy cooks that's like saying you can chop down a tree with a pocket knife.)

Some people use a food processor for puréeing soups. Now, food processors are wonderfully useful items in any kitchen but they are not the first choice for puréeing soups; they aren't even the second choice. They do not make purées from soupy vegetables. No matter how long you process your soup, it will never achieve that fine texture you're looking for. The effect will be gritty and bitty, even if the taste is perfectly good.

For puréeing soups, you need a blender. They're cheap and easy to wash up, and are also useful for milk shakes and other drinks, and for making mayonnaise, spice mixes, and fruit purées. Invest in one and you won't regret it. More to the point, for the purposes of this chapter I am assuming that you own one.

If you do like a bit of rough texture in your soup, please, I repeat, do not think that a food processor will do the job. Use your blender, but when putting in the soup, leave a ladleful or two behind in the saucepan. Mash up that ladleful with a spoon or fork, crushing it roughly. Now purée the remaining soup in the blender and mix it well with the soup in the pan. This will give you the requisite fine texture with a few added bits thrown in for variety. I promise you that this gives better results than any food processor. Indeed, I have never had a satisfying soup made in a food processor.

One final note: in the recipes that follow, I have suggested adding sherry (when called for) after the soup is already cooked and puréed. This is because I invariably make puréed soups well in advance and then reheat them thoroughly before serving. If you are making your soup soon before serving, add the sherry to the stock for the initial stage of cooking. You should also try doing this if you want the flavour of the wine to be less pronounced.

So much for preliminaries. Here is a basic puréed soup which will show how the procedure works, followed by a number of other recipes for your experimental excitation. But remember, throughout this chapter, that the best puréed soups are those that you improvise yourself.

Leek and Potato Soup

Leeks and potatoes form one of the most venerable partnerships in Western cookery, one of those simple synergies that get used in numerous ways. Potatoes are mild in flavour, while leeks – a member of the *Allium* family, which also includes onions and garlic – are sharp and aromatic. Put the two together, in just about any form, and you have one of the great flavour combinations.

When making this soup – which is similar to every leek-and-potato you can think of, including Vichyssoise – I always make too much of the base so that I can use it for other things. A list of suggestions follows the soup recipe.

500 g (1 lb) leeks, white part only
250 g (8 oz) baking potatoes
1 thick pat of butter
salt and pepper
450 ml (16 fl oz) chicken stock
milk or single cream

Cut the leeks in half lengthwise and rinse as necessary to remove dirt. (Sometimes they need extensive cleaning, sometimes none at all.) Chop into shreds and set aside. Peel the potatoes and slice thinly. Heat the butter gently in a large saucepan and add the leeks and potatoes. Cook, stirring, for a couple of minutes – just long enough to soften slightly without colouring. Now add the stock, bring to the boil, and simmer, partly covered, until the vegetables are really soft (around 40 minutes).

The base may be seasoned with just about anything. Here are some suggestions:

mixed herbs (e.g. herbes de Provence)
fresh dill
mild curry powder
garlic
ginger (particularly good)
lemon grass

This quantity of base provides enough soup to feed 8 people. If you don't need that much, remove some with a slotted spoon, leave it to cool, then transfer the base to freezable plastic containers. Cover tightly and freeze. (Or store in the fridge for up to 3 days.)

To finish the soup: put the potato-leek base in the blender and blend until completely puréed. You may need to add some milk to enable it to blend properly.

The texture may be either coarse or fine; I prefer it fine. For an extra-fine texture you can pass it through a sieve, but this is too much like hard work. Return to the saucepan, season with salt and pepper, and add milk to bring it up to the right consistency. A few minutes before serving, reheat it gently.

LEEK AND POTATO BASE

Here are some things you can do with leftover base. If frozen it should be thoroughly thawed.

1. Squeeze out excess moisture and mix with a beaten egg. Thicken with a little flour if necessary. Form it into patties and fry in butter as an accompaniment to chops or chicken.

2. Put it in a buttered gratin dish with a little cheese, dot with butter, and bake in a 230°C (450°F, Gas 8) oven for 25–30 minutes, until golden and bubbling. A little cream may be mixed in for a richer effect.

3. Use it as a base for baking chicken.

4. Reheat it gently in a heavy saucepan or double boiler, and serve as a vegetable dish.

5. Use it to thicken a braised dish (see braising chapter, page 45).

That is the basic puréed soup. Here is a small selection of some others that I have made successfully. I hope that you will use them as nothing more than ideas to get your own imagination in gear, and to see how many different things you can do with this basic, classic technique.

Courgette Soup with Chili

The lower figure for chilis will give a spicy but quite mild soup, suitable even for children. The higher figure is altogether riskier. This quantity of stock leaves you with a very thick base, which is then thinned out with a lot of milk. The ratio of milk to stock could easily be reversed.

1 clove of garlic
5–10 slices of fresh green chili
250 g (8 oz) onion
500 g (1 lb) courgettes
250 g (8 oz) potatoes
1 bay leaf

½ tsp dried thyme
25 g (1 oz) butter
300 ml (10 fl oz) stock
400–450 ml (14–16 fl oz) milk
75 ml (2½ fl oz) dry sherry

Chop or slice the dry ingredients (except the bay leaf and thyme). Melt the butter in a saucepan and cook slowly as in the master recipe, then add the stock. Part-cover and simmer as in the master Leek and Potato recipe on page 255. Purée and add the milk and sherry.

Parsnip, Apple and Onion

Please note: the combination of parsnips and apples gives this soup a firm push in the direction of sweetness. Some people (myself included) like the sweetness while others do not. If you want to sharpen it, add a tablespoon or so of vinegar along with the milk and sherry.

250 g (8 oz) parsnips
500 g (1 lb) apples
500 g (1 lb) onions
1 clove of garlic
a thick pat of butter
1/2 tsp whole cumin

1/2 tsp whole fennel seeds
2 whole cardamom pods
500 ml (18 fl oz) stock
400–450 ml (14–16 fl oz) milk
75 ml (2 1/2 fl oz) dry sherry

Trim the parsnips and peel them if necessary; cut out the woody cores. Peel and core the apples. Chop both with the onion (peeled) and garlic. Melt the butter in a saucepan and cook slowly with the spices as in the master Leek and Potato recipe, then add the stock. Part-cover and cook as in the master recipe. Purée and add the milk and sherry.

What I like best about the following soup – apart from the fact that it tastes great – is its pure white colour. To attain this, you have to be sure to use only the white part of the leek. It helps also to use white pepper instead of black, but that may be carrying things a little too far for lazy cooks.

White Soup – Leek and Cauliflower

250 g (8 oz) leeks
100 g (4 oz) floury potatoes
1 medium cauliflower (around 600 g/1 1/4 lb) trimmed weight
2 thick pats of butter
750 ml (1 1/2 pints) chicken or vegetable stock, or a combination of the two
300 ml (10 fl oz) milk
1 tsp lemon juice

Chop the green ends off the leeks and discard or use for flavouring stock; clean the white bits if necessary and slice or chop thin. Peel the potatoes and slice or chop thin. Trim the leaves from the cauliflower and cut the head into small pieces – around 1 in in size is good, but don't bother getting out your tape measure. Heat the butter in a large saucepan and add all the vegetables, and cook gently for a few minutes. Pour in the stock and bring to the boil, then simmer till everything is very soft. Purée and return to the pan. Bring back up to a gentle simmer, add the milk and let it come up to heat, and then add the lemon juice just before serving. NB: It's important not to let the soup boil once the lemon juice has gone in, as the combination of acid and heat will curdle the milk.

Avocado soup is now something of a cliché. But it's popular because it's good, and very easy; and best of all, it needs no cooking. Here is a version I like, in which the expensive avocado is combined with cheaper cucumbers and onions. Instant, tasty. What more can you ask? There's only one problem with avocados, and that is that some of them are lousy. The best by far are the rough-skinned Hass variety. If you can't get them, use another – but make sure it is perfectly ripe or the soup won't have much flavour.

Avocado Soup

1 small onion
1/2 a large cucumber (around 250 g/8 oz)
4 ripe avocados, preferably the Hass variety

a few dashes of chili sauce
juice of 1–2 lemons
around 500 ml (18 fl oz) chicken stock
60 ml (4 tbsp) single cream

Chop the onion. Peel the cucumber, remove the seeds, and chop. Put the onion and cucumber in the blender. Scoop out the flesh from the avocados, then add to the blender with the chili sauce, the juice of 1 lemon, and a little salt and pepper. Put in around 50 ml (3 tbsp) of stock just to loosen up the mixture and blend till it's perfectly smooth. Taste for lemon – if there isn't enough, add some more and purée again. Now pour the sludge into a bowl or jug that's just large enough to hold it; cover tightly and refrigerate for up to 2 hours. Before serving, stir in the remaining stock and swirl in the cream if you're using it. Serve immediately.

Using lots of milk and cream makes for a very rich, filling result. It is very slightly trickier to do it this way because you have to complete the simmering of the vegetables in a minimum of stock – otherwise the soup will be too thin. Here is an example.

Celery and Cabbage with Thyme

1 large head (around 600 g/1¼ lb) celery
200 g (around 7 oz) white cabbage
100 g (around 4 oz) onions
2 thick pats (around 25 g/1 oz) butter
1 sprig of fresh or 1 tsp of dried thyme
around 500 ml (17–18 fl oz) chicken or vegetable stock
around 250 ml (8–9 fl oz) milk
around 200 ml (7–8 fl oz) single cream

Trim the ends from the celery but do not discard the leaves; they will go into the soup. Wash it as necessary and cut into very thin slices – really the thinner the better, but ¼ in maximum. Trim the cabbage and chop it the same way, again aiming for very thin pieces. Peel the onion and chop it as you please. Melt the butter in the saucepan and put in the vegetables and thyme, then cook for a few minutes to soften.

Now add the stock. I can't specify quantities precisely, but there should be just enough to cover the vegetables. Bring the mixture to the boil and then turn the heat right down, covering the pot partway so that just a crescent of steam can escape. Cook this way for

30–40 minutes

till the vegetables are good and soft, and stir it every so often. You will also want to check that it's not cooking too rapidly or the vegetables will brown. Now purée and return to the saucepan.

You will now have what looks like a thick sludge. And now you can add all that milk and cream, seasoning as you go with salt and pepper. Add enough of the white stuff to bring the soup up to the thickness and creaminess you want. You might use less than specified above, or you might use more. If you're feeding large numbers, you might also want to add stock. In my experience this quantity will serve 6 generously, 8 less generously. If you're having a light main course, use it to serve 6.

Tomato soup is one of the great soups, and this tomato soup has a number of things to recommend it. One is that it's made from tinned tomatoes, so anyone with a well-stocked larder can make it at a moment's notice. The second is that it takes even less work than most puréed soups: the vegetables are pre-digested, as it were. Third, it is delicious. The sun-dried tomatoes add a real wallop of extra flavour, so don't exclude them if you can help it. NB: there are two ways of making this soup, with cream or without. If you choose to leave the cream out, use extra virgin olive oil instead of butter for the initial cooking. And you might consider putting in a little potato as a thickener, since the soup will otherwise lack a certain amount of body.

Tomato Soup with Ginger and Tarragon

1 medium onion (around 3 in in diameter)
3 cloves of garlic
2 slices of peeled ginger, around ⅛ in thick
3 sun-dried tomatoes
2 thick pats of butter or 2 tbsp extra virgin olive oil
three 400 g (14 oz) tins Italian plum tomatoes
a few leaves of fresh tarragon or 1 tsp dried (or 1 tsp herbes de Provence)
700 ml (just over 24 fl oz) chicken stock or milk
2 tbsp dry sherry
3–4 tbsp double or single cream

Coarsely chop the onion, garlic, ginger and sun-dried tomatoes. Heat the butter or oil in a saucepan and cook them for a few minutes, then open the tins and dump them in. Add the tarragon, a little salt, and plenty of pepper, and let the tomato mixture bubble gently for 40 minutes or so. If you like, you can now put it through a sieve to remove the seeds. I don't bother. Instead just plop the red goo into the blender and purée it. (Can be made well in advance to this point.)

When you're around half an hour from serving, taste the mixture. If it needs more tomato oomph, add a small squirt of tomato purée. If it doesn't, just pour in around 500 ml (18 fl oz) of stock or milk, add the sherry, stir it, and taste again. You can add more stock or milk if the soup seems too thick. Now bring it up gently to heat, making sure it doesn't boil. Just before serving, swirl in the cream (if using). This goes well with slices of good toast, which can be brushed with a little melted butter or olive oil if you feel the need for even more richness in an already-rich dish. (And there's nothing wrong with that.)

The soup above, being unthickened, it is a fairly light dish. You can do the same thing but add much more body by combining the tomatoes with red lentils. Here's how.

Tomato Soup with Red Lentils

125–175 g (4–6 oz) red lentils
1 medium onion (around 3 in in diameter)
3 cloves of garlic
2 slices of peeled ginger, around ⅛ in thick
3 sun-dried tomatoes
2 thick pats of butter or 2 tbsp extra virgin olive oil
three 400 g (14 oz) tins Italian plum tomatoes
a few leaves of fresh tarragon or 1 tsp dried (or 1 tsp herbes de Provence)
around 1 litre (2 pints) chicken stock or milk
2 tbsp dry sherry
3–4 tbsp double or single cream

Wash the lentils and remove any discoloured bits. Proceed exactly as in the previous recipe but add the lentils with the tinned tomatoes. This soup will need more thinning out because of the thickening provided by the lentils – but that means it can feed more people. If you want to add some real zing to it, include

1 dried red chili, de-seeded

in the basic mix.

The next soup, based on one of my all-purpose ingredients, is unthickened, unusual, and unbeatable. It takes a highlight flavouring and turns it into the star of the show: background and highlight all at once. The quantity of spring onion is phenomenally high, and this makes the soup fairly expensive if that commodity is out of season. But you can substitute ordinary onions for all or part of the spring onions; using ordinary onions only will give a much sweeter soup. And while the spring onions take a lot of chopping, it's worth both the trouble and the expense.

Garlic, Ginger and Spring Onion Soup

around 900 g (2 lb or so) spring onions and/or onions
4 cloves of garlic
4 slices of ginger, peeled
2 thick pats of butter
around 400 ml (14 fl oz) chicken or beef stock
75 ml (3 fl oz) dry sherry
around 400 ml (14 fl oz) milk

Trim the spring onions and slice into thin discs; if using ordinary onions, peel them and chop or slice very thin. Chop the garlic and ginger together. Melt the butter in a large saucepan and let the onion, garlic and ginger cook gently for a few minutes, then add the stock, sherry, and a judicious amount of salt and pepper. Bring to the boil, turn down the heat, and simmer gently for a good long time – at least 45 minutes. The aim is to bring out the sweetness of the onion, which only happens with long cooking. Purée the mixture and return it to the pot.

When you're getting ready to serve, add the milk and stir in thoroughly. Taste to see whether it's the right consistency, and add more milk if desired.

Spinach Soup with Nutmeg and Parmesan

500 g (1 lb) potatoes
two 300 g (10 oz) packets of frozen spinach
1 tsp freshly grated nutmeg
around 400 ml (14 fl oz) chicken or beef stock
75 ml (3 fl oz) dry sherry
around 400 ml (14 fl oz) milk
2–3 tbsp freshly grated Parmesan

Cook the potatoes and spinach as in the recipe for Leek and Potato Soup, but get the spinach going first as it will have to defrost in the pot. Add the potatoes when it's fully defrosted, which should take around 15 minutes. Add the nutmeg with the potatoes, cook for a few more minutes, then add around half the stock and the sherry. Cook till everything is soft, then purée and return to the pan. Thin out as you prefer, bearing in mind that the potatoes will make this a very thick mixture. When the soup is in the serving bowls, sprinkle a little Parmesan on each one. This would go well with a slice or two of *ciabatta* or another good, crusty bread.

If you're feeling penurious, try the next soup. But try it on a Friday or Saturday night, when you won't have to face anyone on the train to work (or, worse still, at your place of work). Garlic gets milder the longer you cook it, but the fearsome amount in this concoction will never leave your breath smelling sweet and fresh – however long you cook it.

This is loosely based on some versions of *sopa de ajo*, Spanish garlic soup, but I think of it as Jeremy Round's soup, in honour of the distinguished food writer who died in 1989. Mr Round was on record as saying that his two favourite foods were potatoes and garlic. And those are the two principal ingredients here.

Potato and Garlic Soup

500 g (1 lb) potatoes
1 head of garlic (around 50–75 g/2–3 oz)
around 75 ml (3 fl oz) dry white wine or sherry
around 400 ml (14 fl oz) chicken or beef stock
around 400 ml (14 fl oz) milk
a good handful of parsley

Gently cook the potatoes and garlic as described in the master Leek and Potato recipe on page 255, taking care not to let the garlic get too brown. Add the sherry and around half the stock, or maybe somewhat more – adding more may help subdue the twang of the garlic. Simmer very gently for a longer time than usual, again with the aim of damping down the garlic flavour: the soup will come to no harm if it simmers for an hour or more. Purée the mixture and add the milk. Just before serving, chop the parsley very fine and mix into the soup, or put some on each serving bowl.

Finally a soup for a special occasion. It's based on asparagus, one of the glories of the spring and early summer, and let's be clear – it will cost you plenty. I suggest making it with the inferior (i.e. cheaper) asparagus that you sometimes see on vegetable stalls. But even then it's expensive. The only thing I can say by way of consolation is that it's delicious and simple. The stock can be either a light chicken stock or vegetable.

Asparagus Soup with Leeks and Lime

1.5 kg (3 lb) fresh asparagus
250 g (8 oz) leeks
2 thick pats (around 25 g/1 oz) butter
750 ml (around 1½ pints) chicken or vegetable stock
1 small potato (optional)
450 ml (around 1 pint) milk
juice of 1 lime
2 tbsp double cream

Wash the asparagus and cut off any white bits from the stem end. Don't worry if you lose quite a lot this way: there's plenty of the green stuff to make up for it. Chop into discs no more than ¼ in long – this is important for getting a good smooth texture. Clean the leeks and chop them into thin discs. Peel and slice the potato, if using. Melt the butter in a large pot and slowly cook the leeks and potato for 5 minutes, then add the asparagus, the stock, and plenty of salt and white pepper. Simmer gently for 30–45 minutes, till every bit of asparagus is well softened. Purée in the blender and return to the pot. Thin out with milk to taste (or use extra stock if you prefer a lighter result), and bring back up to heat. Stir in the lime juice and cream (if using) just before serving, and garnish if desired with spring onion or parsley.

Since this is by definition a summer soup you can also serve it cold. Let the purée cool to room temperature, stir in the lime juice, and store in the fridge for at least 3 hours. Blend with cold milk or stock, stir in the cream (if using), and dig in.

I hope these recipes will suffice to convey the idea I'm trying to get at here. Making puréed soups is just about the easiest thing in the world. And once you've mastered the technique, a whole universe of simple starters will open up to you. Make them freely, make them often. Your dinner guests will love you for it.

A FINAL WORD

I am a sucker for puréed soups. Everything about them – taste, texture, and ease of preparation – thrills me to pieces. But I recognize equally that good soups can be made without a blender. And some people prefer to have a chunky soup, at least on occasion. Funnily enough, these take more time to prepare than puréed soups because you have to pay attention to the chopping. The vegetables have to be chopped roughly the same size, and it must be the right size: not so small that they'll disintegrate, not so large that they'll have trouble fitting on the average soup spoon. If you want to do it this way, aim at dimensions of no more than

½ in square

or thereabouts. Cook them in exactly the same way as described in the master Leek and Potato recipe on page 255, but simply omit the puréeing stage. And they can be cooked as long as you like, though anything over

1 hour

will produce something more closely approximating to vegetable mush than to a clear soup with vegetables in it.

Another problem with chunky soups is that the quality of the stock will be more apparent: a soup made with fresh stock will be noticeably better than one made with cubes. You can get partway round this problem by adding further flavourings – garlic, herbs, spices – with a heavy hand. A pungent mayonnaise (Provençal *aïoli* or *rouille*) will also do much to mask the cubist flavour. But there's no denying that your best stock – if you can be bothered to make one – should be used in clear, chunky soups.

Assembled Salads

Salads have been revolutionized in recent years, if that term can be used without embarrassment for something that sits on a plate. What I mean is that salads are now recognized to be more than lettuce and tomato tossed with a vinaigrette. The concept now embraces endless variety, and nowhere is this seen better than in the French *salade composée*. The title of this chapter is an approximate translation of that term.

Assembled salads can combine meat, fish, vegetables, fruits; the ingredients can be raw or cooked, or a combination thereof, and can be dressed individually or collectively. They can be served as a starter, or as a main course if the meal is light (or the starter very filling). Some can be used in the traditional manner, as an accompaniment to the main dish, though they're much better as a separate course. In all cases they are one of the lazy cook's greatest allies.

One of the attractions of assembled salads is that they aren't temperature-specific. With most, you can do the cooking well in advance and serve the dish straight from the fridge, or warm, or at room-temperature. Or you can do the cooking at the last minute and serve the dish hot. Or you can use a combination of all three.

Where the classic French *salade composée* consists of ingredients laid side by side on the plate, assembled salads can be constructed in many ways. One technique that I like is to build the salad in layers, each possessing a flavour and texture that contrasts with its neighbours yet contributes to a harmonious total effect. This takes hardly any time, and it's ridiculously impressive. Not all ingredients, however, lend themselves to layering. And there's no shame in serving the salad as French cuisine serves its *salades composées*. Or the main ingredient can nest in or on a little pile of greens. See how your ingredients work together and then make your own decision. The final arrangement will be determined by aesthetics, engineering, and your own level of enthusiasm for fiddling around with food.

If you are presenting the salad in layers, don't neglect the virtues of bread. Though optional in most recipes for layered salads, bread is necessary in a few of them to complete the picture of contrasting tastes and textures. The bread can be just about anything as long as it's (a) good and (b) the right size for the other ingredients. If you're using large slices of floppy grilled red pepper, you'll need large slices of bread. On the other hand, if the only bread you have is small, you can simply cut the pepper into smaller pieces. The bread can be either served as is or toasted, depending on the textures of the other foods in the dish. Again, aim for a range of contrasts between crunchy and yielding. And needless to say, you can also serve bread on the side rather than as part of the salad.

A final word on the subject of presentation: don't get too fussy about it. Yes, it is nice having a plateful of food that's arranged with care and discernible purpose. But it is much more important that everything taste good. If you are, like me, one of those people who just can't seem to get things to look right, don't worry about it.

Just to give you an idea of the kind of razzle-dazzle you can pull off with assembled salads, bear with me while I describe in detail the very best dish of this type that I've ever eaten. It was served not as a salad but as a main course, and it was made at Clarke's restaurant in Kensington Church Street, London W8. The cooking at Clarke's has less to do with fancy or elaborate sauces than with taking flawless materials and putting them together in nice ways after careful, simple cooking. This approach is the essence of the assembled salad.

The dish at Clarke's was a main course of grilled halibut, courgettes, red peppers, aubergines, and a salad of mixed leaves. On one side of the plate, the leaves were piled in a neat little tumble. Partly overlapping them were the courgettes and aubergines, a few slices of each, perfectly grilled. The halibut, as perfectly cooked a piece of fish as you will ever see anywhere, came next: resting half on, half off the grilled vegetables. Finally, a few diamonds of grilled red pepper lay on top of the fish. Each element had its own distinct flavour but all the elements mingled and complemented each other beautifully. This was the assembled salad to beat all assembled salads.

I am not suggesting that you try to duplicate this dish. For all its simplicity, making the dish was a highly labour-intensive proposition – and cooking of that precision rarely falls within the abilities of the true lazy cook.

More important, I think it's a mistake to think in terms of recipes when you're making assembled salads. In this enter-prise, as in most areas of lazy cooking, improvisation is the essence. The idea is not to go out thinking, 'Tonight I will make a salad of X, Y and Z,' but to see what's available and then put together the salad in an interesting way. This approach is summarized by Paula Wolfert in *The Cooking of Southwest France*, where she describes one salad as 'an informal assembly of good things to eat together'. That encapsulates neatly the aim of this chapter.

Because assembled salads depend so much on improvisation with the materials that happen to be available on a given day, I shy away from presenting hard and fast recipes. Doing that would stifle the improvisatorial impulse, and be untrue to the real character of this kind of cooking. Recipes tend to look fixed and regulated; assembled salads are spontaneous and anarchic.

What follows instead is a different approach. The first (and longest) part of this chapter is a list of some of the best ingredients for assembled salads. The list is my personal choice, and by no means exhaustive.

Next comes a list of ten of the assembled salads that have succeeded for me. These are nothing more than suggestions, and are intended solely to spark off your own ideas. Once you've got the hang of it, you can make your own combinations. And I guarantee that they'll be just as impressive as mine.

INGREDIENTS

Aubergines

Aubergines are one of the best ingredients for assembled salads. Buy the smaller ones if you can get them, and give them a good tap to check on quality: if the vegetable sounds hollow inside, it will not be firm, dense and flavourful.

PREPARATION AND COOKING

Aubergines need no more preparation than slicing, and sometimes they don't even need that. My favourite cooking technique for salads is pan-grilling (see page 103), using slices around

¼ in thick. They can also be sautéed or grilled. Whole aubergines can be roasted, steamed, or grilled, then scooped out of the skin and mashed either roughly or to a fine purée.

GOOD PARTNERS

Just about anything, but especially other vegetables; fresh herbs; olive oil and/or vinegar; sharp cheese.

Avocado

A good avocado is a thing of beauty; a bad one is enough to make you wonder how anyone ever thought of eating the things at all. Buy only the nobbly-skinned Hass variety, and don't use them till they're good and ready.

PREPARATION AND COOKING

For a swell-looking salad you really want to remove the fruit from its skin and the stone from the fruit. And you want to do this in a way that leaves the avocado unbruised and unsquashed. And this, sadly, takes a bit of care and attention. I do it as follows. First cut the avocado in half. Then remove the stone. Then, using your fingers and a small, very sharp knife, peel off the skin as gently as possible. With luck, and a bit of practice, you will be able to do this easily. But remember, *please*, that avocados discolour very quickly once they're exposed to the air. So you should have everything else ready, and on the plates, before you start messing around with the avocado. As soon as it's peeled and prepared, serve the salad. Avocados do not need cooking.

You may serve the avocado just halved, peeled and stoned. But it's much nicer to look at if you slice it or dice it, and this is worth doing (as in the recipe on page 293). Again, do this just before serving.

GOOD PARTNERS

Anything sharp or smoked makes a good partner to avocado. Smoked fish, a good assortment of salad leaves, raw cucumber or fennel or capsicums. But don't let very strong flavours overwhelm the relative delicacy of the avocado.

Capsicums (Red, Yellow, and Green Peppers)

One of the best ingredients for assembled salads and often good enough to serve on their own. What's nice about them is, first of all, their diversity: each colour has its own flavour, ranging from the acidic zing of the green to the deeper, mellower robustness of the red. They also look impressive on the plate, with their vivid colours, and are therefore an easy way of impressing guests. But choose your guests carefully: capsicums can be ridiculously expensive. And choose the peppers carefully too. They should be firm and bright-skinned, with not a trace of softness or wrinkling anywhere. In Italy and Spain, where vegetables are grown for flavour rather than appearance, capsicums tend to be on the small side – and somewhat misshapen. Don't be put off if yours look like that. This may be a sign of higher quality than you get in the picture-perfect blandness produced in Holland.

PREPARATION AND COOKING

All capsicums can be served raw, of course, but they are better when cooked – grilled, roasted, or pan-grilled. See pages 184 and 107 for detailed instructions on the latter two cooking methods. If you're roasting or grilling them, you can either leave them whole for cooking or remove the stems and seeds. Pan-grilled peppers should be cut in pieces that will enable them to cook fairly uniformly in the pan. When they're cooked, remove the skins (if this is appropriate) and serve them hot, or leave them to cool and refrigerate, covered, till needed.

GOOD PARTNERS

Just about everything: smoked or cured fish; greens; smoked or cured meat; other vegetables; sharp cheese; vinaigrette and other acidic flavours.

Cheese

Cheese has a place in assembled salads, though the range of suitable cheeses is not a large one. I tend to use three cheeses in salads: Parmesan, mozzarella, and fairly mature goat's cheeses.

PREPARATION AND COOKING

Most cheeses for a salad are best when served cool (*not* straight from the cold fridge) and uncooked. The exception, a cliché of modern bistro cooking, is a whole small goat's cheese. These can be heated in the oven, grilled, or pan-grilled, and then served either hot or pleasantly warm. Mozzarella should be sliced or cubed, Parmesan shaved off a whole hunk into ultra-thin crumbly wafers, and goat's cheeses served whole (if small) or in slices (if large).

GOOD PARTNERS

Ripe, red tomatoes; salad greens; cured or smoked meats; pan-grilled or roasted vegetables.

Courgettes

An excellent choice, especially in summer. Their problem is that they tend to release a lot of water, which may make other ingredients soggy. To combat this, salt them following the technique for aubergines (page 193). Or cook them quickly and fiercely, especially by pan-grilling (see page 104). This cooks out more of the water than other methods – or at least takes everyone's mind off the water that remains.

PREPARATION AND COOKING

Clean, top and tail, and cut into discs, matchstick threads or thin slices. Cooking can be by steaming, parboiling, stir-frying, grilling, or pan-grilling. Particularly good when pan-grilled (see page 104) or charred (see page 172).

GOOD PARTNERS

Any other vegetable, but especially aubergines, onions, capsicums; vinaigrette; cheese, either mild or sharp.

Cucumber

Cucumbers release a lot of water which may ooze out into other ingredients. But as long as you take care with them, and treat them properly, they make a mild, fresh contrast to other flavours. If using slices straight from the whole cucumber, add them at the very last minute. For ease of eating with a knife and fork, it's best to peel them — but this is optional if you're in a rush.

PREPARATION AND COOKING

(1) Slice thin and add immediately to the salad. (2) De-seed, slice thin, and sprinkle lightly with salt. Leave for 30 minutes, then dry thoroughly. (3) Proceed as in (2), but sauté or steam the slices lightly before serving hot or warm.

GOOD PARTNERS

Any other vegetable; raw fish; fresh herbs.

Eggs

A green salad served with a poached egg on top is one of the best of all simple dishes. Unfortunately, lazy cooks do not go in for egg poaching. Though simple in result, the fine points of the technique make this a forbidding enterprise except for the experienced. If you make good poached eggs, serve them in salads. If you don't, stick to boiled eggs. Eggs make for a fairly rich salad, so figure on 1 per person unless the salad is intended for use as a main course.

PREPARATION AND COOKING

Use the freshest eggs you can find, and boil them till *just* hard-boiled. I get best results by starting a cold egg in cold water, bringing it to the boil with the lid on, then turning down the

heat and simmering the egg gently for exactly 8 minutes.
Overcooked eggs are a drag: don't just let them bubble while
you take a bath. Cool them in cold water, crack immediately,
and leave in the fridge till you're ready to prepare the salad.
Slice on an egg slicer, one of the most useful of all kitchen
gadgets.

GOOD PARTNERS

Red, ripe tomatoes; salad greens; vinaigrette or mayonnaise;
salsa; smoked fish.

Fennel

This is perhaps my all-time favourite in the assembled salad
line. You can serve fennel either raw or cooked, and the
cooking can take numerous forms. When buying fennel look
for the smaller heads (which are more tender and less stringy),
and avoid those that have a dried-out or brown exterior.
Bright, crisp-looking leaves (the feathery bits on top) are also a
good sign; and they can be finely chopped to serve as a garnish.

PREPARATION AND COOKING

(1) If using raw, trim the top and base; discard any tough outer
layers; and slice very thin across the grain. (2) If cooking them,
you can: pan-grill in thick or thin slices (see page 104, and
recipe below); stir-fry in thinner slices; parcel-roast (see page
180); or roast in an open oven (see page 183).

GOOD PARTNERS

Any other vegetable; raw fish; smoked fish; sharp cheese; fresh
herbs; any vinaigrette.

Fish, Cooked

There are a lot of saladistic possibilities using cooked fish, but
one qualification must be made. Not all types of fish are good
cold or at room temperature. And if they can't be eaten that
way, they can't be used so easily in a salad. Good eaters in their

cold state include salmon, monkfish, and most shellfish. And incidentally, please don't forget about the humble anchovies, sold packed in oil in those tiny little tins. Many people prefer the type sold in salt, but these are harder to find and require more preparation. A tin of anchovies will add exuberance to just about any dish.

There is another way into the salad plate where fish is concerned, and that is to prepare everything in advance except the fish. Then you cook the fish and put it on the plate and serve the dish immediately. This is the approach used in the salad described earlier that I ate in Clarke's restaurant. I have used the same approach, just to give an idea of how this can be done at home, in the recipe on page 297.

PREPARATION AND COOKING

Whatever fish you're using, and however you're using it, you should aim to serve neat slices or slabs rather than an unwieldy, bone-laced hunk. This will probably mean fillets rather than cutlets, and thinner pieces rather than thick ones. A good weight per portion is anything from 50–100 g (2–4 oz), depending on what else you're serving, and you should ask the fishmonger to weigh the slices if necessary. Cook them by steaming, microwaving, flash-roasting (see page 139) or pan-grilling (see page 109).

GOOD PARTNERS

Almost anything crunchy; salad leaves; pan-grilled vegetables, including potatoes; bread; a sharpish vinaigrette or *salsa* (see page 323).

Fish, Raw

Only sea fish can be eaten raw, and it's mostly the expensive ones that take best to this treatment: salmon, tuna, halibut, turbot. But mackerel can also be eaten raw. With all raw fish, the fish itself must be of the most dazzling freshness or your guests will look round for a sick-bag when the plate is set before them.

PREPARATION AND COOKING

Shred, dice very small, or slice very thin. This is fiddly work – lazy cooks might hesitate to undertake it. Try getting the fishmonger to do the preparatory work for you. And remember: assembled salads are for dinner parties. A little extra effort is worthwhile if you want to impress everybody.

GOOD PARTNERS

Almost anything crunchy; creamy dressings; fresh herbs (especially sorrel and chives).

Fish, Smoked

Smoked fish can be expensive (salmon, eel, halibut), mid-expensive (cod and haddock), or cheap (mackerel). In practice, unfortunately, the expensive items work best in assembled salads. Any of the three mentioned above, served on a plate with a green salad, makes a starter worth killing for. When you go down the price scale, the options are more difficult, and not as universally appealing. But it can be done. Smoked mackerel is too dry to be really appealing on its own, but if you tart it up sufficiently you will be eating well – and saving money.

PREPARATION AND COOKING

The expensive fish need little more than unwrapping and plating. Cod or haddock should be cut into neat portions and either poached for 5 minutes in barely simmering milk, or flaked to make a tartare. This is what I've described in the recipe on page 291. The same can be done with mackerel.

GOOD PARTNERS

With expensive fish you don't want assertive flavours. A green salad or cooked salad, dressed in a vinaigrette that tends towards the oily end of the flavour spectrum, is a good bet. Mid-priced fish and mackerel can take something a little more gutsy, including pan-grilled vegetables (see page 103).

French Beans

These are a top choice for salads because they're easy to prepare, easy to cook, and delicious. What's more, they go well with just about anything, and they can be served hot, warm or at room temperature.

PREPARATION AND COOKING

Wash, top and tail the beans. They can then be steamed, boiled in salted water, charred (see page 168), cooked *à l'étuvée* (see page 160), or microwaved.

GOOD PARTNERS

Looking over the list of ingredients in this section, I can't see a single one that wouldn't go well with French beans. But think in particular of fish, raw, cured or cooked; other vegetables; salad greens; mushrooms .

Fruit

Fruit is a useful but tricky member of the assembled salads club. If you use it right, it can be delicious. If you use it wrong, it is too sweet and too overpowering.

As a rule I use only two fruits in assembled salads: citrus and melons. Anything else starts to make the starter look like a dessert. In no circumstances should the fruit be cooked. Oranges are usually my first choice in the citrus line, especially the big sweet navels from Spain or Morocco. But pink grapefruits can also be used to good effect, as I have learned from Nico Ladenis's *My Gastronomy*.

PREPARATION AND COOKING

Citrus: Cut into slices or, if you feel energetic, into individually peeled segments. Peeling is essential with grapefruit, which has thick skins between the segments. This is a chore but essential. Do not serve whole, unpeeled segments: they will not release any flavour into the mélange and will look kind of clunky to boot.
Melon: Cut in slices or wedges or chunks.

GOOD PARTNERS

Citrus: poultry, fresh or smoked; smoked fish, especially salmon; salad leaves; vinaigrette.
Melon: *prosciutto* or other salt-cured meats.

Leeks

I love leeks, especially the small, young, tender variety, and I often serve them as the centrepiece of an assembled salad. The big ones need longer cooking, which can produce a mushy result when you're trying to make a nice picture on the plate. But they are worth using, especially for wintertime salads with which you want to produce a fairly hefty, robust, satisfying first course.

PREPARATION AND COOKING

Clean well and cook whole. The small ones can be steamed, pan-grilled, braised, microwaved, cooked *à l'étuvée* (see page 157), parcel-roasted (see page 180) or boiled. Poaching in stock is also a good option, producing a well-flavoured liquid as an added bonus. The big ones should be steamed or boiled. In all cases, drain leeks well whenever you cook them in liquid. Then, when they've cooled off, mix with a vinaigrette if you're using one. If the leeks are going to sit for a while after cooking, they may need further draining.

Meats, Smoked and Cured

Lazy cooking and pre-prepared meats go together like the proverbial horse and carriage. Someone else, in Britain or France or Italy or Spain, has done all the work for you. All you have to do is combine their products with other ingredients. Only one word of warning is needed here: buy well. Most of the pre-sliced salami, ham and sausage sold in plastic wrapping comes from the low end of the quality spectrum, and deficiencies will be apparent in a salad.

PREPARATION AND COOKING

No cooking here, obviously. On the preparation side, all that's needed is separating the slices and arranging them on the serving plates. You can make nifty little parcels if you wish, rolling up salami or fluffing *prosciutto* into floral curlicues, but I prefer just to lay them on the plate and put the other stuff on top. You do what you want.

GOOD PARTNERS

Good bread; sharp flavours, whether from vegetables in a vinaigrette or pickled vegetables; mushrooms; salady stuff; melon or orange.

Mushrooms

I love mushrooms in all their forms, cultivated or wild. The only exception is raw cultivated, which to me lack flavour. But if you use them well, they are a versatile and easy component in salads.

Fresh mushrooms can be either cultivated or wild; the latter have more flavour, on the whole, but are more expensive. Incidentally, I am not greatly impressed by cultivated oyster mushrooms: high cost for little apparent gain in flavour. I'd rather have a good cultivated mushroom (especially one of the organic brown-capped specimens which are increasingly available) any day of the week. **Wild** mushrooms can be *ceps* (Italian *porcini*), *chanterelles*, or any other exotic varieties you happen to come across in the market. **Dried** mushrooms are more difficult for salads, as they often lose the firm texture that's essential in such a simple preparation. The big exception here is the Chinese black mushroom. These expensive little numbers have a deep, concentrated, almost smoky flavour which I actually prefer to their fresh counterparts. Use them in moderation or your bank manager will hate you. There's a recipe using them on page 298.

PREPARATION AND COOKING

Mushrooms must be well cleaned. The **cultivated** type are grown in carefully controlled conditions and can usually just be wiped down with a damp cloth. Break the stems off or cut just below the level of the cap. Cooking: microwave, pan-grill, sauté. **Wild** mushrooms can usually be relied upon to have a goodly supply of sand and earth, and they can be a pain in the neck to clean properly. Cooking: microwave, pan-grill, sauté. **Dried** mushrooms need a good soak in warm or hot water for 20–30 minutes, till they feel soft throughout, and will usually need careful cleaning once reconstituted. Soaking with the gill side down facilitates the removal of grit, which is the only drag about cleaning them. Squeeze them gently while still in the water to get the last bits of grit out, then remove them and pat them dry. Cooking: microwave, pan-grill, sauté, steam or poach gently.

GOOD PARTNERS

Bacon or another smoked meat; green vegetables, including salad leaves; capsicums (peppers), grilled or roasted; smoked or cooked poultry; sharp cheese; vinaigrette or another sharp dressing; Chinese flavourings (especially soy sauce).

Onions, White

Onions are cheap, delicious, and versatile; all these qualities make them a first choice for using in salads. But you have to proceed with caution. Raw onions have a strong flavour, beloved of many but just too powerful for others. I personally am one of the doubters, and I have had to struggle to find the right way of using the raw bulb in salads of any description.

I do not like raw white onion in great quantities: the taste tends to drown other flavours, and the effect on one's breath is drastic and long-lasting. But the sweeter, milder varieties are good when raw. If they are raw, don't use too much: you'll shout down the other flavours. Otherwise cook them in any of the ways described below.

PREPARATION AND COOKING

Steam, grill, pan-grill, stir-fry; they're especially delicious char-red, releasing a deep, nutty sweetness that bears no relation to the raw onion taste. For the sake of presentation it's nice to keep the onions in neat, whole slices. But if they're well cooked, they can also be served in shreds. *If using them raw*, consider slicing them thin and then steeping them for up to 8 hours in equal quantities of extra virgin olive oil and good vinegar, perhaps with some herbes de Provence or fresh herbs (e.g. sage or thyme) thrown in. This dilutes some of the sharpness and is utterly delicious.

GOOD PARTNERS

Other strong-flavoured vegetables; sharp cheese such as mature Cheddar or Parmesan; fried bread; potatoes.

Onions, Red

Red onions have a milder flavour than the white ones, and are altogether better for using raw. Indeed, this is the best way to preserve their colour, which is easily lost (heat breaks down the colouring compounds) in cooking. And the colour alone is a good reason for using them, especially when you're trying to wow your friends with a beautiful presentation.

PREPARATION AND COOKING

As for white onions, but bear in mind the loss of colour that can result from cooking. They too take well to marinating in oil and vinegar, though again with some loss of colour. Slice as thin as possible.

GOOD PARTNERS

As for white onions, but also try with salad leaves, smoked fish, creamy cheeses.

Onions, Spring

These are one of my favourite standbys for assembled salads. They're versatile, easy, and delicious – and they look pretty, whatever you do with them.

PREPARATION AND COOKING

Serve them raw, either whole or cut into discs (easy) or shreds (impressive-looking). Or you can grill, pan-grill, stir-fry or microwave them. Like round onions, they're especially delicious when charred outside, sweet and soft inside. If the onions are good enough, use as much of the green as possible for variety in flavour and colour. If you're cooking them, leave them whole, which makes life a lot easier, or cut them in half lengthwise. Then cook by your chosen method and either leave as they are or cut them into ¼ in lengths. If using them raw, slice into thin discs and sprinkle on top of other ingredients.

GOOD PARTNERS

Just about anything, but especially other vegetables, smoked or cooked poultry, potatoes.

Potatoes

These are a little tricky in salads as they have to be of a type that's good when served cold or at room temperature. That means either the waxier varieties or small new potatoes. I prefer those that come from Cyprus or, especially, Egypt. They cry out for a vinaigrette or mayonnaise to heighten their flavour, and for strong-tasting ingredients to set off their relative blandness. And they will make your salad fairly substantial: don't serve more than a couple of ounces if the salad is a starter to a full meal.

You can serve hot potatoes for a first course, as in the renowned French bistro dish of potato salad with *saucissons chauds*. Somehow I've never quite been able to justify it, either from the meal-planning or the laziness point of view.

PREPARATION AND COOKING

If you're serving them cold or at room temperature, steam or boil only: any hard crust formed by cooking in fat will soften and defeat the purpose. If they'll be served hot, steam, boil, or pan-grill.

GOOD PARTNERS

Anything with a sharp, acidic flavour, such as vinaigrette; sharp cheese (e.g. Parmesan); tomatoes; red or spring onions; smoked meats, especially bacon or ham.

Poultry, Fresh

Birds make a versatile and delicious salad. Most can be served either hot or at room temperature, so you can do the preparation well in advance. And they're equally well suited to humble dinners and the fancier variety. Use chicken when you're feeling poorer, duck or quail when you want to spend extra money. Just remember that you don't want to serve too much bird or it will overwhelm the other ingredients (as well as your guests' appetites).

PREPARATION AND COOKING

Chicken can be either leftovers or a dish you've prepared specially for the occasion. Roast, poached, steamed and pan-grilled are all good for serving as salads; it can be in slices or chunks; and you can either serve it plain or with a dressing. Don't serve it on the bone, however, as it will be more difficult to eat with the rest of the salad.

    Duck is a doozy in assembled salads. Use the breast only, preferably those expensive breasts from France which are sold, wrapped in plastic, by many supermarkets and higher-quality butchers. Flash-roast or pan-grill them, and leave them to cool. Then slice them as thin as possible and give each eater 5–6 slices with the rest of the salad. Do try not to serve them too cold, as this will dampen down the flavour somewhat.

    Quail is the only exception to the boneless rule for poultry. It should be cooked by pot-roasting (see page 39) and served as soon as possible in a 'nest' of greens. Your guests won't mind eating this diminutive beastie off the bone: they'll be embarrassingly impressed by the fact that you've served it in the first place.

GOOD PARTNERS

Any kind of greens, whether salad leaves or cooked vegetables; potatoes; fresh herbs; vinaigrette.

Poultry, Smoked

Smoked poultry, like smoked or cured fish and meats, is easy to prepare. And when it's good, it's very good. Lazy cooks should take advantage of it.

Having said that, I should add immediately that some smoked poultry products are better than others. Smoked chicken in particular can turn out dry and chewy, and has to be lubricated with something oily or creamy for best results. Duck breasts are better, in my view, and perfect for salads. Quail sells well for novelty value alone and is worth trying at least once.

PREPARATION AND COOKING

Smoked poultry needs no further cooking. Chicken should be boned and cut up either in slices or chunks; if you're mixing it with a dressing of some kind (e.g. mayonnaise, yogurt, or something creamy), small chunks are best. Quail should be jointed. Duck breasts need nothing more than slicing, on the bias, into very thin pieces. Do not remove the skin from any of these items: much of the smoky flavour is concentrated there, and if your guests don't eat poultry skin they can remove it themselves.

GOOD PARTNERS

Salad leaves; pan-grilled vegetables; mayonnaise, vinaigrette, or something creamy; citrus fruits.

Salad Greens

Let us not forget that salads are traditionally made with uncooked leaves of lettuce or some such material – and that they too have their place in the assembled version. Leaves can create presentation problems, since they don't lie in neat rows or layers, but you'll avoid the problems if you tear them into small pieces and heap them up in the centre of the plate.

The leaves to use in assembled salads are the ones you would use in any salad, namely those that have real flavour. Avoid Iceberg and the insipid round lettuces that fill the shelves of most markets. Go instead for: radicchio, frisée, arugula (rocket), endive, watercress, young spinach, batavia, lamb's lettuce (mâche), oak leaf.

PREPARATION AND COOKING

Green salads must be spotlessly clean and completely dry. The cleaning should be done in a sink or bowl full of cold water, the drying in a salad spinner. (If you don't have a salad spinner, buy one. In the meantime, make do by shaking the cleaned leaves violently in a colander and then wrapping them well in kitchen towels.)

By definition, salad leaves need no cooking. But some of them (especially endive and radicchio) can be pan-grilled, and endive can be braised (see page 162) or cooked à l'étuvée (see page 157). I am not a great fan of grilled radicchio myself, and for saladistic purposes I would rather eat endive raw than either grilled or braised.

GOOD PARTNERS

Just about anything, but especially: other vegetables; raw, grilled, smoked or cured fish; sharp cheese in moderation.

Tomatoes

A good tomato salad is one of the best things you can eat. Indeed, a good tomato on its own has few peers: sprinkle on a little salt, a little pepper, and you're eating well. But this incomparable luxury is all too rare in this country because good tomatoes are hard to get hold of. For cooking I usually use tinned Italian plums; for salads, only fresh will do. If you can't get really good ones, use something else altogether. Or use sun-dried tomatoes in small quantities, as in my recipe below for Pan-grilled Aubergine with Sun-dried Tomatoes and Mozzarella.

PREPARATION AND COOKING

Cut out the core, then slice or dice or chop in rough chunks. Tomatoes can be charred (see page 167), but if you've got a good one it seems a shame to do anything to it apart from seasoning. Sun-dried tomatoes should be drained from their oil (see page 341) and then sliced or minced.

GOOD PARTNERS

Just about anything, especially salad greens and other vegetables. Apart from the obvious choices: sharp cheese; smoked meats

TEN ASSEMBLED SALADS

OK, now for some recipes. At the risk of repeating myself, I must say yet again that these are nothing more than suggestions: dishes that have worked well for me on at least one occasion, and which I would not hesitate to serve again. But the assembled salad I improvise tomorrow may be better than any of them. And the same goes for the salad you cook for your next dinner party.

Pan-grilled Fennel and Red Pepper

This recipe uses pan-grilling, my favourite cooking technique, for both the principal ingredients. It can be served at any temperature you like, from blazing hot to cold. If serving 'cold', however, do remove it from the fridge at least 30 minutes before serving. Any vegetable suitable for pan-grilling is suitable for a salad of this type. Fennel and peppers just happen to be a combination to which I'm particularly partial.

4 small red peppers
4 small bulbs of fennel
3–4 tbsp extra virgin olive oil
around 1 tbsp balsamic vinegar
5–6 sprigs of fresh coriander or parsley

Preheat the grill pan (see page 84). Cut the peppers in half, deseed, and trim them to form pieces that will lie roughly flat in the pan. Eat the trimmings. When the pan is hot, brush the peppers with oil and get them cooking. See page 107 for guidelines on cooking times. While they're cooking, trim the fennel well and reserve any feathery green leaves from the top. Eat the trimmings. Slice around ¼ in thick. When the peppers are done, remove to a plate. Brush the fennel with more oil and put them on the grill. Cook for 2–5 minutes per side, depending on how soft you want them. I like them nicely browned and soft right through to the centre, but still retaining quite a bit of bite.

To serve, simply arrange the vegetables on a plate and dribble on a little extra oil plus the vinegar. Mince the fresh herbs, sprinkle them on, and dig in. If you want to make this even more substantial, serving it as a main course, grill or toast some good bread and lay the vegetables on top of it.

Smoked Fish Tartare with Red Onions in Vinegar

This recipe is inspired by one in Raymond Blanc's *Cooking for Friends*. Naturally, my version is simpler than his – and that's saying a lot. The whole thing can be prepared well in advance, but the onions must be done that way or they'll taste too strong.

1 medium red onion
1 tbsp extra virgin olive oil
1 tbsp red wine vinegar
250 g (8 oz) smoked cod or haddock
a 2 in length of cucumber
a few large sprigs of parsley or coriander
2 tbsp double cream or Greek yogurt
juice of ½ a lemon (a generous tbsp or more)

At least 1 hour before serving, cut the onions in half lengthwise and each half in the thinnest slices you can manage. Put them in a non-reactive bowl (i.e. glass or ceramic) and toss well with the oil, vinegar, and salt and pepper to taste. Toss them from time to time.

In the meantime, make the tartare. Skin the fish and remove every single bone, then chop it into small pieces. (Raymond Blanc calls for tiny dice, but this is hard work.) Peel and de-seed the cucumber, and chop into similarly minuscule pieces (dicing is easier here). Mix the fish and cucumber with the chopped herbs, yogurt and lemon juice, and season well with salt and pepper. If you like, you can pack the tartare into individual ramekins for serving. Otherwise just scoop out neat balls of the stuff on to serving plates, surround it with the onions, and serve with a slice of good bread.

Tomatoes with Parmesan and Cucumber Raita

This recipe came about by accident one evening, when an unexpected dinner guest turned up. The combination may seem peculiar, but it is light, simple, and very refreshing for a summer lunch. It is only worth making with really good tomatoes.

a 4 in length of cucumber
100 ml (around 3½–4 fl oz) low-fat fromage frais or yogurt
4–5 leaves of fresh mint
½ tsp paprika
1 small clove of garlic, minced or crushed
2 large, ripe tomatoes
1–2 tbsp extra virgin olive oil
a hunk of Parmesan

If you don't like cucumber peel, remove it. Otherwise just cut the cucumber section in half lengthwise and scoop out the seeds. Chop into fine dice (around ⅛ in square) and dry them as well as possible on a kitchen towel. Mix with the *fromage frais* or yogurt, the mint and the garlic; season with salt and pepper to taste. Leave in the fridge for 30–60 minutes to allow the flavours to blend.

Just before serving, remove the core from the tomatoes and slice them around ¼ in thick. Arrange them around the edges of your serving plates and dribble a tiny bit of oil on each plateful. Season with salt and pepper. Using a vegetable peeler, shave off a few thin pieces of Parmesan and scatter or crumble them over the tomatoes. Divide the cucumber raita between the plates, placing a shapely dollop in the centre of each, and sprinkle with the paprika. Serve immediately.

Smoked Halibut and Avocado

The smoked halibut in this simple recipe can be replaced, if necessary, by smoked salmon or even by raw halibut. (Come to think of it, raw halibut would probably be even better than smoked.) Assemble the salad at the last minute to preserve the freshness of the fish and the colour of the avocado. NB: this is a very light starter, small but elegant. Follow it with something substantial like a braise or a robust pasta dish.

3–4 fresh chives
2 tbsp Greek yogurt or sour cream
250 g (8 oz) smoked halibut

2 ripe avocados, preferably Hass
juice of ½ a lemon

Snip the chives into tiny pieces and mix with the yogurt or sour cream. Divide the fish between 4 large plates, aiming to make a neat layer of single slices. Now cut the avocado in half and remove the stone. Working carefully with a small, very sharp knife, peel it and slice thin but keep each half intact. Lift carefully on to the centre of the plates and brush with lemon juice. Dribble or brush the yogurt mixture on to the fish and give each plate a generous grinding of black pepper plus a little salt. Serve immediately.

Goat's Cheese and Pan-grilled Leeks on Bruschetta

Goat's cheese in a salad must be one of the great culinary clichés of modern times. But who cares about clichés when the taste is so good? This version was inspired by a dish I ate – courtesy of someone else's credit card, I hasten to add – at the famous three-star Troisgros restaurant in Roannes. It has come a long way from its inspiration, and entirely in the direction of simplicity. The cheese can be any type you prefer – British or French, mild or soft. If it's a small, hard variety, you can grill it for a minute or so just to warm it through.

4 small leeks
2–3 tbsp extra virgin olive oil (or more as needed)
3–4 tbsp good vinaigrette
4 large slices of good bread, any type
4 small goat's cheeses or 4 slices from a large cheese

Heat the grill pan over a medium heat. Trim the leeks, discarding the green parts, and wash thoroughly without splitting them. (Young leeks tend not to have as much grit between layers as older specimens, so you should be able to get away without splitting.) Dry the leeks thoroughly and brush with oil. Grill them, turning regularly, until just done (around 5–8 minutes). Remove from the grill pan and leave to cool. (May be prepared in advance up to this point.)

When you're ready to eat, reheat the grill pan. Using a very sharp, thin knife, cut the leeks into thin discs (around ¼ in should be the maximum); try to keep the discs intact. Brush the bread with more oil and cook on the grill pan till toasted and crisp. Put the toasted bread on your plates. If you're grilling the cheese, brush each piece with oil and cook for 30 seconds on each side. Put the cheeses on the bread, top with leeks, and dribble some vinaigrette on each slice. A topping of fresh herbs (parsley, basil or mint, for example) would not go amiss here. Serve immediately.

Smoked Chicken with Grapefruit and a Lemon Vinaigrette

I wouldn't say that smoked chicken is one of my favourite preparations for that bird: usually the meat is on the dry side. But it's pretty good when served with something to counteract the dryness. And it's a godsend for lazy cooks, since all you have to do is slice it up and serve it forth. This is a great item for a summer lunch or as a starter for a dinner party. Since the breasts look best in a salad, I've suggested using them only. Reserve the legs for your dinner the next day. But if you're serving more than 4 people, use the whole bird.

juice of ½ a lemon, or more as needed
1 small sprig of fresh thyme or ¼ tsp dried
4 tbsp extra virgin olive oil
1 large grapefruit, pink (first choice) or white
2 breasts from a smoked chicken
1 bunch of watercress

An hour or so before you plan to eat, mix the lemon juice and the thyme and leave them so the flavours can blend for a while. You can add the oil at this stage if you want to. Half an hour later, get to work on the grapefruit. Peel it, then remove the skin from each section and pick out any seeds that lurk annoyingly within. (This is a pain, but essential.) When they're all peeled, cover them in a bowl and refrigerate till needed.

Now cut the chicken in slices as thin as you think will hold together. If the chicken breast seems very dry, ¼ in will probably be the thinnest you can get.

Mix the vinaigrette if you haven't done so already, and season well with salt and pepper. Wash and trim the stems from the watercress and mix with the grapefruit. Toss gently with 1 tbsp of the lemon juice and oil. Divide the chicken slices neatly around the edges of 4 plates and dribble the remaining vinaigrette over them. Put a heap of grapefruit and watercress in the middle of each plate, and serve immediately.

Pan-grilled Aubergine with Sun-dried Tomatoes and Mozzarella

This ultra-simple salad utilizes some classic ingredients from Italian cooking. There's next to no cooking involved, and the whole assembly can be layered to make an attractive package on the plate. As long as the raw materials are good, you'll make a hit every time you serve it.

2 medium aubergines
2 medium courgettes
3–4 tbsp extra virgin olive oil
1–2 Italian mozzarella cheeses
4 small or 2 large spring onions

4 anchovy fillets
4 sun-dried tomatoes
2–3 tsp balsamic vinegar
fresh herbs to garnish (optional)

Preheat the grill pan over a medium heat. While it's heating up, trim the aubergines and slice them around ¼–½ in thick. They can be cut either lengthwise or into discs, and can be a little thicker if you like. Do the same with the courgettes. Brush the aubergines well with oil and get them cooking. When they're ready to turn (see page 103 for cooking times), brush again with oil and sprinkle with a little salt. Turn and continue cooking. When they're done, remove to a plate and blot with paper towels to remove any excess oil. Cook the courgettes in the same way (see page 104 for cooking times) and repeat the blotting procedure. They can now be kept happily for a couple of hours.

While the aubergines and courgettes are cooling, slice the cheese around ¼ in thick or cut it into small chunks if you find this easier. Mince the spring onion, anchovies, and tomatoes together.

To serve, put the aubergines on the plates and sprinkle on the minced stuff in as even a layer as you can manage. Put on a single layer of courgettes, followed by a single layer of mozzarella slices, then sprinkle on the vinegar and a few energetic grindings of black pepper. Sprinkle with the herbs and serve immediately with good bread. You can add a clove of garlic to the minced ingredients for a more pungent taste.

French Beans, Raw Spinach, and Pan-grilled Salmon

This salad presents warm, cold and hot ingredients – one raw and two cooked – on the same plate. The contrast of temperatures accentuates the contrast of flavours and textures, and the dish is not a difficult one to produce for guests as most of the preparation is done well in advance.

250 g (8 oz) French beans	*1 tbsp extra virgin olive oil*
250 g (8 oz) young spinach	*1 tsp soy sauce*
4 small pieces of salmon fillet	*juice of ¼–½ a lemon*

Cook the beans till *barely* done either by boiling them in a large pot of well salted water or by charring (see page 168) or ordinary stir-frying. Keep them warm in the cooking vessel. Wash the spinach very thoroughly, dry well, and cut out any tough ribs; keep in the fridge till needed. When you're ready to eat, preheat the grill pan over a medium heat and cook the salmon on one side only (see page 109). While it's cooking, toss the spinach leaves with the olive oil and soy sauce, and put them, with the beans, on serving plates; season with salt and pepper. The cooked salmon should go either on top of the greenery or on the side, and then be sprinkled lightly with lemon juice; you may need less or more, depending on your taste for lemon acidity.

Potato, Asparagus and Bacon

The idea of pouring freshly-fried bacon strips (*lardons*) over a green salad came originally from French cuisine, and has been taken up enthusiastically all over the place. There's a reason for this: it's good. Here is a variation using potatoes and asparagus, both served hot-to-lukewarm. This would be a perfectly adequate main dish for a summer lunch in the garden. Try to use Jersey Royals, one of the great delicacies of the potato world, which have their season at the same time as English asparagus.

500 g (1 lb) new potatoes, the smaller
  the better
500 g (1 lb) asparagus
200 g (6oz) streaky bacon

1 tbsp balsamic vinegar
10–15 chives
a small handful of parsley

Boil the potatoes and keep them hot in the pot by draining and putting the cover on. Trim the asparagus and cut on the bias into 2 in lengths. Boil it till just cooked, proceeding as follows: put in the stem pieces first, then a minute later add the tips. Boil rapidly for another 4–6 minutes and drain well. While the asparagus is cooking, cut the rind off the bacon and slice it into matchstick-sized pieces. Fry it rapidly in a nonstick pan, without oil, till it's done the way you like it – for the purposes of this dish, a fairly crispy result is best. When done, turn the heat off but leave the bacon in the pan.

When the asparagus is cooked, drain it well on kitchen towels. Slice the potatoes around ¼ in thick and put them on the plates. Put the warm asparagus on top or around the sides. Put the vinegar in the pan with the bacon, heat it briefly, then divide it between the serving plates: it should be scattered over the bacon and, if possible, the asparagus. Mince or snip the herbs into tiny pieces, scatter them over the plates, and serve immediately. This is a really delicious dish.

Double Mushroom Salad with Pan-grilled Spring Onions

This mycophile's delight takes a bit of time to prepare, and calls for two cooking methods – stir-frying and pan-grilling. But it is worth the effort for a special dinner party.

4 good handfuls of mixed salad leaves
8 dried Chinese black mushrooms
4 large or 8 small spring onions
2–3 tbsp extra virgin olive oil
½ tsp balsamic vinegar
1 tsp lemon juice (around ¼ of a small lemon)
½ tsp soy sauce
250 g (8 oz) cultivated white mushrooms, at least 1 in in diameter

Wash the salad leaves and dry thoroughly; keep in the fridge till needed. Put the dried mushrooms in a small bowl and cover with hot water. Turn them so the gill side faces down, and leave to soak for 15–20 minutes, or until the caps are well softened without a hint of resistance to the touch. Clean out any remaining grit, trim off the stems with a small, sharp knife, and set aside.

Top and tail the spring onions, and cut 1in or so of the green part from each one; mince or cut the green in thin discs and set aside, covered, till needed. Heat the grill pan over a medium heat. Brush the main section of spring onion with oil and pan-grill for 4–5 minutes, till lightly blackened outside and barely softened inside. Put the pieces in a shallow bowl and toss with the balsamic vinegar.

Heat another tablespoon of oil in a small frying pan. Cut the reconstituted mushrooms into ¼ in slices and fry them gently for a few minutes, till they're very hot and thoroughly softened; adding a few tablespoons of the soaking water will speed this along and add extra flavour. Remove to a bowl and toss with the lemon juice and soy sauce, plus a few grindings of pepper.

When you're ready to serve, reheat the grill pan. Clean the fresh mushrooms and brush the gill side with oil. Pan-grill at a medium heat, with the gill side down, for 2 minutes; then brush the caps with oil, turn, and continue cooking until a small sharp knife penetrates easily to the centre of the cap. (This can take anywhere from 2–5 minutes.) While they're cooking, divide the salad leaves between your serving plates and put the dried mushrooms on top. Sprinkle on the green tops from the spring onions. Put the grilled spring onions on the plates. As soon as the fresh mushrooms are cooked, put them on the plates and serve immediately. Slices of good bread make a perfect accompaniment here.

The Obligatory Chapter on Desserts

The end of the meal is my least favourite part. A sweet tooth, luckily, is one of the few food vices that I have been spared. Most of the time, I'm just as happy going without sweets at the end of a meal. Or with doing as the Italians usually do and just having fresh fruit or fruit with a bit of cheese.

Of course, like most people I'll make an exception for the sublime fantasies served in a first-rate restaurant. These concoctions have absolutely nothing to do with real life, which is partly what makes them so wonderful. It also means, however, that they have nothing to do with lazy cooking. Lazy cooking, whatever else you might say about it, is solidly grounded in real life. The lazy cook does not bake cakes, simmer custards, or make puff pastry.

But many greedy people don't consider a meal to be complete unless it ends with something sweet. Moreover, puddings are *de rigueur* at dinner parties, even if they're positively to be shunned most days of the week. So here is a short section on sweets.

The best speedy option for sweets is also the best for your waistline: fresh fruit, whatever's good that day, served on its own or, with little extra time and trouble, in the form of a fresh fruit salad.

On occasion, however, you want to produce something a little fancier to add bounce to the end of the meal. When I'm trying to do that, I use fresh fruit again. But instead of serving it on its own, I cook it in ways that are simple and easy, yet unfailingly impressive. What follows below is a sampler of my favourite techniques along those lines. I've also included a section on shortcrust pastry, the only form of pastry-making that lazy cooks should even consider.

One of the great advantages of these techniques for lazy cooks is that the fruit needn't be perfectly ripe. Ripeness in fruit means two things: the perfect texture and the perfect balance between sweetness and acidity. And unripe fruit lacks sweetness above all else. When you cook it, you enhance what sweetness is there. If you add sugar in cooking, the fruit's tartness is effectively masked. For all the recipes in this chapter, therefore, you don't need to go out searching for a perfect apricot or nectarine. And this in turn saves you time.

CLAFOUTIS

Clafoutis is one of the world's best puddings. The idea of the dish could not be simpler: you make a pancake batter, pour it over fruit in a baking dish and bake it in the oven. Then you let it cool off and serve it either warm or at room temperature. It takes all of 10 minutes to prepare, and it never fails to win smiles and compliments from anyone who eats it.

To see why *clafoutis* is the perfect pudding for lazy cooks, you need only look up the recipes for the dish in a dozen cookbooks. If you do that, you'll find the same basic procedure but wild variations in the details. Some cooks add butter to the batter, some add cream; some use a lot of flour while others use just a little. In short, this is a dish that works well however you make it. That's why I like making it, and why you too will like it once you've mastered the basics.

Another nice point about *clafoutis* is that it can be made sweet, not very sweet, or positively *un*sweet. All you do to control the sweetness is adjust the amount of sugar you put in the batter. With the calories you lose by making a fairly tart *clafoutis*, you can afford, calorically speaking, to serve the dish with cream, whipped cream, or *crème fraîche*.

The final selling point for *clafoutis* is that it can be made with a variety of fruits. A classic *clafoutis* is made with cherries, but that is by no means the only one you can use. See below for a list of other possibilities. And needless to say, you can combine two or more of these in a single dish. This trick is especially useful if you're making *clafoutis* in large quantities (i.e. a large baking dish) and can afford to throw in the fruit with a free hand.

Here is a basic recipe for *clafoutis*. It is designed to produce a result that's low in added sugar and heavy on the fruit.

Clafoutis *with Cherries*

2 tbsp flour	*275 ml (10 fl oz) whole milk*
3 tbsp sugar	*500 g (1 lb) fresh cherries*
2 eggs	*1 thick pat of butter*

Mix the flour and sugar in a clean, dry mixing bowl. Break in the eggs and beat well, then pour in the milk and beat till thoroughly blended. This will be much easier to do if you use a wire whisk. Allow the batter to stand for 30 minutes or so while you prepare the fruit.

Preheat the oven to

180°C (350°F, Gas 4)

Wash the cherries under cold water, and stone them if you feel like puttin' on the Ritz. Stoning cherries only qualifies as lazy cooking if peeling grapes also qualifies. In other words, you can skip this stage if you want to. As far as I'm concerned, stoning is only necessary when the Pope is coming to dinner. Your guests will have to remove the stones themselves after each cherry. I have not heard any complaints about it from less exalted dinner guests.

Smear the butter generously round the bottom and sides of a baking dish around 8 x 10 in in size. Put the cherries in, making sure they're distributed evenly. Pour on the batter in a gentle stream, so the cherries don't roll all over the bottom of the dish, and bake the *clafoutis* in the middle of the oven for

35 minutes

checking halfway through to make sure it isn't browning too fast. If it is, move it to a lower shelf in the oven. If it hasn't browned enough by the end of 40 minutes, move it to a higher shelf for a further 5 minutes. Remove from the oven and leave to cool.

When it's cooled off for 20–25 minutes, you can dust it, if you like, with

1–2 tbsp caster or icing sugar

before serving. I usually skip this, and no one seems to miss the extra sugar. But the light dusting does look nice, and can be a good addition to the flavour if the *clafoutis* itself isn't very sweet.

Clafoutis can be served very warm, warm, or at room temperature; it is good whichever option you go for, and I use all three of them depending on circumstances. In general, it's best to allow a minimum of 30 minutes' resting time before serving. But one of the dish's great advantages is the way it fits into just about any cooking schedule. Because it can easily sit for a few hours, it's a good dish to make in advance and then get out of the way. On the other hand, if you're cooking other dishes in the oven you can bake the *clafoutis* first and take advantage of the oven's heat to cook everything else. Or you could, say, flash-roast some fennel and red peppers for your starter, then do the *clafoutis*, then flash-roast some chicken legs as the main course. This would give the *clafoutis* around 1 hour of resting time between baking and serving, which is just about the right time if you want to serve it warm.

Those are the bare bones of *clafoutis*. You can jazz up this basic recipe by adding one or more of the following *to the batter*:

a large pinch of cinnamon (around 2 ml/¹/₈ tsp) or a piece of cinnamon stick
1 tsp grated or minced lemon zest, around 2 x 3 in peeled size
1 tsp grated or minced orange zest, around 2 x 3 in peeled size
1 tsp clear honey
1 tbsp liqueur – Cognac, Armagnac, Calvados, Cointreau, Grand Marnier
2–3 drops of vanilla essence
1 tbsp cocoa powder
1 tsp powdered ginger

You can also make the *clafoutis* richer by substituting cream for some of the milk in the batter. Personally I prefer to serve the cream separately, allowing my guests to decide for themselve whether they want the additional calories. If you're uncon-cerned about such niceties, use

225 ml (8 fl oz) whole milk and
50–60 ml (around 2 fl oz) single cream

in the basic mix.

VARIATIONS

Here are some of the fruits from which I like making *clafoutis*:

apples	*peaches*
apricots, fresh or dried	*pears*
fresh figs	*plums*
grapes	*prunes*
nectarines	*raisins*

If you're using large fruits, you can prepare them in large or small pieces. Peeling is unnecessary, and with most fresh fruits leaving the skin on helps the pieces keep their shape. The only exception here is any kind of pear, such as Comice, that has a tough, chewy skin. The skin will become even tougher and chewier after 40 minutes of baking.

Large fruits such as apples and pears can be cut into 1in chunks or just cut in half. **Dried fruits** such as prunes or apricots can be soaked for 30 minutes in hot water or just stoned and put straight into the pan. (I think it's worth the minimal extra trouble to stone them.) **Small items** like raisins and grapes should, naturally, be left whole.

When using large fruit, the batter should come around a third to three-quarters of the way up the sides of the fruit, so some of it will be exposed to the full oven heat and brown slightly on top. This is not very different from cherry *clafoutis*, as the cherries float in the batter. Indeed, one of the visual attractions of the dish is that the pieces of fruit sort of peek up through the browned batter and create a nice contrast of colours. If you've left the fruit unpeeled, which I recommend for everything except tough-skinned pears, try to make sure the peel side is facing upwards. It takes better to the oven's heat.

Clafoutis made with two or more fruits is a very good thing. I don't usually use more than two at a time: the flavour is more harmonious that way. Here are three of the combinations I like best:

peaches and pears	*pears and apples*
cherries and apricots	

You can, of course, mix three fruits if you want to. I just don't think it's necessary.

PASTRY

Shortcrust pastry is the only truly simple pastry to make, but there is one important proviso here: you must have a food processor or it is tedious and time-consuming. I never used to make it at all until I got a food processor, and even then my pastry-making had to wait for the simplest and most foolproof procedure I have ever seen. This is the recipe in Joyce Molyneux's *Carved Angel Cookery Book*, one of the best food books of recent years. Ms Molyneux's basic recipe is reproduced here with thanks, and is followed by a number of suggestions for using the delicious stuff. The suggestions are my own.

Shortcrust Pastry

275 g (10 oz) flour
½ tsp salt
1 large pinch of sugar

225 g (8 oz) butter, chilled and cut into
small pieces
8–9 tbsp cold water

Combine all the ingredients except the water in the bowl of your food processor. Process until it resembles small breadcrumbs.

Gradually add the water to form a firm dough, one that gathers itself into a ball around the shaft of the processor blade. Gather up into a ball, wrap in clingfilm, and leave to rest for at least 30 minutes in the fridge before using.

I got this right the first time I made it, and so will you. The only slightly tricky point is knowing when to stop adding water. You shouldn't process the mix any longer than is absolutely necessary, but it must form a cohesive mass or it will be too crumbly. Generally speaking, when it starts looking more like a ball and less like separate bits of dough, it is ready to come out.

Now that you have your dough, chilled for 30 minutes, you can do all sorts of lazy things with it which impress the hell out of your friends. And there's nothing lazier than simple discs of dough, rolled thin and baked in the oven. Here's how.

Pastry Discs

Preheat the oven to 180°C (350°F, Gas 4). Take a lump of dough weighing around

25 g (1 oz) or a little over

This will be a lump around the size of a golf ball. On a spotlessly clean, smooth-surfaced table – or a marble pastry board, if someone's given you one for Christmas – roll out the dough to a thickness of around

⅛ in or even less

You can, if you don't mind the amorphous shape, just transfer the whole sheet to the baking sheet. In my experience, no one ever objects to this. It doesn't look a restaurant-style dessert, but then your guests won't be paying for their meal.

If you're more fastidious than I, get out a cookie cutter or some other round, hollow utensil. The size is up to you, but it should not be bigger than 6 in in diameter. I often use an old yogurt or cottage cheese tub (around 4 in in diameter) and cut around the edges with a small, sharp knife; this works as well as a purpose-built cookie cutter.

Transfer each disc to a nonstick baking dish and prick it all over with a fork. Pricking allows the air underneath to escape as it expands. If you didn't prick, the expanding air would deform the pastry. (There will probably be some deforming anyway, but it doesn't greatly matter.)

For a deeper colour you can paint the pastry with a wash, usually made from

a beaten egg
milk
cream

or a combination of egg and milk. Sometimes I do this, sometimes I don't. It's not really necessary if you're just going to be hiding the pastry anyway, under a heap of strawberries or apple slices, but it is definitely a good method for guaranteeing a deep brown glaze.

When the pastry is rolled out and on the baking sheet, whack it into the oven, using a shelf around two-thirds of the way up, and bake until lightly golden-brown in colour – around

12–15 minutes

Transfer the discs to a flat rack – I use the rack from a roasting pan or grill, which should be cleaned and dried if necessary – and leave them to cool while you continue rolling, cutting, and baking as many discs as you need.

The discs are now ready to top with something delicious. They can be topped with just about anything, including savoury things (they make a nice base for smoked fish or vegetables in an assembled salad – see Chapter 8 for more on this angle), but since we're talking about desserts in this chapter, here is a list of toppings I like, to spark off your imagination.

berries of any description, including strawberries, blueberries, raspberries, and
  preferably topped with cream
baked fruits (see below)
grilled fruits (see below)
plain slices of banana, preferably topped with cream
fruit salad of any description, preferably topped with cream
fruit purées, made with either fresh or frozen fruit

Whipped Cream

Whipped cream is one of the all-time great foods – grossly unhealthy if you eat too much of it, but a rare balm for tormented souls if you regard it as an occasional luxury. It makes a perfect partner for crispy pastry and any of the fruit preparations described above. And it is simple to make as long as you follow three rules.

1. Use the right kind of cream.
2. Everything to be used in whipping – cream, bowl, beaters – must be very, very cold. I put bowl, beater, and cream in the freezer for 30 minutes or so before whipping.
3. Don't beat the cream too long or it will turn to butter.

Buying the right cream can be trickier than it sounds. If your shop sells whipping cream (and most do), it is always a safe bet. Whipping cream has a fat content of 35 per cent, which is just about right for whipping. If you can't find it, buy both double and single cream and mix them in the following proportions:

anything from 1:1 to 4:1 (double to single)

Obviously, the result will be lighter if you use a higher proportion of single cream. That's not to say that whipped cream will ever be a slimmer's friend, but it's something. In any event, the important point is that you shouldn't whip double cream on its own. It's too vulnerable to butter-ification.

You can make your dessert with 2 discs, one serving as a base and the other on top. If you do this, sprinkle the top disc with caster sugar or cinnamon sugar, and plop on a sprig of fresh mint to serve as decoration. The contribution to the flavour won't be earth-shaking, but it will look nice.

Or you can do something slightly more complicated with the pastry: roll it around pieces of raw fruit and then bake it for a while. This is a trick I picked up from a book called *Loire Gastronomique* by Hilaire Walden. In the Loire they use their splendid apples for a traditional dish called *bourdains*. You can do the same thing with any good eating apple, and here's the recipe.

Bourdains

4 good apples
½ the recipe for shortcrust pastry (see page 308)
4 tsp jam or fruit conserve: strawberry, apricot, plum (optional)
milk, cream or egg for wash

Core and peel the apples, and cut a slice off the bottom of each so they sit easily on the baking sheet. Divide the dough into 4 pieces and, working quickly, roll out one of them to form a roughly square shape ⅛ in thick, as in the pastry recipe (page 308). The square should be around 7 x 7 in, but don't worry if it's a bit bigger or smaller – or if it's not exactly square. If you're using jam or conserve, spoon it neatly into the hollow where the core used to be.

Now put the apple on the centre of the square and fold up the 4 corners, pinching the edges to seal them and neatening it as far as possible. (Don't worry if the package looks a mess: it will look fine when it's cooked.) Refrigerate that apple while you repeat the procedure with the others. They can all stay in the fridge for up to 30 minutes or so.

When you're ready to bake, brush the pastry with wash. You'll need a teaspoon or so, and for this recipe it is worth using a wash because the colour deepens so impressively. Immediately pop them into a medium oven, i.e.

180°C (350°F, Gas 4)

and bake them for exactly 45 minutes. Remove from the oven and serve warm or at room temperature, with a creamy topping if desired.

NB: the apple inside the pastry will collapse to around a third or half of its normal size. This is entirely normal, and nothing to worry about.

If you want to use whole fruit, you can do the same thing with a pear or a peach. Or you can cut the fruit into smaller pieces, and use

apples
pears
bananas
fresh figs
peaches
nectarines

Cut the fruit into pieces around

1 x 2 in

and wrap them in proportionally smaller squares of dough. Naturally, the cooking time will be shorter – probably around

30 minutes

I am particularly fond of banana rolls cooked this way.

Once you've got the hang of making shortcrust pastry you will find your own favourite ways of using it. These are just a few ideas to get you started.

BAKED FRUIT

Baked fruit dishes follow the same procedure as *clafoutis* but omit the batter, using the fruit on its own or with a rich mixture of milk, cream, and extra flavourings. They are therefore even easier and lower in calories, and they can be jazzed up in a number of ways to add extra excitement.

If you're feeling rushed or lazy, you can just toss the fruit with sugar and juice or cream to produce a jumbled look in the pan. If you layer it carefully, the result will look more like a gratin. And indeed, this is much the same dish in principle as a vegetable gratin (see page 185), but with a sweet rather than savoury effect. In all their guises, I am crazy about them. Here is the basic procedure for baked apples, followed by suggestions. Incidentally, this has little to do with traditional baked apples, which are made with the cooking variety. Using dessert apples eliminates the need for large quantities of added sugar, and I – following the example of French cooks – prefer it that way.

Baked Apples

6 small apples (around 450–500 g/1–1¼ lb)
juice of ½ a lemon
juice of 1 small orange (around 2 tbsp) or the same amount of apple juice
1–2 tbsp sugar
1 thick pat of butter

Preheat the oven to 200°C (400°F, Gas 6). Core the apples and peel them if you wish. I never bother. Cut them in half lengthwise and then into slices around ¼–½ in thick. Toss well with the fruit juice and half the sugar; as long as the slices are thoroughly coated with juice (to prevent discolouring), you can leave them to macerate for a couple of hours.

When you're ready to cook, butter a baking or gratin dish and put in the apples. Again, you can just throw them in or lay them in to form neat layers. Sprinkle on the remaining sugar and bake in the upper third of the oven for anywhere from

25–40 minutes

till the apples are soft inside and a light brown on top. If they haven't browned on top, slide them under a really hot grill for a couple of minutes to finish them off. You can serve them hot or at room temperature, with cream or whipped cream for a really luxurious effect.

Baked apples can be jazzed up by adding one or more of the following *to the fruit*:

a large pinch of cinnamon (around 2 ml/⅛ tsp)
1 tsp grated or minced lemon zest, around 2 x 3 in peeled size
1 tsp grated or minced orange zest, around 2 x 3 in peeled size
1 tbsp liqueur – Cognac, Armagnac, Calvados, Cointreau, Grand Marnier
2–3 drops of vanilla essence

And instead of using apples you can substitute any of the following:

apricots, fresh or dried	*peaches*
bananas	*pears*
fresh figs	*plums*
nectarines	*prunes*

The cooking time will be roughly identical whatever fruit you use, but some will not brown as well as others. Don't worry: you can hide any deficiencies in the colour with illiberal quantities of cream.

Or you can cook the fruit *with* cream, either double or *crème fraîche*. This changes it completely, and is deeply satisfying on a cold winter night. If you do it this way, don't serve extra cream with the dish unless you're ready for a seriously rich dish. Here's the basic procedure, suitable for any of the fruits above.

Creamy Baked Fruit

6 small apples (around 450–500 g/1–1¼ lb)
juice of ½ a lemon
juice of 1 small orange (around 2 tbsp) or the same amount of apple juice
2 tbsp sugar
1 thick pat of butter
75 ml (5 tbsp) double cream

Prepare the fruit and the baking dish as described for Baked Apples. Measure out the cream, and whisk it if it is very thick; this will make pouring easier. Pour the cream over the fruit, trying to ensure that it covers as much of the surface as possible. (You can spoon it over the uncovered bits if coverage is incomplete.) Sprinkle on the remaining sugar and bake for

35–40 minutes

till the fruit is soft and lightly browned. Again, stick it under a hot grill if you want to brown it more deeply. The combination of caramelized brownness and sweet cream is delicious. Serve hot or at room temperature.

Using this method sometimes causes the cream to separate. This happens to me around one time in ten. I don't know why it happens on some occasions and not on others, but if you want to avoid the danger altogether, add the cream after

20 minutes

and continue cooking till done.

GRILLED FRUIT

The techniques described above for baking fruits can be applied almost without alteration to grilling fruits. The methods are similar. And hardly anything could be simpler.

Whichever fruit you're using, the technique is the same. Preheat the grill while cutting the fruit in half or into slices. Spread the fruit out on a baking dish or roasting pan, and sprinkle the cut surfaces with

around 1 tsp sugar per piece of fruit

Then stick the tray under the grill and cook the fruit till it's bubbling on the top and hot all the way through. Cooking times can range from

5–15 minutes

depending on the heat of the grill and the ripeness of the fruit. You can also add any of the flavourings listed above for baked fruit, if you want to get fancy, and can spread on around

1 tbsp of cream per piece of fruit

That's all there is to it. Here is a list of my favourite fruits for grilling.

apricots, fresh or dried	*peaches*
bananas	*pears*
fresh figs	*plums*
nectarines	

All of these should simply be cut in half except for bananas, which can be either left whole (my favourite routine) or cut into thick slices.

COMPÔTES

The other fruit dessert that I serve regularly is the compôte, in which pieces of fruit are simmered gently in a stock (sugar) syrup. This is one of the simplest desserts you can make, and it never fails to please.

The first step is to make the syrup, and this is the same whatever fruit you're using. For 500 g (1 lb) of fruit take

125 g (4 oz) sugar, enough to fill a measuring cup to the 4 fl oz mark
225 ml (8 fl oz) water

and put them in a saucepan. Bring to the boil, then turn down the heat and simmer the mixture till the sugar has completely dissolved. The syrup is now ready to use. NB: this is actually a large quantity of syrup for a pound of fruit, but it's much easier to make too much and then just use what you need than to try to get the quantities exactly right. And sugar is cheap.

You can also flavour the syrup in various ways. Here are some suggestions:

a large pinch of cinnamon (around 2 ml/⅛ tsp) or a piece of cinnamon stick
1 tsp grated or minced lemon zest, around 2 x 3 in peeled size
1 tsp grated or minced orange zest, around 2 x 3 in peeled size
1 tbsp liqueur – Cognac, Armagnac, Calvados, Cointreau, Grand Marnier
2–3 drops of vanilla essence
2–3 cloves
1 tsp powdered ginger

Once you've got your syrup, you are ready to put any fruit in it. Here is a list of my favourites for compôtes.

apples
apricots, fresh or dried
bananas
berries of any description, especially
    strawberries and raspberries
fresh figs
grapes

mango
nectarines
peaches
papaya
pears
plums
prunes

Dried fruits should be soaked first in hot water, plus a little liqueur (Cognac, Armagnac, Calvados, Cointreau, Grand Marnier) if you have some, for 20–30 minutes. Apart from that, the procedure is the same for all of them:

Wash and dry the fruit, and prepare it as necessary. Peeling is obviously essential for bananas but is strictly optional with fruits that have edible peels or skins. If you're cooking for a dinner party, however, and want to make an impression, then peeling may be worth the few extra minutes it takes.

Notes on peeling: (1) **Apples, pears** and other fruits go brown fairly quickly when the skin comes off. To counteract this tendency, rub the cut surfaces well with ½ a lemon. Or toss them in lemon juice as each piece is peeled. (2) **Peaches** and **nectarines** are easier to peel if you slip them into boiling water for a few seconds.

When the fruits and syrup are all ready, get the syrup simmering gently. I like doing the cooking in a large frying pan, which tends to cook the fruit more evenly (and with less need for stirring) than a saucepan. NB: the syrup should not be allowed to boil at a high heat or it will start to caramelize, and this is not what you're looking for in a compôte. Put the fruits in and cook, uncovered, for around

3–15 minutes

stirring gently every few minutes if the fruit is not in a single layer in the pan.

Unfortunately, it's not possible to be more precise about cooking times: these will be determined by the size of the pieces and the type and ripeness of the fruit. As a rule it's always best to start testing very early in the proceedings; the aim is always to get the fruit softened but not disintegrating, and a goodly hint of 'bite' is infinitely better than a potful of sugary mush.

The only exceptions to these timing guidelines are berries, which are small and soft and therefore need just a few seconds in the syrup. They won't get completely cooked, but they don't need to.

It's easy to test for doneness by sticking a small, sharp knife into a piece of the fruit. The knife blade should slide in easily; if it does, the fruit is done. Remove it with a slotted spoon, draining the pieces well, and put them in a nice serving bowl. You can then spoon on as much of the syrup as you like.

Better still, you can use the syrup to cook another batch of a different fruit. This will produce a multi-coloured, multifarious compôte of real elegance. I think it's best to cook one fruit at a time. You don't have to worry about different cooking times this way, which simplifies matters considerably for lazy cooks. And you can then either mix the fruits together in the bowl or produce a layered effect, which looks especially impressive if there are three or more layers. Here are some combinations that go well together:

peaches, bananas and strawberries
apples, apricots and papaya
figs, grapes, and pears

Compôtes are at their best, in my opinion, when served warm or just above room temperature. And they can be decked out with all manner of adornments. The first choice is something creamy, which can be

single or double cream
crème fraîche
Greek or Bio yogurt

Each diner can spoon these on to his or her own plate, or you can add the cream in the serving bowl. I think it's better to let each diner do the spooning. They can also be garnished with fresh herbs, especially

mint
basil

for an extra accent of flavour. Following a hint from *Ken Hom's Cuisine: East Meets West,* you could try stirring the herbs into the compôte a few moments before taking it off the heat. Cinnamon can be sprinkled on top if it hasn't been added to the syrup, and so can the merest hint of fresh-grated nutmeg.
For further complexity of flavour you can add a tiny bit of 'sauce' to the finished dish. Here is one such 'sauce', an

all-purpose sharpening of the compôte sweetness. It should go on when the fruits are fully cooked, and should do nothing more in the pan than heat through. And incidentally, if you add a tablespoon of sugar it is also good for fruit salads. It is enough for a pound or two of fruit and goes well with just about anything, but particularly with apples and bananas.

Fruit Sauce

juice of 1 lime (a generous tbsp or so)
1 generous tbsp sugar (optional)
1 generous tbsp balsamic vinegar
1 tsp crème de cassis *or ruby port*

Mix all the ingredients well.

Five All-Purpose Flavours

In the Introduction I said that there are certain things I use almost constantly in my cooking. Here is more information on the 5 most important.

SALSAS

Few preparations have risen to greater prominence in trendy-menu-speak than *salsa*. In Spanish and Italian the word means sauce; in menu-speak it means a cold sauce, usually oil-based, which contains one or more chopped ingredients. The chopped stuff may be either raw or cooked.

Salsas are popular because they're easy, versatile, and – when well made – pungent and delicious. The best known are *salsa verde* and *salsa cruda*. These form the basic idea in the recipes that follow.

But it is among *salsa's* many virtues that the basic idea provides nothing more than a starting point for experiment and innovation. You can make 100 different *salsas* by varying proportions and by adding or subtracting an ingredient here or there. As Diana Kennedy says in *The Cuisines of Mexico*, 'There is no end to the variety of sauces; they just depend, very often, on what is available.' In California, whose innovative cooks and chefs have done so much to promote the virtues of *salsas*, the list of possible ingredients is almost endless. You should experiment to your heart's content, secure in the knowledge that what you make will at worst be palatable, and at best be unforgettable.

The best known *salsa verde* is based on oil, usually olive oil. If you're making this type, the oil should have real flavour. The best extra virgin olive oil is always your best bet, but you should experiment with combinations of olive oil, plain oil, and Chinese-style sesame oil (the latter in small quantities). Water-based *salsas* have no oil and are therefore not as thick and rich. This type is more like a fresh relish than a sauce, and it certainly has its place. See below for a basic recipe.

You can eat *salsas* with just about anything, animal or vegetable, and it's always a welcome addition to the meal. Its secret,

I think, lies in the fine contrast of flavours and textures. However you make a *salsa*, it almost always has at least one ingredient that gives a good dose of acidic zing. Usually this is counterbalanced by other ingredients that are blander but fruity.

SERVING

I've noticed a peculiar problem when I serve *salsa* to dinner guests. *Salsas* are concentrated preparations, packing a lot of gustatory punch into a small package. A serving can be measured in tablespoons, or teaspoons. So you make them in small quantities even for a dinner party of 6 or 8 guests.

Yet for some reason, few of my friends seem to notice how little of the stuff there is. As a result, they almost inevitably take too much of it. And I, the kind of old-fashioned host who never helps himself to anything till the last guest has filled his or her plate, usually end up scraping the bottom of the *salsa* bowl. My friends are not rude, or greedy; they simply don't understand that where *salsa* is concerned, small portions are beautiful.

There are three solutions to this problem. One is to make much more *salsa* than you need. This is no bad thing, but with those *salsas* that aren't as fresh the day after making, you're wasting some good chow. The second is to inform your guests as politely as possible that they don't need much of it. (I usually say, when using this ruse, 'The *salsa* is very pungent, so go easy on it.' Sometimes it works, and more often it does not.) The third is to exercise what people in the catering trade call 'portion control'. Serve the *salsa* yourself, putting it on each guest's plate rather than letting them help themselves. This means you'll also have to put the other dishes on the plates, at least in the first-helping stage. But it will guarantee that you get some *salsa* for yourself.

TIMING

Since the *salsas* I'm talking about here are uncooked and served cold (really at room temperature), they're easy to co-ordinate with the rest of your meal. But you do have to decide whether to make them in advance or at the last minute, and there's something to be said for both approaches. If you make the *salsa* just before serving, each of the strong flavours will hum its own individual tune. If you make it in advance, the flavours will form a harmonious ensemble. Also: the acidic ingredients (vinegar, capers, citrus or olives) will have a chance to subdue somewhat the pungency of any oniony ingredients (including garlic) that you may have added.

Which you prefer is a matter of taste. Try it both ways to see the difference, then decide for yourself which you like best.

TEXTURE

The same open-endedness applies to texture. Michael Field, one of the great American cookery writers, believes that all solid ingredients in a *salsa verde* must be chopped very, very fine. I agree that *salsas* do work perfectly when they're done that way, but there's also something to be said for leaving more texture in the *salsa* by chopping rather coarse. Again, try it both ways. To begin with, however, use the classic approach and chop everything into tiny little bits.

Basic *salsa verde* is one of those preparations that don't really need a recipe: you add enough of each ingredient till the whole mess looks right, then you taste and see if anything's missing. But here's the lowdown, just to get you started. These quantities are enough to serve with a whole chicken, or a couple of pounds of cold beef. In other words, they're quantities for company. Make less if you're eating alone or *à deux*.

Basic Salsa Verde

3 tbsp capers
a large handful of parsley
1 medium clove of garlic
1 large spring onion or a thick slice from a small onion
90 ml (6 tbsp) extra virgin olive oil
juice of ½ a lemon

Chop the capers, parsley, garlic and onion. Mix with the remaining ingredients and season with salt (go cautiously, as the capers are quite salty) and plenty of black pepper. Either serve immediately or let the mixture stand for a maximum of 3 hours.

If you had no other *salsa* than this one, you would probably never get tired of it. But some people would say that no *salsa* can be made without anchovies. For the quantity above, use

6–8 anchovy fillets

well drained. Chop them with the other solid ingredients and mix in well.

Here is a list of some of the plain dishes that I serve with *salsa*:

fish: steamed, flash-roasted, pan-grilled
lamb chops
cold roast beef
roast chicken
boiled beef, hot or cold
grilled vegetables (see page 103)
baked onions
cold leftover potatoes
starchy foods: pasta, rice, pulses – even good brown bread
crudités

After you've made the basic *salsa* once, start out trying your own variations. The scope for invention really is limitless, but here, to get you started, is a list of 10 main ingredients that always work well:

TEN BASIC *SALSA* INGREDIENTS

1. Capers (or green olives)
2. Fresh herbs: parsley, coriander, basil and mint are my favourites
3. Vinegar – wine, sherry, or balsamic
4. Garlic

5. The onion family – white, red, spring; chives, shallots; raw, blanched, grilled
6. Chili – fresh, pickled, dried, in sauce; raw or grilled
7. Citrus fruits – lemon, lime, orange; juice or zest
8. Tomato – fresh, sun-dried, tinned
9. Capsicums (peppers), any colour; raw, roasted or grilled
10. Unorthodox additions: ginger, avocado, fresh horseradish, cucumber, beetroot

As you see, some ingredients can be used in several different forms. Tomato, for instance, can be fresh, dried, or tinned. You could even add a tiny dash of tomato purée to perk up an otherwise drab sauce. Capsicums are particularly versatile.

If it's silly to give a recipe for basic *salsa*, it's even sillier to give a long list of the variations. This is a sauce you should re-invent each time you make it. For recipe-lovers, however, here are a few permutations that happen to have worked particularly well for me.

Using raw peppers – both sweet and hot – lends a pleasant zing that goes particularly well with fish. Please note, when using raw sweet peppers, that the *salsa* shouldn't be made until the last minute. If it's made in advance the peppers will release a lot of water, which in turn will make the *salsa* too thin.

Red Pepper Salsa Cruda

1 medium red pepper, or 1 small red and 1 small green pepper
1 small handful of parsley (or fresh coriander)
110 ml (4 fl oz) extra virgin olive oil
1 tbsp balsamic vinegar
2 good dashes of chili sauce (optional)
1 tbsp lemon juice

Chop all the solid ingredients and mix with the liquid ones. If the mixture is too thick for your taste, add more olive oil.

If you use cooked peppers instead of raw, the flavour of the *salsa* becomes much mellower and smoother. Here is a good way of using up leftover roasted peppers (see page 184) and goes well with fish, chicken, or lamb – or with just about anything, for that matter.

Roasted Pepper Salsa *with Basil*

1 large or 2 medium roasted red peppers (see page 184)
a small handful of basil
1 spring onion or 2 large shallots
75 ml (5 tbsp) extra virgin olive oil
30 ml (2 tbsp) balsamic vinegar
juice of ¼ of a lemon

Remove the skin and seeds from the peppers, and chop them into tiny pieces. Chop the basil and onion or shallot into pieces around the same size, and mix with the remaining ingredients. Season with salt and pepper, and serve within 20 minutes of preparation.

'Puttanesca' sauce for pasta is one of the all-time greats. Using the same ingredients for *salsa* is a nice variation that is not far removed from the classic approach. This is powerful stuff, suitable for hearty dishes like a pasta salad, lamb, or plain lentils.

Salsa *'Puttanesca'*

2 anchovy fillets   *1 clove of garlic*
2 tbsp capers   *½ a dried red chili*
2 large red, ripe tomatoes   *3 tbsp extra virgin olive oil*
8–10 green olives

Chop all the solid ingredients and mix with the olive oil.

Here is a variant using similar ingredients, but with the emphasis on anchovies. This is only for people who really love those diminutive fishes.

Anchovy Salsa

10–12 anchovy fillets
1 tbsp capers
½ a dried red chili

3 tbsp extra virgin olive oil
1 tsp Worcester sauce
1 tsp red wine vinegar

Chop all the solid ingredients and mix with the liquid ones.

Make this next *salsa*, which is really a Chinese dipping sauce, an hour in advance so the flavours have a chance to blend. It is particularly good with pan-grilled chicken or beef.

Chinese-flavoured Salsa

4 thin slices of ginger
2 small cloves of garlic
1 spring onion, white part only (around 6in in length)
¼ of a small dried red chili or 2–3 drops chili sauce (optional)
1½ tbsp soy sauce
1 tbsp dry sherry
1 tsp oyster sauce
1 tsp sesame oil
1 tbsp peanut oil
1 generous tsp red wine vinegar
a small handful of fresh coriander

Chop the first 4 solid ingredients and mix with the liquid ones. Allow to sit for an hour or more. Just before serving, mince the coriander and mix it in.

Olives are another surefire *salsa* winner. If you're worried about calories, you could substitute good stock or the braising liquid from beef or celery for some or all of the oil in this recipe.

Olive and Coriander Salsa

12 green olives, preferably with herbs and garlic
1 shallot or ½ a small onion
4 tbsp extra virgin olive oil
1 tbsp balsamic vinegar
plenty of black pepper
a small handful of fresh coriander

Combine all the ingredients except the coriander and let them sit till needed. Just before serving, chop the coriander and mix it in. Good with grilled pork or other meats, and with chicken.

The next recipe is inspired by a *salsa* I tasted at the Sydney Street Restaurant, London SW3 (now defunct). They used jalapeño peppers. I have adapted it for use with dried red chilis, which are more widely available. NB: the beetroot must be cooked but *not* pickled.

Beetroot and Chili Salsa

100 g (4 oz) cooked beetroot
2 spring onions, all of the white part and half the green
1 dried red chili (around 1 in in length)
60 ml (4 tbsp) extra virgin olive oil
1 tsp wine vinegar
1 tbsp lemon juice (around ½ a lemon)
1 pinch of dried thyme

Peel the beetroot and chop it very fine, or even into a purée if you wish; this will be easiest in a food processor. Put it in a small mixing bowl. Chop the spring onion into smallish pieces, then add to the beetroot. Roll out the seeds from the chili and crumble it up, then chop or pound it as fine as you can get it. Add to the beetroot. Stir in the other ingredients and leave to blend for an hour or more before serving.

This *salsa* also benefits from the addition of a small handful of fresh chives or coriander, stirred in at the last minute.

OIL-LESS *SALSAS*

You don't need olive oil in your *salsas*, especially if you're trying to watch calories: the same flavours can be used on their own for a much lighter result. This is a Mexican-style *salsa*. Eat it with meat, fish, pulses or rice.

Salsa Mexicana

2 ripe, red tomatoes
2 small green chilis
1 small onion or 2 shallots

juice of 2 limes or 1 lemon
a few leaves of fresh coriander

Chop the tomatoes coarsely, discarding the seeds if you wish. De-seed the chilis (optional) and chop finely with the onion or shallots. Mix with the citrus juice and coriander and serve immediately. The citrus can be replaced by water if you like, or (less traditionally) by light chicken stock.

Here's a *salsa* that gets perked up by the addition of whole roasted cumin. It's also good with 3–4 tbsp of olive oil if you're not worried about calories. Roasting spices is easy, and it deepens the flavour of the *salsa*.

Salsa *with Cumin*

a large handful of parsley
3–4 spring onions
juice of 1 large or 2 small lemons

2–3 drops of chili sauce
salt and pepper
1 tsp whole cumin

Finely chop the parsley and spring onions, and mix with the lemon juice, chili sauce, and salt and pepper to taste. Just before serving, heat the cumin for 20–30 seconds in a small pan over a medium heat. When the seeds just start to take on a deep colour, and to smell really delicious, pour them into the *salsa* and serve immediately. This goes particularly well with an oily fish like mackerel or herring.

GARLIC, GINGER AND SPRING ONION

This trio, one of the basic flavourings in every region of Chinese cooking, is perfect for lazy cooks. It can be used to perk up almost any dish, and it is so surprising that your dinner guests will exclaim with delight at your cleverness for using it. For the sake of brevity, I will refer to the combination as GGS.

When spring onions are unavailable, or expensive, or of poor quality, ordinary onions can be substituted. Their flavour is slightly different from that of spring onions, but they'll do very well in a pinch.

The proportions can be varied as you like, but it's important not to get too high a ginger content. A little ginger goes a long way, and an excess can overpower the flavours not only of the other two ingredients but of anything else you put in the dish. As a rule of thumb, here is a basic 'recipe' for using the trio:

Spring onions: 1 large or 2 small
Garlic: 1 large or 2 small cloves
Ginger: 2 peeled slices, each around the thickness of
   cardboard

Depending on how you're using the mixture, the ingredients may be minced, shredded, coarsely chopped, or mashed with a mortar and pestle. The ginger should be peeled first. All the ingredients may also be cut into thick pieces if you're using GGS in a stir-fry or a braised meat dish such as Braised Beef with Chinese Flavours (see page 60). Some recipes in other books call for using the white part (bulb) only. I like the colour and flavour of the green part, so I tend to use the whole thing.

TIPS ON BUYING

The key is finding fresh ingredients which have not been sitting around too long. **Garlic** should be hard as a rock, without a hint of give. Larger cloves are easier to deal with. **Spring onions** should also be hard, and the green shoot should be a deep green with no hint of yellowing or dryness. Brown, wet shoots are a sign of improper storage. The thicker onions are easier to deal with but have a stronger flavour – sometimes closer to leeks than spring onions.

Ginger is somewhat trickier to buy well than the two other members of the trio. (Ironically, this is in some measure the by-product of ginger's popularity: as more and more people demand it, it is increasingly likely to be found in shops that don't sell enough for the rapid turnover that ensures fresh supplies.) Ginger must have a maximum of freshness and a minimum of fibres. Freshness is indicated by three qualities: density, hardness, and a firm, smooth skin. Pick up the piece you're considering and heft it in your hand. If it feels heavy for its size, that's the first hurdle: it hasn't lost too much water weight through evaporation. Now give it a good squeeze between thumb and forefinger. If it's rock-hard, you're still OK. Finally, check out the skin. If it's pleasantly smooth with no hint of wrinkling (also an indicator of evaporation), your prospective purchase has met the three freshness criteria. If these three criteria aren't met, the ginger is not worth buying and you should make other plans for your meal – or go to another shop.

Fibres are unconnected with freshness; they indicate that the ginger (which is a rhizome, an underground stem) was picked when fairly well advanced in age. The older it is, the stronger and thicker the fibres. And the fibres will make the ginger harder to slice or mince to the desired thickness. There's no way to test for fibrousness except by breaking a piece off, but generally, if you buy ginger that's good and fresh, you won't have too big a fibre problem. Very fibrous ginger is fine, incidentally, for marinades and for soups or braised dishes. Only when it will be cooked for a very short time is fibrousness a real problem.

Ginger keeps well as long as it's stored properly. Wrap it in plastic and keep it in the vegetable compartment of your fridge. I've stored ginger this way, with no perceptible loss of quality, for up to a month.

USES

How do lazy cooks use GGS? The question is: How don't they use it? Numerous suggestions are given elsewhere in this book. Here are a few more.

MARINADES

Good in both Eastern- and Western-style marinades. Use the quantities given above per 225 ml (8 fl oz/1 cup) of liquid, which may include any of the following:

wine   *plain oil*
dry sherry   *extra virgin olive oil*
vinegar   *stock*
soy sauce   *brandy*
oyster sauce

GGS on its own is enough for the marinade, but you may add one or two other herbs or spices. Suggestions:

parsley   *chili (fresh or dried)*
fresh coriander   *lemon grass*
thyme (fresh or dried)

GGS also makes a good partner with the flavours of any citrus fruit, especially lime or lemon.

Barbecue Sauce

For an instant barbecue sauce, double the quantity of GGS in the master formulation and combine it with:

1 green or red chili, fresh or dried

Chop the mixture as finely as you can manage (this will be much easier in a food processor). Now add:

a 400 g (14 oz) tin of tomatoes
1 tbsp Worcester sauce
1 tbsp soy sauce
1 tbsp dry sherry

1 tbsp vinegar
1 tsp sugar
2 tbsp plain vegetable oil
lots of freshly ground pepper

If using a food processor or a blender, process until thoroughly blended. If blending by hand, chop the tomatoes as well as you can manage (this is a pain in the neck) and mix with the other ingredients.

The flavour of this sauce can be deepened by frying the GGS and chili in the oil and then adding the other ingredients, and reducing by around a quarter over a very low heat. This is optional, however. The quantities here are enough for a few pounds of ribs, chicken pieces, or any other meat for that matter. Marinate the meat in the sauce for at least a few hours, then use it to baste the meat while it's cooking. The meat may also be cooked in the oven.

Barbecue Basting Sauce

If you don't have time to marinate, GGS can be used as in a basting mixture for barbecued (or grilled) fish, meat or vegetables. For 500 g (1 lb) of meat, chicken or fish, combine the quantity in the master Barbecue Sauce formulation with

4 tbsp vegetable oil or extra virgin olive oil
1-2 tbsp vinegar, dry wine, dry sherry, or lemon juice

Just before you start cooking, brush one side of the meat or fish or chicken with this basting sauce and start cooking with that side facing the heat. Baste at least once while that side is cooking, then baste the other side when you turn it over and once more before cooking is finished. The flavour of the GGS will be very strong, but no one is likely to complain. (If you're worried about complaints, use half the quantity in the master formulation.)

RICE, PASTA, PULSES

Starchy foods blend beautifully with GGS. The quantities above will amply flavour 2 servings of any pulse or rice dish. First cook the GGS slowly, in around 1 tbsp of oil or butter, until it's softened but not coloured (around 3–5 minutes). Then proceed as follows.

Rice

Cook the GGS in a small saucepan. Add 150 g (6 oz, enough to fill a measuring cup to the 6 fl oz mark) of plain long-grain rice. Stir it to coat, then put in salt, pepper, and 250 ml (9 fl oz/1⅛ cups) of water or (preferably) good stock. Bring to the boil, then turn down the heat, cover, and simmer at the merest whisper of heat for 20–25 minutes. This makes rice interesting even for people who normally hate the stuff.

Pasta

This is a side dish only, a good alternative to noodles with butter and cheese. Cook the GGS either in advance or while the pasta is cooking. When you're ready to serve, toss the pasta with the cooked GGS and some extra butter or oil if you're not worried about calories. A dribble of cream is also a good idea. If you add some squid or sliced monkfish to the GGS and cook for a few minutes more, this dish turns into an instant main course.

Pulses

There are two approaches here. One is to add the cooked GGS when the pulses are done, simply stirring them in immediately before serving. This will give them a very sprightly flavour. If you prefer to subdue their flavour somewhat, use the second approach: When the GGS has finished with its initial cooking, add the pulses and then whatever liquid you're using to cook the pulses. Cook in the usual way.

SOUPS

The quantity in the master formulation is perfect as an addition to the base for a puréed soup. GGS goes well with most green vegetables, with starchy vegetables, and with tomatoes. See the basic instructions in the soup chapter (page 241), and add the GGS when you give the vegetables their preliminary cooking.

STUFFINGS

GGS can be used in just about any stuffing for poultry. Use the quantity above for around 500 g (1 lb) of stuffing.

The GGS can also be used on its own, to stuff poultry under the skin. The quantity above should suffice for a whole chicken of around 1.5 kg (3 lb), but you could easily add more. All you do is loosen the skin and poke the GGS under it with your fingertips. The same technique can be used for chicken pieces, or for turkey, guinea fowl, duck or poussins. The mixture will taste even better with a tiny bit of fresh or dried chili mixed in before stuffing.

VEGETABLES

GGS can be added to just about any of the dishes given in the vegetable chapter (page 153). It will add real class to any stir-fry of vegetables. And it is particularly delicious with mashed potatoes. Here's the way to do it:

Cook the potatoes in your own preferred manner with the garlic, peeled, added to the cooking water. While the spuds are draining, heat a tablespoon or so of extra virgin olive oil or butter in the cooking pot. Add the ginger and spring onion and sauté them gently for a minute or two. When the spuds are drained, return them to the pot and mash well. Now add milk, cream, more butter or oil – or whatever you like with mashed potatoes.

SPICE PASTES

Spice pastes are simple to make and a useful friend to have sitting around in the fridge. It's worth making them in fairly large quantities, as the effort is no greater than that of making a tiny spoonful. And once you've got a pot waiting for you, you can use it to jazz up boring evening meals. Here is an example using GGS with an assortment of other flavours from both East and West.

1 tsp cumin	*¹/₂ tsp allspice berries*
1 tsp coriander seeds	*the basic GGS recipe (see page 332)*
1 tsp black peppercorns	*90 ml (6 tbsp) peanut oil*
1 tsp fennel seeds	*45 ml (3 tbsp) wine vinegar*

If the spices are whole, grind them in a coffee grinder or mortar and pestle (no prizes for guessing which is easier). Now mix them with the GGS mixture, which should all be very finely chopped. Blend in the oil and vinegar and keep sealed in the fridge. This will stay in tip-top form for up to 2 weeks. Stir it into braises, soups, or stir-fries.

HERBES DE PROVENCE

Herbes de Provence is a mixture of rosemary, thyme, bay, basil and savory. Sold in packets or sometimes in bags, it is one of the greatest of all-purpose flavours. If you've looked through other chapters of this book, you will have noticed that every other page contains at least one reference to the stuff.

I love herbes de Provence first of all because it tastes good, and second of all because it comes ready-mixed. Lazy cooks shy away from recipes that call for taking one teaspoon of this, half a teaspoon of that, a quarter teaspoon of something else. With herbes de Provence, you don't need to poke around in the spice rack. The mixing and blending have all been done for you. And because the mix is so versatile and delicious, it can be used on almost any food, whether vegetables, fish, fowl or red meat.

Herbes de Provence is sold in packets by delicatessens and supermarkets. The cheapest and best place to buy it is in France, where it's sold in large bags. If you're buying a few of them, keep one bag in the spice rack and store the others – wrapped in a well-sealed plastic bag – in the freezer. Dried herbs do not have an indefinite shelf life and should be kept away from air, heat and light.

When using herbes de Provence, remember that a little goes a long way. Dried herbs, having lost all their moisture, are always stronger and more concentrated in flavour than fresh.

Herbes de Provence Seasoning Mix

Here is a basic herbes de Provence mix for use on meats which are to be grilled, fried, or roasted.

2 tbsp salt
1 tbsp herbes de Provence
1 tsp freshly ground black pepper

Combine the ingredients and sprinkle lightly on the meat. If it's going on meat for grilling or chopping it must be used sparingly: the mixture should cover the surface thoroughly but should not be too thick. If the mixture is going on meat for roasting, you can and should use more of it, rubbing on as much as will stick to the surface. A piece of meat left to sit with the coating will absorb some of the flavour.

If you pound the peppercorns with a mortar and pestle instead of grinding them in the peppermill, you will end up with a coarser mix which is particularly good for steaks and roasts. This is similar to the effect of *steak au poivre*, where the large nuggets of pepper fairly burst in the mouth.

Meat Marinade

2 tbsp Dijon mustard   *1 tbsp dry wine or vermouth*
1 tsp herbes de Provence   *salt and pepper*
4 tbsp vegetable oil

Mix all the ingredients. Smear on the meat. This is enough for around 6 chops or one small joint. Double the quantity for a large joint like leg of lamb or shoulder of pork.

Herbes de Provence Mix for Curing Fish

Gravadlax, salmon cured with a seasoning mix based on fresh dill, has become a popular dish in recent years. Here is a variant based on herbes de Provence. The quantity given will cure 2 sides of fresh salmon each weighing around 500 g (1 lb); the salmon must be very fresh, as it will stay in the fridge for a day or more.

12 g (enough to fill a measuring cup to the ³/₄ fl oz mark) coarse salt
1 tbsp herbes de Provence
1 tsp black pepper
¹/₂ tsp sugar

Blend the ingredients and use them to coat the flesh side of 2 filleted sides of very fresh salmon. Wrap well in cling film or aluminium foil and leave to cure in the coldest part of the fridge for at least 24 hours and up to 3 days, turning from time to time. To serve, slice on the diagonal. Serve with Greek yogurt and a little salad of cucumber and spring onion.

Herbes de Provence Barbecue Sauce

1 medium onion
2 cloves of garlic
1 tbsp herbes de Provence
110 ml (4 fl oz) oil
1 tbsp tomato purée
2 tbsp Worcester sauce
50 ml (2 fl oz) dry wine, dry sherry, or wine vinegar

Blend the onions and garlic in your food processor till they are smashed to a pulp. Add the remaining ingredients and process again for 30 seconds or so. If possible, leave for 1-2 hours before using.

Herbes de Provence Vinaigrette

Since this will keep indefinitely and even improve with time, the recipe here is for a large quantity of dressing. Use more garlic if you like.

1 small clove of garlic
1 tbsp Dijon mustard
225 ml (8 fl oz) vegetable oil, or half plain oil and half extra virgin olive oil
50 ml (2 fl oz) wine or sherry vinegar
1 tbsp herbes de Provence

Crush or mince the garlic and mix with the remaining ingredients. If you wish, you can strain the vinaigrette before adding it to your salad. (Most of the flavour will have seeped into the dressing anyway.)

Only one word of warning is needed regarding herbes de Provence. All dried herbs lose their freshness after 6 months or so, and this is no exception. Store it away from light and heat, and if you find that you have some left over after 6 months, throw it away and buy another pack. You won't regret the waste, which in any event is minimal if you use the stuff as often as I do.

SUN-DRIED TOMATOES

Sun-dried tomatoes have become intolerably fashionable in recent years. Lazy cooks who are wary of trendiness would be fully justified in treating these things with suspicion.

Well, almost fully justified. Trendy or not, sun-dried tomatoes are delicious things. They come mostly from Italy or California, where the ample summer sun gives tomatoes real flavour. The tomatoes are picked when fully ripe, laid out on enormous racks, and dried, as their name implies, in the heat of the same sun that made the fruit so good in the first place. Drying them evaporates the water and leaves behind the essence of the tomato flavour, with delicious undertones of smokiness as well. A few pounds of fresh tomato are needed to produce a few ounces of sun-dried.

Sun-dried tomatoes are sold in two ways: either in olive oil or just dried, on their own. If you buy the oil-packed type, no further treatment is needed. Obviously, it's easier to buy them in this form. These are sold in jars and are widely available, but the best tend to come from Italian delicatessens. Make sure the tomatoes are packed in extra virgin olive oil for the best flavour. The received wisdom on the dry type states that they must be soaked in boiled water for anything from 20 minutes up to a few hours, and if you're using them for a salad or stir-fry then the received wisdom is correct. If you're using them in a dish that will be cooked for a long time, presoaking is unnecessary.

USES

Sun-dried tomatoes are another of those foods that can be used in almost any way. They add clout to tomato soup, tomato sauce, or just about any other dish calling for well-cooked tomatoes. Finely minced or shredded, the oil-packed type can also be used in salads, *salsas* (see page 323), pasta sauces, sandwiches, or lightly cooked vegetable dishes. The dry-packed type can be added, without further preparation, to a wide range of braised dishes, pulse and grain dishes, and even soups. Here is a plain lentil dish that benefits immeasurably from their company. You can make it with any lentil that still has its hull intact.

Lentils with Sun-dried Tomatoes

2 slices of smoked bacon
1 medium onion (around 100 g/4 oz)
2 unsoaked sun-dried tomatoes
1 heaped tsp herbes de Provence

1 tbsp tomato purée
250 g (8 oz) green lentils
around 1 litre (2 pints) chicken stock

Cut the bacon into thin, matchstick-width shreds and the onion into somewhat thicker shreds (around ¼ in thick). Cut the tomatoes in half lengthwise and then crosswise into the thinnest shreds you can manage. Put the bacon in a large saucepan with a small splash of water and heat it gently for a couple of minutes to start rendering out the fat. Add the onion and cook, stirring, for a minute or two. Then add the tomatoes, tomato purée and herbs, and mix well. Put in the lentils, mix again to coat with bacon fat, and then pour in the stock. Bring to the boil, then turn down and simmer gently, partly covered, till the lentils are done – around 30–40 minutes.

Sun-dried Tomato Vinaigrette

You can make this in large quantities and keep it in the fridge, tightly covered, for weeks. If making in advance, don't add the pepper and garlic until just before serving. This quantity will dress 500 g (1 lb) of cooked vegetables or a smallish green salad for 2 people. It's particularly good with cooked vegetables, however – especially those cooked by charring (see page 167) or pan-grilling (see page 103).

3 tbsp extra virgin olive oil　　　　*1 small sun-dried tomato*
1½ tbsp wine or sherry vinegar　　　*1 thin slice of garlic*
1 tbsp lemon juice　　　　　　　　*salt and pepper*

Mix the oil, vinegar and lemon juice. Chop the tomato and garlic as fine as you can get them and add to the liquid. Season with salt and pepper to taste. NB: if you're making large quantities, you could do this in a blender so the tomato will be pulverized.

Here's a sandwich of ordinary ingredients made sublime by the addition of sun-dried tomatoes. If you omit the bread and serve the ingredients on a plate, you have an instant starter for dinner parties. Or you could substitute *bruschetta* (Italian toast) made with *ciabatta* or Greek *daktylla* bread and make your party dish more substantial. These quantities make one sandwich.

Mozzarella Sandwiches with Sun-dried Tomatoes

2 slices of bread or 1 pitta bread	*2 leaves of basil*
4 thin slices of Italian mozzarella	*1 tsp extra virgin olive oil*
1 small sun-dried tomato	*freshly ground black pepper*

Toast the bread if you wish to, but otherwise just lay on the slices of cheese. Chop the tomato into tiny chunks or thin shreds and scatter the pieces over the cheese. Tear the basil into small pieces and put it on, then sprinkle with the oil and grind on the pepper. Dig in. Or, if you're feeling supremely self-indulgent, omit the oil from the interior and instead brush the outsides of the sandwich with 1–2 tbsp of it. Then fry the sandwich in a nonstick pan till the cheese is melted and the bread nicely browned. This makes a perfect hangover lunch.

A final word on sun-dried tomatoes, passed along by Ken Hom, who gave me my first (and best) jar of the things. When the jar is finished, use the fragrant red oil as a sauce for pasta. A single tablespoon will sauce 125 g (4 oz) of dry pasta. Add a handful of chopped parsley and maybe some garlic, and you will be dining like a king – without having to work at it.

BALSAMIC VINEGAR

Balsamic vinegar is made in the northern Italian province of Modena by a process that, traditionally, takes many years. The process begins with a single grape variety, the Trebbiano. This is boiled down to a sugar-rich syrup and then aged in wood, giving what Marcella Hazan (in *Marcella's Italian Kitchen*) calls a 'deep, charred brown colour'. For a succinct but detailed account of the manufacturing process, you can't do better than Marcella Hazan's book or Claudia Roden's *The Food of Italy*.

Traditional balsamic vinegar is fantastically expensive, and highly prized by the Italian families lucky enough to own some. Incontestably superior, it cannot, to my knowledge, be bought in this country. Even in Italy it is a rarity, each tiny bottle being treasured by the owners and doled out by the drop on special occasions. And if it *is* available here, at some shop frequented by the very-well-monied classes, I would not recommend buying it except in extraordinary circumstances. Have you won the Pools recently?

What we *can* buy is a cheaper substance that's aged for a much shorter time, typically 3–6 years. First brought to Britain by Italian delicatessens, it is now widely available. Purists will tell you that it's a pale imitation of the real thing, and they are undoubtedly right. But the imitation is delicious stuff. It's not exactly cheap, £3–£5 for a small bottle, but it's worth every penny. I use it constantly, and that's why it's mentioned on almost every page of this book.

Balsamic vinegar has a deeper flavour than ordinary wine vinegar, simultaneously sweet and spicy. In theory it should not be heated too much, as its complex aromas and flavours are highly fugitive, and should be used in moderation. I agree with the theory. But sometimes I use it in hot sauces, and sometimes I use huge amounts. No one has ever complained about either infraction.

SALADS AND VEGETABLES

Balsamic vinegar makes wonderful vinaigrettes, either on its own or with other acidic ingredients. For very flavourful salad ingredients (e.g. frisée lettuce or endive), try using a dressing made of nothing more than

1 part balsamic vinegar
5 parts extra virgin olive oil

But it also goes well with a sharper form of acid, especially citrus. Here's another good salad dressing:

1 tbsp balsamic vinegar
6 tbsp extra virgin olive oil
1 tbsp lemon or lime juice
a pinch of chopped fresh herbs

The sweetness of balsamic vinegar also goes well with walnut and hazelnut oils, even though these are French in origin.

When you're pan-grilling or charring vegetables, a judicious sprinkling of balsamic vinegar provides all the dressing you need. Don't put it on till the vegetables have finished cooking, and figure on around

1–2 tbsp per 500 g (1 lb) of vegetables

I don't usually add butter to plainly cooked vegetables, but I'll make an exception if the vegetables in question are French beans or courgettes and the butter is mixed with balsamic vinegar. Melt a little butter gently, whisk in the vinegar and some fresh herbs, and pour it over the steaming vegetables. The sweetness of the vinegar goes just as well with butter as it does with extra virgin olive oil – the obvious partner.

MEAT, POULTRY AND FISH

Plainly pan-grilled, grilled or roasted meats benefit immensely from a dash of balsamic vinegar. Use it in the liquid for deglazing roasts, or just sprinkle or brush it on to individual portions. The sweetness of the vinegar is a treat with smoky barbecue flavours of any kind. I like it particularly with chicken, but it's also great on barbecued fish. Or on raw fish, for that matter. If you want a simple starter for an elegant dinner party, try this out. The quantities here will feed 4.

Salmon or Halibut Tartare with Balsamic Vinegar Marinade

300 g (10 oz) skinless fillet of salmon or halibut
2–3 coriander seeds
8–10 chives or 1 spring onion
2 tbsp extra virgin olive oil
1 tsp dry vermouth or dry white wine
1 tbsp balsamic vinegar

Cut the fish in dice around ¼ in square or in ¼ in slices and put the pieces in a bowl. Crush the coriander and mince the chives or spring onion. Mix with the remaining ingredients, season with salt and pepper, and pour over the fish. Let the fish sit for at least 30 minutes and up to 2 hours. Serve with toast.

A Picnic Tip

Cook some chicken by grilling, roasting (see page 19), or flash-roasting (see page 117). When cool, pack it into tightly sealable plastic boxes. For each piece of chicken put in 1 tsp of extra virgin olive oil and 1 tsp of balsamic vinegar. Season with salt, pepper and fresh or dried thyme. Close the container. By the time you get to the picnic spot, the chicken will have been thoroughly doused in the marinade. I brought this dish to my wife in hospital an hour after the birth of our third child, and she declared that she had never eaten anything better.

FRUIT

It was *Marcella's Italian Kitchen*, by Marcella Hazan, that tipped me off about the perfect marriage between balsamic vinegar and strawberries. She uses 1 tbsp of vinegar per 500 g (1 lb) of berries, plus 2–3 tbsp of sugar. Mix the berries and sugar first, an hour or so before serving, and let the mixture sit till needed. Add the vinegar just before serving, toss, and serve. This is one of the greatest desserts I've ever eaten, and easily one of the simplest.

Since then I have experimented with other uses of balsamic vinegar in fruit desserts, and have found that it's pretty good with just about anything. Use it to macerate fruit, as in Marcella Hazan's recipe; mix it with the cream or yogurt you spoon on to a fruit salad; or see page 320 for a simple 'sauce' containing the stuff. It's particularly delicious when added to the liquid in a cooked fruit compôte. Use no more than a tablespoon per 500 g (1 lb) fruit.

Or, for something completely different, you can use balsamic vinegar in a drink based on citrus fruits. This summer cooler is suitable for drinking on its own or with a tot of vodka if you're so inclined. These quantities are per serving.

Balsamic Cooler

juice of 1 large orange (around 100 ml/scant 4 fl oz)
juice of ½ a lime (around 1 tsp)
½ tsp balsamic vinegar
25 ml (scant 1 fl oz) vodka, or to taste (optional)

Mix the juices and vinegar well. Add the vodka if using. Pour over plenty of ice in a tall glass. Turn on the radio. Sit down.

Acknowledgements

My thanks go first of all to *Cosmopolitan* and the Weekend *Guardian*, and especially to my editors there: Marcelle d'Argy Smith and Matthew Fort. When you're forced to cook, for whatever reason, you gain the experience that is the *sine qua non* of culinary competence. I have spent the last few years cooking for *Cosmo* and the *Guardian*, and many of the ideas developed here arose from that work. My thanks to Marcelle and Matthew for giving me the opportunity, and to Matthew – a better cook than I – for sharing knowledge, opinions, and amity in general.

If experience is the first pillar on which my cooking abilities rest, the second consists of the hundreds of cookbooks I have read or looked at. Out of those there is a handful to which I return constantly. These books are the work of exacting cooks who seek the best way, not just a good enough way, of preparing a particular dish. Their precision makes life easier for us lazy types, even if we don't follow their recipes to the letter. Many fine books are mentioned in the text, but I must single out those by Julia Child, Marcella Hazan, and Nico Ladenis. About food in its broader senses I have learned most from M.F.K. Fisher, Jane Grigson, and Harold McGee.

I owe special thanks to the friends and relations who ate what I cooked while writing *The Lazy Cook*. In normal circumstances it is unfair to ask people whether they like what you've cooked for them. When you're writing a cookbook you have to ask, and many people endured this grilling on numerous occasions. While I cannot thank them individually, I hope they know who they are.

I am deeply indebted to Bob Birchenall and the late Phil Fairman of B & M Seafoods, London NW5, for their expert advice. My editor at Bantam Press, Georgina Morley, showed endless patience in waiting for the manuscript and sympathetic skill in editing it. Annie Lee copy-edited the book with remarkable care and diligence. Anne Curtis, Jonathan Goodman, and Gail Simmonds gave different types of help and advice which they know all about.

I owe an incalculable debt to Emma Dally, my long-suffering wife and chief taster. At the ends of countless tiring days, Emma waited patiently for dinner while I scuttled around the kitchen with scales, spoons, pen and paper, and a tape measure. She didn't object when I scrutinized and sometimes poked at the food on her plate. She gave opinions thoughtfully and honestly, even though all she wanted to do was eat. And she endured countless meals with a companion who, absorbed in analysing what had gone wrong, was often incapable of normal conversation. No one should have to put up with this. She did.

Finally I thank my mother, Norma Solway Ehrlich. Neither of us knew it at the time, but I learned to cook by standing in the kitchen and watching her work. This instruction-by-osmosis had less to do with specific techniques than with the basics of good cooking: preparing sound ingredients, observing their behaviour in the pot, and paying attention to how they look and taste on the plate. These irreplaceable lessons form the third pillar of what I know about food; without them I would not have learned so early or so well. My debt is acknowledged both here and in the dedication to this book.

Index